Ksenia

RLM ˙AN 2021
– 5 FEB 2021
A + L Mc Faul
Genevieve.

mup

Katherine Howard

Katherine Howard

The Tragic Story of Henry VIII's Fifth Queen

JOSEPHINE WILKINSON

JOHN MURRAY

First published in Great Britain in 2016 by
John Murray (Publishers)
An Hachette UK Company

1

© Josephine Wilkinson 2016

The right of Josephine Wilkinson to be identified as the Author
of the Work has been asserted by her in accordance with the Copyright,
Designs and Patents Act 1988.

A CIP catalogue record for this title is available from the British Library

ISBN 978 1 444 79626 1
Trade paperback ISBN 978 1 444 79627 8
Ebook ISBN 978 1 444 79628 5

Typeset in Bembo by Palimpsest Book Production Limited,
Falkirk, Stirlingshire

Printed and bound by Clays Ltd, St Ives plc

John Murray policy is to use papers that are natural,
renewable and recyclable products and made from wood
grown in sustainable forests. The logging and manufacturing
processes are expected to conform to the environmental
regulations of the country of origin.

John Murray (Publishers)
Carmelite House
50 Victoria Embankment
London EC4Y 0DZ

www.johnmurray.co.uk

In memory of my grandparents, Olive and George

Contents

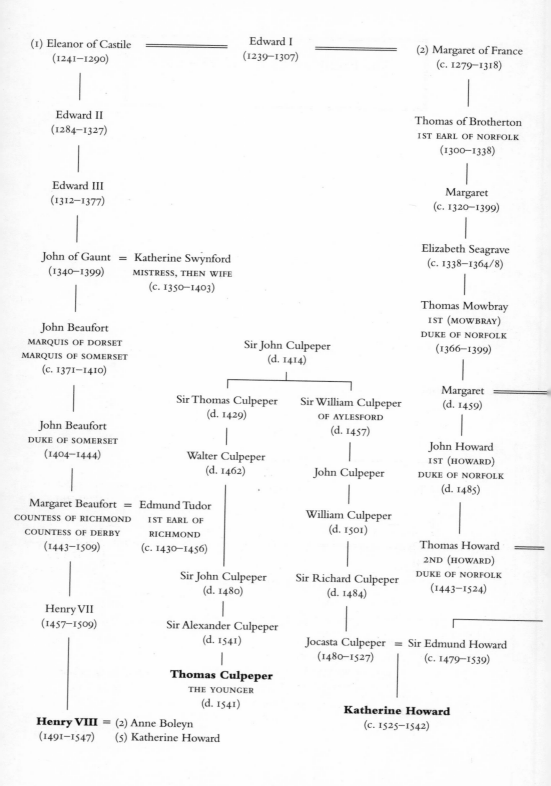

(1) Eleanor of Castile ═══════ Edward I ═══════ (2) Margaret of France
(1241–1290)   (1239–1307)   (c. 1279–1318)

Edward II   Thomas of Brotherton
(1284–1327)   1ST EARL OF NORFOLK
                                                   (1300–1338)

Edward III   Margaret
(1312–1377)   (c. 1320–1399)

                                                   Elizabeth Seagrave
John of Gaunt = Katherine Swynford   (c. 1338–1364/8)
(1340–1399)   MISTRESS, THEN WIFE
               (c. 1350–1403)   Thomas Mowbray
                                                   1ST (MOWBRAY)
John Beaufort   Sir John Culpeper   DUKE OF NORFOLK
MARQUIS OF DORSET   (d. 1414)   (1366–1399)
MARQUIS OF SOMERSET
(c. 1371–1410)   Margaret ═══════
                  Sir Thomas Culpeper   Sir William Culpeper   (d. 1459)
                  (d. 1429)   OF AYLESFORD
John Beaufort   (d. 1457)   John Howard
DUKE OF SOMERSET   1ST (HOWARD)
(1404–1444)   Walter Culpeper   John Culpeper   DUKE OF NORFOLK
                      (d. 1462)   (d. 1485)

Margaret Beaufort = Edmund Tudor   William Culpeper
COUNTESS OF RICHMOND 1ST EARL OF   (d. 1501)
COUNTESS OF DERBY   RICHMOND   Thomas Howard
(1443–1509)   (c. 1430–1456)   2ND (HOWARD) ═══════
                          Sir John Culpeper Sir Richard Culpeper DUKE OF NORFOLK
                          (d. 1480)   (d. 1484)   (1443–1524)
Henry VII
(1457–1509)   Sir Alexander Culpeper
                          (d. 1541)
                                             Jocasta Culpeper = Sir Edmund Howard
                          Thomas Culpeper   (1480–1527)   (c. 1479–1539)
                          THE YOUNGER
                          (d. 1541)
                                             Katherine Howard
Henry VIII = (2) Anne Boleyn   (c. 1525–1542)
(1491–1547) (5) Katherine Howard

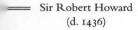

The Family of Katherine Howard

~

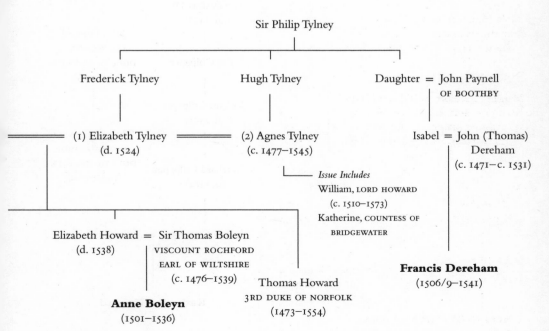

Sir Robert Howard
(d. 1436)

Sir Philip Tylney

Frederick Tylney

Hugh Tylney

Daughter = John Paynell
OF BOOTHBY

(1) Elizabeth Tylney
(d. 1524)

(2) Agnes Tylney
(c. 1477–1545)

Isabel = John (Thomas)
Dereham
(c. 1471–c. 1531)

Issue Includes
William, LORD HOWARD
(c. 1510–1573)
Katherine, COUNTESS OF
BRIDGEWATER

Elizabeth Howard = Sir Thomas Boleyn
(d. 1538)   VISCOUNT ROCHFORD
                 EARL OF WILTSHIRE
                 (c. 1476–1539)

Anne Boleyn
(1501–1536)

Thomas Howard
3RD DUKE OF NORFOLK
(1473–1554)

Francis Dereham
(1506/9–1541)

Prologue

~

AT A FEW minutes before nine in the morning, a small cortège
left the queen's lodgings in the Tower of London and
made its way across the courtyard. The queen was escorted by the
constable of the Tower, attended by her almoner and four ladies.
She wore a grey damask gown lined with fur over a scarlet kirtle
and an ermine mantle, while an English gabled hood completed
the outfit.

They went through the huge twin towers of the Coldharbour
Gate into the inner ward, passing the imposing mass of the White
Tower on the right. Some fifty or so metres ahead stood the scaffold. Less than six feet high, it was draped in black and strewn
with straw.

The queen climbed a small flight of wooden steps and turned
to face the crowd of onlookers, no more than a thousand people,
and addressed them. She explained that she had come here to die.
She acknowledged the justice of her fate, accepting the verdict
found against her. She prayed for the king, praising his goodness
and mercy, before expressing the hope that, if anyone would take
up her cause, they would judge the best. She then took her leave
of the people, asking them to pray for her.

At that moment her ladies stepped forward and removed her
mantle. She lifted off her hood, passing it to one of the ladies,
who gave her a white coif. This she placed on her head, tucking
her abundant hair neatly inside so it would not inhibit the stroke
of the blade. One of her ladies bandaged her eyes and the queen
bade them a final farewell. All four ladies, once hostile, were now

I

overcome with emotion as they withdrew to the back of the scaffold.

The queen knelt upright on the straw, and it was obvious to all who watched that she was not bound or restrained in any way. Quietly, she began to pray: 'Jesu receive my soul; O Lord God have pity on my soul; to Christ I commend my soul.'

The last words she heard were those of the headsman, who called upon his assistant to 'fetch my sword'. Anne Boleyn instinctively turned her head, at which point the executioner swung his heavy weapon, brought it down and removed her head with a single stroke. It was a momentous event. Anne Boleyn was the first Queen of England ever to be executed; none could have imagined that she would not be the last.

I

A Calamitous Childhood

~

Who goith A borrowing, goith a sorrowing[1]

E DMUND HOWARD, KATHERINE'S father, is one of those
men whose passage through life, although apparently charted
for him by kindly destiny, nevertheless founders at every turn until
his story becomes little more than a catalogue of failure.

Still, his origins were, on the surface at least, promising. He belonged
to a great family whose fortunes had risen and fallen on the tides of
war, illustrious marriages, changing royal dynasties and treason. They
would regain their prestige only through long and dedicated service
to the new Tudor regime. The year of his birth is not certain, although
it can be narrowed down to 1478–80.[2] His position in the family as
the third son of Thomas Howard, Earl of Surrey, meant that he would
be eclipsed by his elder brothers and would receive scant, if any,
inheritance; little would be expected of him.

Edmund Howard's first significant appearance in the historical
record occurs in June 1509 when he took part in the jousts that
formed part of the celebrations for the coronation of Henry VIII
and Katherine of Aragon. Edmund attended alongside his brothers,
Thomas and Edward; Sir Thomas Knyvett, his brother-in-law;
Richard, the brother of the Marquis of Dorset; and Charles
Brandon, esquire. All were 'gorgeously apparelled, with curious
devices, of cuts and of embroideries, as well as their coats, as
in trappers for their horses, some of gold, some in silver, some in
tinsels, and diverse other in goldsmiths work, goodly to behold'.[3]

Two years later, Edmund became a member of the Middle Temple, indicating an intention to go into law. Here, as custom dictated, he was, 'pardoned of all offices' before receiving 'liberty to be in commons and out of commons at his own liking'.[4]

The Howards were noted ship owners, so it should be no surprise that Edmund's next appearance was as captain of the *Gryt Herry Imperyall* in February 1513.[5] However, it was on land that Howard was to make his most significant mark, at the Battle of Flodden Field in September of that same year. Edmund Howard, as marshal of the host,[6] commanded the right wing of the vanguard. At the head of 500 Lancashire men and 1,000 Cheshire men, he encountered the Chamberlain of Scotland, Alexander, Lord Hume, with his company of 8,000 pikemen. Many of Howard's men fled in the face of this fearsome sight, leaving their leaders to fend for themselves.

The Scottish force managed to get close enough to Howard to cut down his standard-bearer and two of his servants. Left to stand alone, Howard was felled three times before assistance arrived in the form of a badly wounded John Heron, who assured him, 'there was never noble man's son so like to be lost as you be this day, for all my hurts I shall live and die with you'.[7] As it was, Howard barely escaped with his life and he was forced to fight his way through the field in order to reach the protection of his brother's vanguard. For his undoubted bravery, Edmund Howard was knighted on the field by his father.[8]

The following year saw Sir Edmund take another ceremonial role when he and his father joined the train of Princess Mary Tudor as she journeyed to France for her marriage to King Louis XII. Edmund asked for, and received, £100 to purchase the necessary items for the jousts and tourneys that were to be held. He was also awarded 40 marks 'for diets at 26s. 8d., for 20 days' beginning on 28 September 1514.[9] Edmund attended the marriage of the French queen and the aged King Louis. For their services, he and his companions received twenty days' wages in hand.

At this point, Edmund was still a bachelor. The list of those men who crossed to France includes the names of their wives, among them the Duchess of Norfolk, the Countess of Oxford[10] and the Marchioness of Dorset, and no lady's name is attached to that of Sir Edmund Howard.[11]

The trip to France had left Edmund in debt to the king.[12] This situation would worsen in September 1515, when he had managed to persuade Henry to lend him a further £100. In his generosity, Henry also gave Edmund silks and cloth of gold worth £618. 7s.[13] Why Sir Edmund required such a large sum is not stated, but by this time he was married to the recently widowed Jocasta Culpeper. The marriage had taken place in 1514 or 1515, by which time the Howards were firmly back in royal favour following their success at Flodden. With his family's name and honour re-established, Edmund Howard, notwithstanding his position as a younger son and his financial difficulties, could be seen as a desirable husband.

For her part, Jocasta Culpeper was also a fine catch, coming as she did from such an excellent lineage. The Culpepers were a large and well-connected clan who could trace their ancestry back to Edward I through his daughter, Joan of Acre, and whose influence spread across the counties of Kent and Sussex and further afield. However, if Edmund thought that marrying into the Culpeper family would bring him the lands and wealth that were denied him by his place in the Howard family, he was mistaken.

As it was, Edmund found himself responsible for a new wife, five stepchildren and an increasing number of his own offspring. While such a situation might have cultivated a sense of duty and responsibility in some men, this was not the case with Sir Edmund Howard. In 1516 he was indicted in the Court of Star Chamber for abusing his position as Provost Marshal for the county of Surrey,[14] although he received no sentence.

The following year, Sir Edmund Howard was called upon to act against the offenders in the notorious Evil May Day riot.[15] A largely racially motivated disturbance, this was unique in London at the time. It was frightening and violent while it lasted, but the unrest soon ran its course; nevertheless, a dithering Cardinal Wolsey belatedly called in the Howards to restore the peace. Edmund's father and brother were among those who presided over the subsequent oyer and terminer, a special commission established to judge the case, while Edmund, as Knight Marshal, supervised the punishments of those found guilty. The ringleaders were 'executed in most rigorous manner, for the Lord Edmond Howard, son to the Duke of Norfolk, & knight Marshal showed no mercy, but extreme cruelty, to the poor younglings in their execution'.[16]

Edmund's earlier adventure on the wrong side of the law had not taught him any lasting lessons, and he was forced to seek pardon after being indicted for instigating riots and supporting 'misdoers' in the county of Surrey.[17] By contrast, later in 1517, he was paid twenty shillings a day for 'taking thieves'.[18] After this, he was appointed to attend Henry VIII during a visit to Calais in 1520,[19] and was selected as one of the jousters under the captaincy of the Earl of Devon.[20]

Two years later Edmund had the chance to taste real war once again when he accompanied his brother, Thomas, Earl of Surrey, to Brittany. Together, they sacked the town of Morlaix and set fire to what remained. After that, he and Surrey moved on to Picardy where they rampaged with equal vigour, pillaging and burning several towns.[21]

However satisfied Edmund might have felt with his military activities, they did nothing to ease his financial situation. Moreover, he had by now acquired a reputation for financial incompetence, an unfortunate characteristic given the steadily increasing size of his family. He and Jocasta would go on to have three sons, Henry, Charles and George, and at least three daughters, Margaret, Katherine and Mary. It is probable, though not certain, that Katherine was born in 1525 at Lambeth, the second of the sisters.

As expected in aristocratic houses, Katherine was not fed by her mother, but by a wet nurse carefully selected according to strict guidelines, such as those laid down by Thomas Elyot. The nurse should be between twenty and thirty years of age, and not a servant. It was essential that she should be free of vice because it was thought that an evil disposition could be transmitted to the child through the milk, an idea that goes back at least as far as Cicero. Similarly, the nurse should be free of illness and deformity, and would possess a 'right and pure sanguine' complexion. The baby would be attended by a woman of 'virtue, discretion and gravity', who would allow no 'act or dishonest tache, or wanton or unclean word' to be spoken in the presence of the child. For this reason, all men were expressly excluded from the nursery.[22]

As Edmund's debts increased, his wife's family refused to come to his aid and he was excluded from any inheritance from the will of his wife's stepfather, Sir John Legh of Stockwell.[23] Sir John's widow, Dame Isabel,[24] took a similar approach, denying her son-in-law the benefits of the Culpeper inheritance.

Edmund's financial position now became so difficult that in 1527 he felt compelled to turn to Cardinal Wolsey, the Lord Chancellor, for help. Afraid to leave his house because of the risk of arrest, he sent his wife[25] to Wolsey with a letter begging the cardinal to grant her an audience.[26] He complained that he was 'utterly undone' and 'so far in danger of the king's laws by reason of debt that I am in, that I dare not go abroad, nor come at mine own house, and I am fain to absent me from my wife and my children'. Edmund was anxious to avoid 'writs of execution' being served against him, as were his guarantors, who also faced arrest or harassment of some sort. He therefore asked Wolsey to show him favour, which kindness 'shall be the save guard of my life and relief of my poor wife and our ten children,[27] and set me out of debt'. Edmund bewailed his social status, which debarred him from earning a living by means of trade; to do so would bring dishonour to himself and his family. Nevertheless, he thought he had found a solution to his dilemma. He had heard that a voyage was being planned to a 'newfound land'. Several ships would be taking part, requiring captains, officers and soldiers. With this in mind, he volunteered his services, assuming Wolsey should 'think my poor carcass anything meet to serve the king's grace in the said voyage . . . glad would I be to venture my life to do the king's service'.

It was about this time that Jocasta died, leaving Katherine and her siblings to the care of a man wholly unsuited to the task. Edmund had been forced to sell off his wife's estates in an attempt to pay his debts, and as a result, the Howards were so impoverished that Jocasta had to be buried from the home of her younger sister, Elizabeth.[28]

Soon afterwards, Katherine gained a stepmother, Dorothy Troyes, the daughter and co-heir of Thomas Troyes, esquire, of Kilmeston in Hampshire. This second marriage brought Edmund manors and their rents, but it would be childless and tragically short. Dorothy wrote her will on 9 May 1530, noting that she was 'sick in body but whole in mind',[29] and died two days later. She made no mention of Katherine or any of the other Howard children in her will.

A widower for the second time, Edmund's straitened circumstances, having eased for a short while, once more became pressing. Even his appointment, in April 1531, as comptroller of the town and marches of Calais does not seem to have helped.[30] Two months after taking up the post, he was writing to Thomas Cromwell, who was now running Henry's legal and business affairs, for help. Cromwell promised to advance Howard's suits to the king. The grateful Howard felt he owed everything to Cromwell, for though he is 'highly kinned', he is as 'smally friended as man may be'; he was 'so beaten in the world' that he knew 'what a treasure is a faithful friend'. The letter was addressed to 'my wellbeloved friend, Mr Cromwell'.[31]

The sorry plight of Sir Edmund did not prevent his marrying again. His third wife was Margaret Jennings, the widow of Nicholas Jennings, who had died in about 1532.[32] If she ever met her stepdaughter, Katherine, it could only have been when the Howards paid a visit to England or, less probably, if Katherine ever travelled to Calais to visit her father.

As it happened, the day-to-day business at Calais sometimes proved too taxing for the new comptroller. He found it difficult to control illegal exports from Calais, causing Cromwell to appoint two men to take the matter in hand.[33] He worried about the precarious state of the town and marches of Calais with respect to victuals, which few could afford to buy.[34] He complained about having to 'follow daily suits in the law', which was, he said, 'small pleasure to me, and great cost, whereof I have small need'.[35]

Notwithstanding these problems, Edmund was only just managing to scrape a living. While his post brought £80 in wages and fees each year,[36] it was not sufficient to cover the expenses. On top of keeping his house at Calais, Edmund was responsible for the welfare of 'seven clerks, four horses and a keeper'.[37]

His election as mayor might have gone some way to easing many of these burdens, but King Henry opposed it. As Lord Husee noted: 'the king will in no wise that my lord Howard be admitted to the mayoralty'.[38]

That Calais was beset with divisions, both political and religious, made it even harder to govern, and Edmund, with his increasingly failing health, found it all too much. He travelled to England, where he acted as chief male mourner at the funeral of his sister, Elizabeth Boleyn, Countess of Wiltshire, who had died on 3 April 1538 and was buried in the Howard vault at St Mary's Lambeth four days later. Sadly, there is nothing to suggest that the occasion brought father and daughter together for the first time in seven years.[39]

Edmund continued to be unhappy with his lot and he expressed hopes of returning to England for good. He longed for a place at court, where he could serve either the king or the queen, 'and have a better living'.[40] In the end, Edmund was succeeded by a Mr Bowes,[41] who was expected to take over the post of comptroller at the end of January 1539. Certain lands were granted to Edmund, but he was to find no new office.[42] Edmund Howard's ill-fated life came to an end only a few months after his return from Calais,[43] when he was about sixty years old.

Edmund Howard, 'smally friended' as he thought he was, and who made so little impact on history, would, nevertheless, make his mark in a way that was to elude his more illustrious brothers.

Like his sister, Elizabeth, the mother of Anne Boleyn, he was destined to be the parent of a queen of England. Such an achievement, however, was to be the only high point of an otherwise unexceptional career, and Edmund himself would play no part in its realisation.

2

Being but a Young Girl

~

EDMUND HOWARD'S PLEAS to Cardinal Wolsey for financial assistance give us some idea of the relative poverty in which the young Katherine was raised. Her father, always in debt and unable to take any meaningful employment, could not provide for his family. Edmund, however, did have several properties and estates to look after, which meant that Katherine's earliest years were unsettled, following her father from house to house as he went about his business, or else being fostered out to various relatives. Here, Katherine was fortunate: her two maternal aunts each had houses in the country, where a child could grow up in a healthy environment. Her mother's elder sister, Margaret Culpeper, now married to William Cotton, had inherited her father's estates at Oxenhoath. Her second aunt, Elizabeth, the wife of Henry Barham, lived in a house called Teston, near Maidstone in Kent.[1] Still, children can thrive in an unsettled existence if they have the love and support of a close family. For Katherine, however, life was to deal a more severe blow than itinerancy: she was only about three years old when her mother died.

The cause, or even the date, of Jocasta Culpeper's early death is not known. It is possible that she died giving birth to another daughter, Jane.[2] If so, the child, like her mother, may not have survived the birth, or perhaps died shortly afterwards, for nothing more is known about her. Another possibility is that Jocasta might have succumbed to the terrible sweating sickness, a serious outbreak of which occurred in 1528 when Katherine was three years old.

Then, in 1531, when Katherine was about six, her father took the comptrollership of Calais, at which point arrangements were made for her to live permanently with her step-grandmother, Agnes, Dowager Duchess of Norfolk.

Agnes Howard, née Tylney, was the second wife and widow of Thomas Howard, Earl of Surrey. Because Surrey had previously been married to Agnes's cousin, Elizabeth, a special dispensation was required to allow the couple to marry. This, however, was granted, and the wedding took place on 8 November 1497, the same year that Elizabeth Tylney had died. Six children from this second marriage survived, among them the future naval commander Lord William Howard, and Katherine, who would marry Henry Daubeney, Earl of Bridgewater.

When Surrey became the second Duke of Norfolk in 1514, the new duchess took a prominent position at court. She acted as godmother to Princess Mary in 1516, and was by her side when the four-year-old princess entertained visitors from France. Agnes of Norfolk became the most important lady in the queen's household after the king's sister. Her sense of loyalty to her then mistress, Katherine of Aragon, meant that she initially disapproved of Henry's attempts to divorce her. One of the grounds for the divorce was Henry's assertion that Katherine, who had previously been married to his brother, Arthur, had not been a virgin when he married her. Later, however, Agnes testified that she had witnessed the newly-wed Katherine and Arthur being put to bed together on their wedding night,[3] and her statement was taken to support the king's case. The duchess's co-operation in the king's 'Great Matter', her exalted social rank and the fact that she was step-grandmother to the new queen, Anne Boleyn, ensured that she would retain her place at court.

As the ceremonies for Anne Boleyn's coronation began, Agnes was among the ladies who took part in the procession from the Tower to Westminster. The following day, she was one of the new queen's supporters during the lengthy coronation service. Later, Agnes would be called upon once more to act as godmother to another royal child when she carried Princess Elizabeth to her christening.

Family business as well as court duties required the duchess to move frequently between her two main residences at Chesworth

Park near Horsham in Sussex, and Norfolk House at Lambeth. It was to the former of these houses that Katherine went to live at the age of six.

Chesworth Park was an almost entirely self-sufficient working farm nestling in beautiful countryside in the heart of the Weald. The manor house dated back to at least the early fourteenth century,[4] and was set in 223 acres of land, which included part of St Leonard's Forest. Surrounded by a moat, the southern arm of which was formed by the River Arun, the house was accessed from the north side, a drawbridge leading through a gatehouse and into the two courtyards beyond. The manor itself was entered through a doorway set into the east wall on the first floor, suggesting that it gave access to a gallery within.

The large timber-framed range was two storeys high and built in the early Tudor style. It comprised a hall, a great chamber, a dining chamber, a chapel and at least twenty other rooms and service buildings. Earthworks to the south-east of the moat could have been the remains of medieval fish ponds. Sadly, by the time Katherine went to live there, the manor had already passed its best and was beginning to show signs of neglect. Over time some buildings were demolished while others, more modern and sturdy, rose in their place.

At Chesworth, according to one account, the young Katherine encountered a life of rigid austerity presided over by the dowager duchess, who dressed in the severe 'nun-like costume of the preceding reign, wearing a hair shirt and playing the lady abbess to a houseful of women and young girls, mostly of mean birth'. She was said to have been 'almost a fanatic in religion', and that she 'sternly closed her doors in the face of the naughty world'.[5] While Agnes was strict when it came to matters such as maintaining good order, this description does not do her justice. She was, in fact, one of the highest-ranking women in England, while her dower rights and thriftiness ensured that she was also one of the richest.

Agnes needed, and could afford, a full complement of household staff. Almost all of them would become embroiled in Katherine's fall some years later. Among them were Edward Waldegrave, a Suffolk man of about twenty years of age, who served as a gentleman-in-waiting, and Roger Cotes, her tailor. Also on her staff were John Benet, Anthony Restwold, Andrew Maunsay, Robert Damport and the elderly William Ashby.

The women and girls of Agnes's household were anything but of mean birth. Several, like Katherine, were related to the duchess, and at least some of Katherine's full and half-siblings had spent time in the duchess's household. Katherine and Malyn Tylney, being related to Duchess Agnes (Malyn was married to Agnes's brother Philip),[6] were Katherine's cousins by affiliation. Anne, the future wife of Katherine's brother Henry, lived in the household at the same time as Katherine.[7]

Other women, although not related to Katherine, were of gentle birth, such as Joan Bulmer, Alice Wilkes, Dorothy Baskerville and Margaret Benet, and would all play a large part in Katherine's life. Many of them were older than Katherine, and much more experienced in the ways of the world.

Katherine was lodged with the other servants in the maidens' chamber, a large dormitory where all the girls and women of the household slept under the supervision of Mother Emet.[8] As was common practice at the time, they usually slept two to a bed, Katherine most often sharing either with Joan Bulmer or Katherine Tylney. As with the ladies, the gentlemen servants shared a dormitory. This was situated in another part of the house and, in theory at least, the two sexes were kept apart. Each night the door to the maidens' chamber was locked, as was presumably that of the gentlemen too. After lock-up, the keys were taken to Duchess Agnes for safekeeping until morning.

The relationship that existed between Katherine and the duchess was simply that of a lady undertaking an obligation towards a younger relative, and was characterised by duty rather than affection.[9] Agnes fed her step-granddaughter, disciplined her when necessary and gave her changes of apparel when the seasons or special occasion dictated, but she had little to do with her beyond that. This was understandable, given the circumstances: Katherine was merely one of many young people to be sent to live at Agnes's home. As a widow, Agnes, by now quite elderly, was busy running a household, managing her estates and a large complement of servants with little practical help.

As with so many others, Katherine was living with the duchess primarily to receive an education, although at a younger age than usual. It was customary for young people of Katherine's status to be sent away from home for schooling and to learn the skills that would allow them to function effectively in their place in society. One famous example of this practice was Katherine's own cousin, Anne Boleyn, who, at the age of twelve or so, was sent to live with Margaret, Archduchess of Austria in the Low Countries. Anne went on to serve at the court in France, where her already considerable accomplishments were further refined.

Katherine learned to read, mainly books of piety, such as saints' lives. She was also exposed to literature that offered guidance; Cato's verses and *Aesop's Fables* were established favourites, both of which had been handily collected by Erasmus. She was taught to write, her letters and words formed by copying from an exemplar; and at least some level of mathematics was necessary if Katherine were to keep track of household accounts.

Other lessons focused on rhetoric, the use of elegant and ornate language, spoken or written with a view to persuasion. To judge by the one surviving example of her handwriting, Katherine was not taught rhetoric to any great degree, or else she did not excel in it. As for social graces, she received lessons in decorum and the art of acting within the bounds of propriety as deemed appropriate to her station, avoiding any improper or offensive behaviour. Katherine would also learn embroidery and tapestry, both suitable skills for a young girl. Since it was considered a wifely duty to make her husband's shirts, she learned blackwork, the embellishment of the neckbands and cuffs of shirts and shifts with black silk.

Katherine received religious instruction, learning by heart the Ten Commandments, the Apostles' Creed and the Lord's Prayer. An important textbook was the Book of Ecclesiasticus, which taught Katherine her place in the world and her position in God's hierarchy: 'All wisdom comes from the Lord, and is with him forever' (1.1) was one lesson this book had to offer. Another was that fathers were all-important: 'The Lord has given the father honour over the children, and hath confirmed authority of the mother over the sons' (3.2). However, Katherine's mother was dead, and her father was living far away with a new wife; she must look to her step-grandmother for the guidance and love she should have received from her parents. Ecclesiasticus also taught her that 'nothing doth countervail a faithful friend' (6.15); and that she would do well to 'open not thine heart to every man, lest he requite thee with a shrewd turn' (8.19). Another lesson was to 'keep thee far from the man that hath power to kill thee' (9.13), a maxim she could never have dreamed would apply to her.

Katherine was expected to marry and to run a great house one day, so she had to be skilled in all the arts of household management. These involved learning to clean, look after livestock, provide clothing for her children, organise meals for her family, preserve whatever foodstuffs her household could produce and arrange for the purchase of those that it could not.

Lessons included cooking, baking and brewing small beer. She would learn to diagnose minor ailments, and formulate and administer medicines. In this respect, she had no better teacher than the Duchess Agnes herself. Like many ladies of her station, Duchess Agnes was knowledgeable about herbs, and had offered advice to her stepson, the Duke of Norfolk, and to Cardinal Wolsey when the sweating sickness broke out in 1528.[10]

Even if Katherine would never personally practise any of the skills she learned from her step-grandmother, she had to be familiar with them so that she could organise her servants and issue appropriate orders. It was understood that, in order to be served, one had to learn to serve, and this was the price for Katherine's education. She attended the Duchess Agnes in whatever capacity the lady saw fit. In this, Katherine's education prepared her for a position that would allow her to take the first steps towards a useful and fulfilled future: service at court.

3

Flattering and Fair Persuasions

~

A T THE DAWNING of the year 1536, the Howards had much
to look forward to. Queen Anne Boleyn was pregnant with
what everyone believed would be a boy. A new Prince of Wales
would secure the succession and preserve the Tudors on the throne
for another generation. The prince would, of course, also be a
Howard: the great-nephew of the third Duke of Norfolk and first
cousin once removed to Katherine.

The first major event in a year that was to be replete with
turning points was greeted with sadness by some and with much
rejoicing by others, particularly Queen Anne. On 7 January
Katherine of Aragon died at Kimbolton, having endured five years
of exile. Separated from the court and forbidden to see her daughter,
the former queen's lonely death ended a life marked by unhappiness and grief.

Events moved on quickly. On 24 January Henry, taking once
more to the tilt-yard, fell from his horse. Dr Pedro Ortiz reported
that the king 'had been two hours unconscious without
speech'.[1] The imperial ambassador Eustache Chapuys, on the other
hand, thought that Henry's accident was not so serious; according
to him, the king, 'being mounted on a great horse to run at the
lists, both fell so heavily that every one thought it a miracle he
was not killed, but he sustained no injury'.[2] Chapuys, however, was
often fed misleading information.

Henry survived his accident seemingly unscathed, but the next
event to excite the court did not end so happily. On 29 January,
the same day that Katherine of Aragon was laid to rest, Anne Boleyn

suffered a miscarriage. The foetus, reported Chapuys, 'seemed to be a male child which she had not borne 3½ months'.[3] Anne wanted to blame the disaster on her uncle, the Duke of Norfolk, who had frightened her when he gave her the news of the king's accident five days earlier. Anne and her uncle had fallen out seriously in 1533–4, with the final breach occurring a year or so later. Now, in this moment of crisis, the abrupt manner he used with her had done nothing to console the anxious queen.[4] Elsewhere, however, the miscarriage was attributed to shock over the news of the king's accident, rather than the way Anne had been informed of it. Added to this was Anne's discovery that Henry was in love with another woman, and this had broken her heart.[5]

For his part, the king was greatly distressed at the loss of his unborn son.[6] Upon visiting the queen, Henry observed heartlessly, 'I see that God will not give me male children'; as he left her chamber, he added, 'When you are up I will come and speak to you.'[7] George Wyatt, writing much later, but taking his information from Anne's ladies and other witnesses, said that Henry had told Anne 'he would have no more boys by *her*'.[8] The full significance of these ominous words would not fully be understood until May and the terrible events that would devastate the court.

While all this was going on at court, Katherine reached one of life's landmarks. Now in her twelfth year, she would soon be old enough to serve as maiden of honour to Queen Anne.[9] Such a position would provide a wonderful opportunity, for the court functioned as a kind of finishing school and marriage market. Katherine could expect to lead an exciting and glamorous life there, her days filled with dancing, music and singing. The court of Henry VIII was renowned for its pageants, such as the famous Château Vert, in which Queen Anne Boleyn had made her stunning debut.

Anne was renowned for dressing well, and her ladies were expected to follow her example. They wore beautiful, colourful clothes, such as the sumptuous crimson damask worn by Anne Bassett, or the lovely taffeta promised to Katherine Bassett.[10] Anne Boleyn had taken the game of courtly love to new heights, turning it into a refined art. Katherine would certainly be a bright ornament in the queen's court, surrounded by courtiers eager to flatter the pretty niece of the Duke of Norfolk.

There was, however, a serious side to court life. Although Queen Anne loved all the court entertainments, she also demanded that her ladies were well behaved and conformed to her exacting standards of propriety. Katherine's education in decorum would be of enormous value in this regard, and she would lead a chaste and virtuous life under her cousin's moral guidance. She would still be allowed to enjoy all the attractions life at court had to offer, but in strictly controlled conditions; her mistress would ensure that her silk-clad feet remained firmly on the ground.

Maidens were required to earn their keep, and their duties included embroidering shirts for the poor and assisting the queen as she fulfilled her various obligations, political, religious and ceremonial. Maidens were expected to be on hand to do anything the queen asked of them. None of this would have daunted Katherine since her tuition under Duchess Agnes's care was intended, in part, to prepare her for just such a life.

There was one possible area of contention, though, and it had to do with Queen Anne's very real concern about the spiritual welfare of her ladies. Anne kept an English Bible in her rooms, and she openly encouraged her ladies to read it any time they wished. However, Katherine was a Catholic; for her, the reading and interpretation of the Bible was the province of priests.

Katherine was almost fully prepared for this exciting new life, but she lacked a certain 'polish'. With this in mind, it was decided that she should receive music lessons, learning to play the virginals and perhaps the lute. Queen Anne was an accomplished player on these instruments, as well as the rebec, an early violin, so she would appreciate and encourage her young cousin's talent. That Katherine was given these lessons, which were by no means inexpensive when the cost of instruments, music books and tutors' fees are taken into account, suggests that she was educated above the basic level usually allowed her by historians.

The search began for a tutor, but it was a matter that required great care. As the advice books of the day were keen to point out, bringing strangers into the household could be fraught with danger. Hugh Rhodes of the King's Chapel advised: 'take good heed of any new servant that you take into your house, and how ye put them in authority among your children'. This warning was sound because, as Rhodes warned: 'youth is disposed to take such as they are accustomed in, good or evil. For if the governor be evil, needs must the Child be evil.'[11] It was vital, then, that Katherine's teacher should be a man of good character who lived according to high moral codes; he should be someone she could look up to, learn from and be guided by.

As it turned out, two men were selected to tutor Katherine: Henry Mannock and Mr Barnes. Of Mr Barnes, nothing is known beyond the simple facts that he taught music and was engaged as a music master to Katherine; later evidence would suggest that he befriended Mannock, if they were not friends already. Henry Mannock, however, is much less of a mystery, and this is due primarily to the impact he had on Katherine's life.

Henry Mannock was a younger son of George Mannock of Gifford's Hall, Stoke by Nayland in Suffolk,[12] very close to the Duke of Norfolk's estate at Tendring Hall. Far from being a menial brought into the duchess's household to help out, Mannock was a Howard retainer. How he came to be engaged as Katherine's music teacher is uncertain; that he was known to Norfolk was undoubtedly in his favour; that he was a cousin of Edward Waldegrave,[13] who was already in the duchess's employ, gave him further advantage. Mannock was well connected and, seemingly, honest and trustworthy. There was nothing in his character to indicate that he would behave in anything other than an appropriate manner when in the company of his young pupil. Sadly, his behaviour after he took up his post betrayed the trust his employers placed in him.

Katherine had not advanced very far with her studies when it became obvious to her that her teacher had more than crotchets and quavers on his mind. She found herself being courted by him as he attempted to beguile her with fair and flattering words. One day, out of the blue, he asked her to allow him to touch her secret parts. Katherine, understandably, did not respond favourably to any of this. Her refusal was ignored, however, and Mannock pestered her for some token that she loved him. Again, Katherine refused. She wanted to know what token she should show him, adding: 'I will never be naught with you and able to marry me you be not.'[14]

In using the phrase 'to be naught' in this context, Katherine was telling Mannock that she would never surrender to his attempts to seduce her. Mannock, however, would not be persuaded. He thought Katherine's apparent unwillingness was calculated to enhance his desire. It was accepted belief – held by women and men equally – that women and girls, even those as young as Katherine, were morally weak. Sexually aggressive, they were responsible for leading men astray. Unable to control their licentious nature, not only did they incite sexual intercourse, they drew great pleasure from it as well. Although Katherine continued to refuse his advances, Mannock saw her rebuffs as consent mischievously concealed behind a veil of playing hard to get: when a woman says yes, she means yes; when she says no, she means yes.

For Mannock, Katherine was easy prey, a view that was encouraged by an incident involving Anne Boleyn that had occurred some years previously. While King Henry was still courting Anne, gossip in certain quarters had it that she and her family were far from respectable. The prophetess, Mrs Amadas, rejoiced when the Tower was painted white, 'for she said shortly after my lady Anne should be burned, for she is a harlot; that Master Nores [Henry Norris] was bawd between the King and her; that the King had kept both the mother and the daughter'.[15] Sir George Throckmorton later expressed a similar sentiment, telling the king that 'it is thought ye have meddled both with the mother and the sister', that is, Elizabeth Boleyn and her daughter, Mary. Henry answered, 'Never with the mother,' at which Cromwell, who was standing by, said, 'nor never with the sister either, and therefore put that out of your mind.'[16] Although such gossip was malicious and largely untrue,[17] the supposed easy reputation of the Boleyn women was perhaps extended to their Howard cousins in the opinion of some people, with Katherine, at only eleven years old, being thought tarred with the same brush.

As she reproached Mannock, Katherine mentioned marriage, which suggests that she was naïve enough to think that Mannock would propose to her, or that he had hinted that he would marry her if she let him have his way. She was unaware that such talk was the sort of empty promise that some young men made. For his part, Mannock had persuaded himself that Katherine was as much in love with him as he was with her. As such, he refused to give up on her just yet; thinking she loved him, it could be only a matter of time before she would give in to him. This is exactly what happened. Having secured her promise that she would let him touch her private parts, Mannock sought out a suitable place of assignation.

Even so, it was a very hesitant Katherine who met her ardent lover in the darkness of the chapel chamber one evening. Her reluctance was so obvious that Mannock felt it necessary to ask her if she would keep her promise. Katherine assured him that she would: 'I am content,' she said, 'so as you will desire no more.'[18] In consenting to Mannock's demands, Katherine had entered into a bargain with him whereby, if she let him have his way, he would honour his side of it and stop pestering her. Katherine then gave in to her tutor's 'flattering and fair persuasions' and 'suffered him at sundry times to handle and touch the secret parts of my body', which 'neither became me with honesty to permit nor him to require'.[19]

Here, honesty meant honour. The relationship between Katherine and Mannock was governed by rigid rules of etiquette and hierarchy, underpinned by values of trust and honour. Her comment that complying with his wishes undermined the honesty of them both shows that Katherine was aware of how far those principles had been infringed and how inappropriate his behaviour was. Although she occupied a higher social position than did Mannock, she being the niece of a duke, he was her teacher. Her position was that of a subordinate; notwithstanding her aversion, she was obliged to submit to his authority. This situation was reinforced by two other factors that placed Katherine at a social disadvantage: she was younger than Mannock and she was a woman.

Nevertheless, social conditioning would later impel her, wrongly, to take responsibility for her actions and to qualify her behaviour by pointing out that she was 'but a young girl' at the time. Katherine, despite her relatively lowly position within the household, understood her place on the social scale even if Mannock was happy to ignore it. Mannock, with no such scruples, accepted Katherine's precondition that he should desire no more. Free now to have his way, he 'felt more than was convenient'. He would go on to boast that he knew a privy mark on Katherine's body.[20]

Katherine was seduced by a young man who took advantage of his position of power within the dowager duchess's household. Her need for protection went unrecognised and her protests and pleading to be left alone were ignored. Far from being an adventurous or gallant lover, Mannock, with his clumsy fumbling and the fact that he chose such a young girl as the object of his advances, reveals himself to be every bit as sexually inexperienced as Katherine. Preying on his innocent pupil, rather than a mature woman, was his way of sowing his wild oats while ensuring that his own naïveté would not be noticed.[21]

Pressed against her better judgement into letting Mannock have his way, Katherine had little choice but to allow him to do as he pleased. Then, her condition that he would be content was ignored. Mannock came back for more, continuing to touch her 'sundry times'. His lack of regard for his pupil's welfare led to incaution and, as was inevitable, Duchess Agnes came upon them.

Agnes had taken every measure to ensure that her female and male servants were kept apart, as was common practice in households such as hers. She had appointed a lady, Mother Emet, as mother of the maidens' chamber, to protect her charges and ensure that decorum was observed. As mistress of the house, Agnes expected her orders to be obeyed; it came as a shock to learn that this was not the case.

Katherine had made no mention of her mistreatment to her step-grandmother or to Mother Emet, although they were in a position to do something about it. Katherine knew that, as a girl, she would be judged the guilty party; she may also have been traumatised by her ordeal, fear itself preventing her from seeking help. However, the reality of her situation was that Mannock had obtained her consent, even if coerced; if taken to task, that was his defence. Certainly, he had taken full advantage of the situation and Katherine, as so often in such cases, appeared willing. Whatever she said or did to the contrary was interpreted as 'interior consent'[22] coupled with the teasing pretence of being uninterested.

This, tragically, was also the view of the Duchess Agnes. When she learned about her step-granddaughter's behaviour, she was furious. Notwithstanding the potential damage to the reputation of her house, virginity was one of the greatest assets a lady in Katherine's position could possess. No well-placed family would allow a son to marry someone suspected of easy virtue, and Katherine's chances of making a good marriage were seriously compromised by Mannock's behaviour. In her rage, Agnes dealt Katherine two or three blows and ordered the couple never to be alone together again.[23]

Regardless of when it began, Katherine's mistreatment at the hands of Mannock took place over a significant length of time, meaning that it coincided with one of the most momentous events in the history of the Howard family: the fall of Anne Boleyn.

Anne, like Katherine, was a niece of the Duke of Norfolk. Her mother, Elizabeth Howard, was the sister of Katherine's father, Edmund. Anne was older than Katherine by some twenty-four years: Katherine was only two years old when Anne caught the eye of King Henry, and she was still only eight when Anne became queen. Yet their lives shared a certain symmetry; each woman would follow the same path that would lead them first to the throne and then to the scaffold.

The events that would sweep Anne to her death came suddenly and with frightening speed. As late as April 1536, Henry continued to show every sign that he was committed to the marriage, and was insistent that Charles V should recognise Anne as his lawful wife. On 18 April the king and Anne scored a major diplomatic coup when Charles's ambassador, Chapuys, was manipulated into acknowledging Anne for the first time in his seven years at court. As she and Henry descended from the royal pew, Anne bowed to the ambassador. Court protocol demanded that he should bow to her in response. This amounted to recognition of Anne by Chapuys and, by extension, his master.

Only a few days after this triumph Henry's attitude towards Anne changed dramatically. The process that would lead to Anne's execution began with a casual remark made by one of her ladies-in-waiting, Lady Worcester. She had been accused by her brother, Sir Anthony Browne,[24] of immoral living, with the implication that the baby she was carrying was not her husband's. Lady Worcester sought to diminish her guilt by pointing out that it was as nothing compared to Queen Anne. The story reached Thomas Cromwell who, hesitantly, revealed it to the king.

This was a serious accusation, and Henry ordered Cromwell to investigate. Cromwell, 'authorised and commissioned by the King to prosecute and bring to an end the mistress's trial',[25] opened his enquiries, over which he took 'considerable trouble'. This led him to uncover evidence against Anne that could, if creatively construed, prove that she had committed adultery. In reality, there was nothing to support such a charge, the only testimony having come from the gossip of an indignant woman and the confession of a terrified man, Mark Smeaton, who spoke under torture or the threat of it.

Soon, however, Anne was found to have committed an even more damning crime, that of 'compassing' or plotting the king's death. The evidence for this lay in words she had exchanged at the end of April with Henry Norris, a gentleman of the privy chamber and one of the king's favourites. Anne had asked him why he had not yet married a lady he was courting, Mistress

Shelton, to which he answered that 'he would tarry a time'. Anne teased him, saying that he looked for 'dead men's shoes, for if aught came to the King but good, you would look to have me'.

This conversation was really nothing more than part of the game of courtly love, which Anne played with distinction. However, the fine line between innocent flirtation and something more serious was easily crossed. Anyone wishing to harm Anne could conceivably find grounds in these activities, but Anne's mention of 'dead men's shoes' brought her within reach of the highly flexible Treason Act of 1534: she had imaged the king's death, and that was an act of treason.

The indictment against Anne read:

> Whereas queen Anne has been the wife of Henry VIII. for three years and more, she, despising her marriage, and entertaining malice against the King, and following daily her frail and carnal lust, did falsely and traitorously procure by base conversations and kisses, touchings, gifts, and other infamous incitations, divers of the King's daily and familiar servants to be her adulterers and concubines, so that several of the King's servants yielded to her vile provocations.[26]

The king's servants referred to were Anne's brother George, Viscount Rochford, Henry Norris, Francis Weston, William Brereton and Mark Smeaton. Four of them faced their judges on Friday, 12 May and were found guilty. Anne and her brother were tried three days later, but the verdict had been decided beforehand. Indeed, Anne had laughed when Sir William Kingston told her that even the poorest of His Majesty's subjects had justice,[27] for she knew the truth of it.

On one bloody morning, 17 May 1536, all five men were executed, beheaded by axe in a public ceremony on Tower Hill. Anne's time had not quite come. On the afternoon of the same day, her marriage to King Henry was declared null and void, and her daughter, Elizabeth, declared illegitimate. Thomas Cranmer, Archbishop of Canterbury, drew up the paperwork but offered no justification for the annulment. Chapuys thought it was on the grounds of Henry's prior relationship with Anne's sister, Mary, which brought him and Anne within forbidden degrees of affinity. He also suggested that Norris was the real father of Elizabeth, showing that he, at least, accepted the adultery charge.[28] Elsewhere, it was put forward that sufficient grounds were found in Anne's earlier romance with Henry Percy, heir to the Earl of Northumberland.[29] It was alleged that they had entered into a precontract, and so Anne had never been free to marry Henry,[30] notwithstanding Percy's emphatic denials to the contrary

Although Anne was no longer Henry's wife, she would still die a queen. Her queenship had been conferred on her by an Act of Parliament, and it would require another Act to remove it. No record exists of any such proceeding.

Anne Boleyn accepted the charges against her and refused to speak against her fate. She did, however, find a means to declare her innocence, swearing to it twice on the Sacrament on the peril of her soul's damnation. She went on to make a good death, going to the scaffold free of guilt in the eyes of God, if not the law.

Anne's story demonstrated, as nothing else could, how easy it was to apportion blame to a woman, however innocent. It showed how narrow was the line separating respectability and censure that women were required to walk. That Anne was queen, while Katherine's status was that of an apprentice-cum-servant, might perhaps have been seen as a mitigating factor, but the warning should have been clear all the same. The consequences for the Howards of Anne's fall were serious. The marriage of Henry VIII to his third wife, Jane Seymour, marked the beginning of a relatively lean period for Katherine's family during which they were eclipsed by the new queen's kin. The birth, in October 1537, of Prince Edward, Henry's first legitimate son and heir, raised the Seymour stock still higher. Katherine's behaviour, even though she was the victim, would do nothing to enhance the reputation and position of the Howards had news of it reached the court. No wonder, then, that the Duchess Agnes was angry.

At some point in 1538 Agnes left Chesworth Park for Lambeth. This was part of the normal itinerant life led by those attached to the court, but, unlike on previous occasions, this move had an air of permanence. She took her household with her to Lambeth which, of course, included Katherine. One notable absentee was Henry Mannock. Whether he had finally been dismissed from his post or had resigned of his own accord is not known for certain, but perhaps can be guessed.

The journey to Lambeth took about three days, which meant overnight stops at inns and taverns. The duchess's train followed Stane Street, the Roman road linking Chichester and London, for part of the way, which they would join near Alfoldean. For Katherine, who had become used to life in the country, Lambeth, although still quite rural, must have seemed very new and exciting.

4

'To play the fool'

~

ONCE INSTALLED IN her magnificent mansion on the south bank of the Thames, life continued as usual for the Duchess Agnes. Soon she was consulting Norfolk and her son, Lord William, regarding 'certain peculations' among the farm servants at Chesworth.[1]

Conversely, for Katherine, Lambeth represented the beginning of a new life. Norfolk House, with its beautiful buildings to explore and cultivated green spaces to lose herself in, offered her a wonderful opportunity to put the past behind her and look forward to a better future.

If, however, Katherine hoped that she had escaped the attentions of Henry Mannock, she was to be disappointed. It was soon discovered that he had followed her to Lambeth, finding work in the household of Lord Bayment nearby. The close proximity of the two households meant that Mannock could visit Norfolk House and continue his pursuit of Katherine any time he wished. Even so, he had to exercise caution, primarily because he had outlived his welcome and, in order to facilitate his curious courtship, Mannock recruited Mistress Isabel and Dorothy Barweke to carry tokens of his affection to Katherine.

All the same, such activity could not be kept secret for long, and gossip that Katherine was once again being pursued by Mannock began to circulate. Soon the observant kitchen staff were whispering among themselves of a secret engagement between the two young people. While this appears to have been treated as a source of amusement by most of the servants, others found the situation unacceptable. Alice Wilkes was particularly upset, and she decided to report what was going on to Mary Lascelles.

Mary had joined Duchess Agnes's household fairly recently. She was the daughter of Richard Lascelles and Dorothy, the daughter of Sir Brian Sandford. Originally a Yorkshire family, the Lascelles had settled in Nottinghamshire during the previous century. Two of Mary's brothers, George and John, would rise to prominence in the service of Thomas Cromwell, whose political and religious outlook the two men shared. These views may also have informed the philosophy of their sister.

Mary Lascelles had previously served Lord William Howard but had transferred to Duchess Agnes's service at about the time of her relocation to Lambeth.[2] Here, Mary was employed as a chamberer, her principal task being to clean and maintain the many bedrooms.

Alerted by Alice Wilkes to the situation that was developing between Katherine and Henry Mannock, Mary became concerned. Taking the matter into her own hands, she confronted Mannock to find out exactly what he thought he was up to: 'Man, what mean thou to play the fool in this fashion? Know not thou that if my lady of Norfolk knew of the love betwixt thee and Mistress Howard she will undo thee?'

Of those who knew about the affair, most took it to be only a trivial dalliance that would finish soon enough. It became a problem only when the idea of marriage between Katherine and Mannock was hinted at. Mary warned him of the dire consequences of his actions, pointing out that Katherine was 'of a noble house and if thou should marry her some of her blood would kill thee'.

Even the threat of violence from Katherine's powerful relatives did not deter Mannock. He refused to heed Mary's wise words of caution. His familiarity with Katherine, and the fact that he had already succeeded with her on a number of occasions without being 'undone', filled him with confidence. 'Hold thy peace, woman,' he told Mary. 'I know her well enough for I have had her by the cunt and I know it among a hundred. And she loves me and I love her and she hath said to me that I shall have her maidenhead though it be painful to her, not doubting that I will be good unto her hereafter.'

Katherine's relationship with Henry Mannock is of considerable importance, not least because it took place in the wake of the fall and execution of Queen Anne Boleyn. The charges that would eventually be brought against Katherine are strikingly similar in nature to those faced by Anne. Their origins lay in what took place between Katherine and Henry Mannock at Chesworth Park and Lambeth.

One vital aspect of their relationship was that they had not had sex, a conclusion that is supported by very good evidence. First, neither of them confessed that they had consummated their relationship. Moreover, that Katherine had apparently promised Mannock her maidenhead shows beyond any doubt that she remained a virgin, although Mannock did believe that she would let him have sex with her in the future.

Mary Lascelles then went straight to Katherine, told her what Mannock was saying about her 'and bid her beware'. 'Fie,' was Katherine's angry reply, stating emphatically that she 'cared not for him'. Clearly Mannock, who obviously had a high opinion of himself when it came to matters of romance, had continued to delude himself and had seriously misjudged his standing with Katherine, as he was about to find out.

Katherine took it upon herself to put Mannock in his place once and for all, which was a very brave thing to do, considering she was only thirteen years old at the time. Accompanied by Mary, she went to Lord Bayment's house. Standing before her former tutor, Katherine was merciless and made it perfectly plain that she wanted nothing to do with him. Mannock could only writhe and splutter that he was so 'far in love with her that he wist not what he said'.[3] It is not recorded how Katherine took his answer or how she replied, if at all.

The confrontation at the home of his employer was not the last time Katherine saw Henry Mannock. Despite the duchess's orders that they were never to be alone together again, the following Saturday 'they two alone' were seen walking in the back of the orchard at Norfolk House.[4] What prompted the meeting or under what circumstances it took place are not known. Perhaps Mannock was making one final effort to win Katherine's heart; perhaps Katherine and her would-be suitor had come to an understanding, she having finally persuaded him that she did not appreciate his attentions and had no interest in him. Whatever the reason, this meeting marked the last time they were seen alone together. As far as Katherine, if not Mannock, was concerned, their encounter was firmly in the past.

There were many attractions at Lambeth to catch the attention of the bright young Katherine. The court at Whitehall, so tantalisingly close, must have attracted her like a moth to a flame. Yet the court, so glittering and glamorous, filled as it was with so many fascinating and important people, bowing and fawning and flirting with the king, also had its dark side. It was only two years earlier that the dazzling and alluring Anne Boleyn had been arrested, tried and executed.

There is nothing to suggest that Katherine and Anne, who did, after all, belong to different generations, were close, or even that they knew each other particularly well. Therefore how far Katherine was affected by her cousin's horrific fate, or even how much she knew about the circumstances surrounding it, cannot be said for certain. It can be speculated, but no more, that she would have been aware of the fact of its occurrence and the official, if not the real, reason why it happened.

Similarly, there is nothing to suggest that Katherine thought King Henry had, in fact, murdered Anne or that she was otherwise afraid of him. Under the circumstances, Katherine would have accepted Anne's fate as somehow justified. After all, the sweet and scheming Jane Seymour had married Henry in what can only be described as indecent haste. She would surely not have done so had she thought it a dangerous business to be Henry's wife. In this, Jane showed greater boldness than Mary of Hungary, the regent of the Netherlands. When she was told of the execution of Anne Boleyn and Henry's marriage to Jane Seymour, she wrote:

> I suppose, if one may speak so lightly of such things, that when he is tired of his new wife he will find some occasion to quit himself of her also. Our sex will not be too well satisfied if these practices come into vogue; and, though I have no fancy to expose myself to danger, yet, being a woman, I will pray with the rest that God will have mercy on us.[5]

Although none could have known it at the time, Mary's words were chillingly prescient.

Since then, on 12 October 1537, Jane Seymour had given Henry the legitimate son and heir he so desperately desired. Tragically, the king's happiness came with a high price indeed: Jane, his 'most dear and most entirely beloved wife', died apparently of puerperal fever a mere twelve days after giving birth. 'Divine Providence,' wrote the unhappy Henry to King François, 'has mingled my joy with the bitterness of the death of her who brought me this happiness.' The court followed the king into a protracted mourning from which it would not emerge until February of the following year.

No matter how much Henry grieved for his lost Jane, sooner or later he would have to think about marrying again. Though disinclined to follow the advice of his Council, the king was fully cognisant of the truth of his situation. He had a legitimate son, certainly, but one was not enough. Henry's own elder brother Arthur, Prince of Wales, had died at the age of fifteen, and another brother, Prince Edmund, had died even younger. The future of the Tudor dynasty had rested on Henry's boyish shoulders then, just as now it rested on the delicate Prince Edward. A Duke of York was needed so Henry 'framed his mind, both to be indifferent to the thing and to the election of any person from any part that with deliberation shall be thought meet'.[6]

The quest for a new queen took place against the backdrop of rivalry between the emperor Charles V and King François I. Were the conflict between them to cease, which was by no means improbable, there was a danger that they would join forces and, at the very least, leave England isolated in Europe. Peace in mainland Europe would make way for the Papal Council to urge a Catholic crusade against Henry. Pope Paul III's aggressive policies were a direct threat to England: he had created Reginald Pole, who vehemently opposed Henry's reforms, a cardinal, and had given financial assistance to rebels in the north. In the face of such threats, an alliance with either the French or the imperial party might prove to be England's best protection.

While Henry found himself with several candidates to consider, his personal preference was for a French bride. Accordingly, he contacted his ambassadors in France to see who was available. Marguerite de Valois, the fifteen-year-old daughter of François I, was one suggestion, although she was 'said to be not the meetest'.[7] Then there was Marie, the eldest daughter of Charles de Bourbon, duc de Vendôme, but unfortunately it turned out that she was promised to James V of Scotland, although the marriage never took place.

At that point news arrived of another lady who was considered to be eminently suitable for Henry. This was Christina, the second daughter of the deposed Christian II of Denmark, who possessed many of the attributes Henry favoured in a lady. She was 'very tall . . . of competent beauty, soft of speech, and gentle in countenance',[8] and she resembled Mistress Shelton, the sparkling and vivacious Madge, a cousin of Anne Boleyn,[9] who had captured Henry's heart only a few years before. Henry's interest was piqued, and he thought that he 'might honour the said duchess by marriage, considering the reports of her'.[10] As negotiations began in earnest at Brussels, Hans Holbein the Younger was sent to paint Christina's portrait. When it was presented to him, Henry, charmed by her sweet face and seductive smile, set his heart on her.

Obviously, it was too early to know how the situation with Christina would develop, but such uncertainty did nothing to subdue the atmosphere of excitement that now prevailed. Spring was in the air. The court, shrouded in melancholy since the death of Queen Jane, suddenly burst into life again. In March 1538 Chapuys[11] noticed that Henry 'has been in much better humour than he ever was, making musicians play on their instruments all day along'. He added that the king 'cannot be one single moment without masks'. The ambassador interpreted this as a clear sign that the king 'proposes to marry again'.

Notwithstanding the developments at court, Katherine's immediate future was uncertain. Following the death of Jane Seymour, the queen's household had not been dismissed. Even though he had no wife, Henry so much loved the company of women that he could not bear to let the queen's ladies go. Instead, he lodged the unmarried maidens in the households of the married ladies and frequently brought them to court, where he amused himself by entertaining them in lavish style. He treated them to great banquets,[12] sent them on holiday and on one occasion he arranged for them to travel to Portsmouth, where they viewed the fleet.[13] It was hoped by some that one of the young ladies might catch Henry's eye and become the next queen.[14]

Whether a place could be found for Katherine among these ladies was looking increasingly doubtful. Her hopes of serving at court as maiden of honour had been dashed by the terrible events that had removed Anne Boleyn. Then, the ascendancy of the Seymours over the Howards ensured that she would be overlooked as ladies were chosen for Queen Jane's household. The death of Queen Jane had not diminished the influence of the Seymours; the new prince was, after all, as much a Seymour as he was a Tudor, and the family continued to ride high in the royal favour. By contrast, the situation in which the Howards now found themselves was less than promising. Katherine's uncle of Norfolk had been absent from court for the best part of two years, occupied with the suppression of the Pilgrimage of Grace, the series of uprisings in the north of England against Henry's reforms, and keeping an eye on the Scots troubled by Henry's religious policies. He had returned to court on occasion, once to act as godfather to the new prince,[15] and less than a month later to serve as high marshal at the burial of Queen Jane.[16] He even managed to return to East Anglia to take personal charge of his own affairs for a while. However, the influence of the Howards, to some extent, diminished. As Katherine walked with Henry Mannock in the orchard of Norfolk House, any hopes she might have cherished for a glittering future at court were as fragile as ever they could be.

5

Francis Dereham

~

KATHERINE'S LIFE AT Norfolk House in the spring and early summer of 1538 carried on much as it had done since the day she arrived. Still only thirteen, her routine was ordered by the demands of her step-grandmother; her day would be divided into periods of service, study or enjoyment of the social activities on offer at Norfolk House. What Katherine knew of the affairs that were unfolding across the river at Westminster can only be surmised. Perhaps the Duchess Agnes kept her up to date with the latest piece of gossip; perhaps she heard whisperings in the servants' quarters about the intriguing goings-on at court; or perhaps she was aware of none of it, and lived in untroubled ignorance.

In the matter of the king's latest venture into marriage, Cromwell continued to press for an imperial alliance. His partiality was obvious to the French ambassador, Castillon who, during his visits to the English court, found Cromwell to be 'so proud and ungracious, that I could not help telling the King one day that I did not seem to be before his Council but that of the Emperor'. Cromwell was so opposed to the French negotiations that Henry reprimanded him, telling him that 'he was a good manager, but not fit to inter-meddle in the affairs of kings'.

Shortly after this, the king recalled the Duke of Norfolk 'whom the lord Privy Seal prevented, as much as possible, from coming to Court'. Court politics changed dramatically: Cromwell, Castillon noted, 'is so snubbed and so suspect for the affairs of France' that few asked the ambassador's advice. However, now that Norfolk had returned, things had changed, 'and now most of the Court visit me, which is a good sign.'[1]

Norfolk took the opportunity afforded by his return to court to visit Norfolk House. For Katherine this particular occasion was to have far-reaching consequences. The duke had seen little of his niece since she was a small child; now she stood before him an attractive young woman of thirteen.

The man to whom Katherine was presented was more than fifty years her senior. He was small, lean and of sallow complexion, his clean-shaven face framed by mid-brown hair dressed in the style of a former age. His whole demeanour spoke loudly of his conservatism and his dogged determination to preserve links with the feudal past. His small round eyes hinted at both his intelligence and his rigidity. In his dealings with others, the duke often showed himself to be kindly, approachable and unassuming. He could affect an informal manner, an easy way with people whatever their class or station, although this usually gave way to his characteristic brusqueness. This familiarity, attractive though it was, concealed the true character of the man: for Norfolk was merciless, calculating and ambitious.

For the present, Katherine was the last thing on the duke's mind. He had come to pay his respects to his stepmother, the Duchess Agnes, and he naturally had estate business to discuss with her. The main topic of conversation, however, was the king's marriage.

The duke's prolonged absence from court had denied him any involvement during the first three months of Henry's search for a new queen. By the time he had returned to court, in May 1538, Henry had already despatched Holbein to make portraits of several ladies. Undaunted, Norfolk began to press for an allegiance with France.[2] In the end, however, his efforts were to be undermined by Henry's indiscretion and heavy-handedness.

Initially, Henry had set his heart on Marie de Guise and he refused to accept that she was not available. The ambassador Castillon was unsympathetic; when asked to intervene, he wondered if Henry would 'marry another man's wife'. Henry remained firm. Everything about Marie appealed to Henry: she was tall, alluring and voluptuous, and as the king himself pointed out, 'he was big in person and had need of a big wife'. In the end, however, he had to concede that Marie was lost to him.[3]

Still, Christina of Denmark remained a viable option, at least as far as Henry was concerned. Unfortunately, there were obstacles to this match too. The usual complications associated with dowries and rights of inheritance proved difficult enough,[4] but Henry also wanted Charles to include England in any future peace treaty with France. He saw this as a way to avoid isolation and it would place him in a position to refuse to support the imminent Papal Council.[5] Charles could find no reason to acquiesce to Henry's demands in that respect.[6] Finally, there was the problem of affinity. As Charles's niece, Christina was also the great-niece of the late Queen Katherine of Aragon, meaning that Henry was related to her within forbidden degrees of affinity. All that was required was a special dispensation to allow the marriage to go ahead. Unfortunately, Henry did not recognise the pope's authority to provide one, while Charles refused to recognise Henry's.[7]

Even if such obstacles could be overcome, Christina had her own reservations. Advised by her council, she would accept Henry's proposal only if he accepted 'the bishop of Rome's dispensation and give pledges'. When asked why she wanted pledges, she pointed out that 'the King's Majesty was in so little space rid of the Queens, that she dare not trust his Council, though she durst trust his Majesty; for her Council suspecteth that her great aunt was poisoned, that the second was innocently put to death, and the third lost for lack of keeping in her childbed'.[8]

Henry's marital record was indeed poor, and it proved damaging to the negotiations, but Henry was not prepared to give up just yet. He had been assured that 'France was a warren of honourable ladies' in need of a husband,[9] one of whom was Marie de Guise's sister, who was described as a 'most beautiful creature'.[10] Another of Marie's sisters was Renée, who had entered a religious order but was not yet professed. Henry asked for their portraits, as well as those of three other ladies, Marie de Vendôme and Anne de Lorraine, François's cousins, and Marguerite de Valois, François's daughter.

With so many ladies to consider, Henry thought it a good idea to ask for a company of them to be sent to Calais, so that he might view them. His ambassador, Francis Bryan, tactfully suggested that such a measure would be 'unreasonable'.[11] Castillon proposed that Henry might send some trustworthy person to report on the ladies Henry had in mind, but the king refused. 'By God!' he said. 'I trust no one but myself. The thing touches me too near.' Castillon, in a manner that was only half joking, asked Henry why he 'did not want to mount the ladies one after the other, keeping for himself the one he found the sweetest? Would the Knights of the Round Table have treated ladies in such a manner?' At this Henry laughed even as he blushed.[12]

This exchange reveals much about the qualities Henry required in his brides. Politics was an important consideration, of course; but it was vital to Henry that his wife should be physically attractive. Like his grandfather, Edward IV, what Henry really wanted was a love-match, something usually denied kings.

In the end, Henry's demands were too high. He had insulted the French by requesting the beauty parade at Calais. He expected, unrealistically, French recognition of his title of Supreme Head of the Church in England. Finally, as he had done with Charles, he demanded unreserved support against any papal–imperial accord. It all proved too much and negotiations with France faltered. Henry's regard for François waned, as did the aspirations of the Duke of Norfolk. By the beginning of August Norfolk had left the court and returned to his estate of Kenninghall. However, not all of the duke's retainers returned home with him. Francis Dereham, a gentleman pensioner or man of rank in receipt of a stipend, remained behind to take up a new position in the household of the Duchess Agnes.[13]

The history of the Dereham family is long, though not as

illustrious as that of the Howards. They emerged to prominence during the time of King John, when three brothers, Richard, Nicholas and Elias de Dereham, are named as witnesses to the foundation deed of West Dereham Abbey, begun by Hubert Walter in 1204.[14] The Derehams, for the most part, would continue to live within the area of Crimplesham and West Dereham in Norfolk, and many of their number are buried in the church of St Mary Crimplesham or in St Andrew's, West Dereham.[15]

Francis Dereham was a descendant of Nicholas de Dereham. His maternal grandmother was a daughter of Philip Tylney, one of the Lords of the Close of Lincoln Cathedral.[16] Tylney's third son, Hugh, was the father of the Dowager Duchess Agnes, making Dereham Agnes's first cousin once removed, while Dereham and Katherine Howard were related by affinity, being first cousins twice removed.[17]

Dereham was the second surviving son of John, or Thomas, Dereham of Crimplesham and Isabel, the daughter of John Paynell of Boothby, Lincolnshire.[18] He was born between 1506 and 1509,[19] making him anywhere between twenty-nine and thirty-two years old when Katherine met him in 1538.

Dereham was of good, though not noble, birth. As a younger son, he would not inherit, but he did own some lands in Norfolk that provided him with an income. Like many gentlemen in his position, however, his best hope of advancement lay in service. Dereham's connections with the Duke of Norfolk, through Duchess Agnes, made it fitting that he should join his household. His closer association with the Dowager Duchess Agnes suited him for service with her also, and so he moved to Lambeth to become the new gentleman usher.[20] This placed him in a position of authority over many of the servants who worked above stairs or in the presence of the mistress.[21]

As Katherine went about her usual duties at Norfolk House, she found herself subject to the orders and supervision of Master Dereham. It was his job to ensure that protocol was respected at all times and if further training was required in correct procedure or etiquette, Dereham would be the one to provide it. If Katherine

were required to serve at mealtimes, it would be Dereham's responsibility to ensure that she carried out her tasks promptly and correctly.
Katherine would even be under Dereham's watchful eye in the
ewery as she washed her hands in preparation for the duties that
lay before her.

Katherine's day was rigidly set out: from nine until eleven in
the morning, she and the other ladies would attend the duchess
in the great chamber and then accompany her to chapel. After
dinner, which was served between one and three, they would
return to the great chamber. Then, as long as there were no gentlewomen visitors to be entertained, Katherine might depart to amuse
herself until five o'clock when she would be called for supper. At
each of these times throughout the day, Dereham would give notice
to Katherine and the other gentlewomen of when and where they
were to attend the duchess. Evenings were spent in the great
chamber for as long as the duchess was present. Dereham's duties
required his attendance here too, since one of his functions was to
mingle with the guests and assist with the entertainments; he was
not allowed to leave the chamber unless asked to do so.

Dereham, therefore, was in regular contact with the female servants as well as his mistress's gentlewomen. Katherine would find
herself in his presence for much of her day, either as she went
about her own duties, or when she was called upon to join her step-
grandmother for prayers, meals, entertaining, or simply to enjoy her
company.

As he eased into life at Norfolk House, Dereham became friends
with another male servant, Edward Waldegrave.[22] That Waldegrave's
family was related to the Mannocks lends a peculiar symmetry to
the events that were about to unfold, giving an erroneous impression of co-ordination and co-operation among the gentlemen of
the household.

Dereham's position and duties necessarily allowed him a certain
level of access to the maidens' chamber. This was a suite of rooms,
including a sitting room and a dormitory, in which the ladies of
the household would pass some of their spare time. Here they

engaged in various activities for their own amusement, such as reading, playing music or practising their needlework, and it was also where they slept. The routine at Norfolk House was much the same as at Chesworth Park: the gentlewomen usually slept two to a bed, and at night, the doors to the gentlewomen's chamber were locked and the keys taken to the Duchess Agnes, who would keep them in her own chamber until morning. The same procedures naturally applied to the gentlemen's chamber; in each of the duchess's houses, female and male servants were kept apart after hours, the younger girls being watched over by Mother Emet. Notwithstanding such precautions, Dereham and other gentlemen found a way to enter the maidens' chamber during the night and entertain the ladies.

In the beginning, Dereham paid court to Joan Bulmer, then separated from her husband William,[23] while Edward Waldegrave's sweetheart was Dorothy Baskerville.[24] They would banquet, with Dereham bringing 'wine, strawberries, apples, and other things to make good cheer' after the Duchess Agnes had gone to bed.[25] One of his duties was to check the leftovers after meals and send anything that could be served again to cold storage. He would then oversee the distribution of whatever remained to the servants according to their food allowance. Dereham was also entitled to his share, and at least some of it went to make the 'good cheer' spoken of by Katherine. Once inside the maidens' chamber, he devised an escape plan: should the duchess suddenly come in and surprise them, he would 'go into the little gallery'.

Soon, however, Dereham lost interest in Joan. Possibly he stepped aside because he saw that Waldegrave had become attracted to her. More probably, Joan's appeal withered in the face of a more desirable match, for now Dereham turned his attention to Katherine Howard. She, however, had no interest in Dereham. She was put off by his behaviour, which she found mischievous and ignorant. She disliked the way he would come into the gentlewomen's chamber early in the morning, where he 'ordered him very lewdly', though never at Katherine's 'request, nor consent'.[26]

Dereham, however, was not to be denied and, like Mannock before him, he resolved to win Katherine over 'by many persuasions'.[27] Katherine's resistance fell upon deaf ears, just as it had with Mannock. Her relatively lowly position, both in the household and in society, allowed Dereham the power and the freedom to silence whatever protests she made. Dereham pestered her as relentlessly as Mannock had done, and he would not be content with bashful groping in the chapel. He forced himself upon Katherine, making her his mistress, with all that the word implied.

As before, Katherine had nobody to turn to. The Duchess Agnes was too busy and distant, not to mention too elderly, to keep a close watch on her charges. That task she had delegated to Mother Emet; but she was of little use, outranked as she was by Dereham. Katherine simply had to endure and, as is so often the case with those who are mistreated and exploited, she accepted that Dereham's behaviour towards her, though unwelcome, was in some way normal.[28]

Dereham was anything but discreet and soon the affair was well known to others in the household. Although he would sometimes lie with Katherine in bed with the curtains drawn,[29] his lovemaking, more often than not, took place in public view. Malyn Tylney saw him lying on the bed next to Katherine while still wearing his jerkin, adding that he would 'put his hand often times to the queen's privy place'.[30] One of Katherine's bedfellows, Katherine Tylney, recalled him lying 'upon the bed in his doublet and hose'. As the night wore on, and Dereham's passion increased, it all became too much for Mistress Tylney, who begged, 'I pray you Mr Dereham lie still.' There was so much 'huffing and blowing' that Dereham's antics became a joke: 'hark at Dereham, broken winded'.[31] Joan Bulmer spoke of Dereham visiting Katherine 'between four or five of the clock in the morning, anytime putting his hand in the bed'.[32]

What was a source of amusement for her companions was not so for Katherine. Not only did she have to put up with night-time visits; Dereham would also seek her company during the day. Joan

Bulmer sometimes caught them in Katherine's bed 'in the afternoon and evening'. Andrew Maunsay also saw them on Katherine's bed, although Dereham was still fully dressed at the time.[33] Robert Damport, a friend and confidant of Dereham's, also saw 'Dereham and Katherine Howard kiss often and lie together upon the bed'. This took place in 'the duchess's bedchamber openly in the sight of diverse people many times'.[34] Another time, Margaret Benet caught the two of them together on Katherine's bed when she 'looked out at a hole of a door and there saw Dereham pluck up [Katherine's] clothes above her navel so that she [Benet] might well discern her body'.[35]

Occasionally, Dereham took to using beds other than Katherine's. Clearly, he had taken to heart Katherine Tylney's plea for a peaceful night. One maiden told Joan Bulmer that she had found them 'in the night in the duchess's gallery alone without any light'.[36] Margaret Benet saw them 'alone at a bedside called Mother Emet's bed'. Benet also mentioned the jakes, or the privy, saying that Dereham would follow Katherine inside and, on at least one occasion, he 'put his private in her hands suddenly'.[37]

Dereham confided to Damport that Katherine 'was sick of the green sickness'. This condition was believed to be connected with the onset of menstruation and had strange effects on young women: 'the flow of blood, which no longer serves for the increase of their bodies, does by its abounding stir up their minds to venery.' As a result, the affected woman would develop strange tastes and abnormal appetites. 'Never did Green-sickness'd Girl long with half so much earnestness for Chalk or Oatmeal,' observed one writer on the subject.[38] More dangerously, the condition brought with it a marked increase in sexual appetite. For virgins, the consequences were particularly serious, for this increased desire could 'bring an indelible stain on their families'. The 'strong inclination' of the young women was easily recognised by 'their eager gazing at men, and affecting their company, which sufficiently demonstrates that nature excites them to desire coition'. The only cure was marriage, where 'those desires satisfied by their husbands, those distempers vanish'.[39] Katherine, of course, was unmarried, but Dereham saw the signs of her affliction and stepped in to effect the cure.

The ever vigilant Margaret Benet overheard Dereham telling Katherine that, 'although he used the company of a woman C [100] times yet he would get no child except he listed [wished to]'.[40] This is an ambiguous statement. It could be that Dereham was referring to contraception, several forms of which were available to men. For instance, a tisane of woodbine leaves taken for thirty-seven days would 'so dryeth up the natural seed of a man, that he shall get no more children'.[41] Alternatively, a man might eat rue with 'a certain spice', or drink teas of dill and hemp. Other herbs, such as nenuphar, a species of water lily, protected a man against 'Venus and fleshly lusts', and therefore would not suit Dereham's purpose. Another method was to have sex in the position considered best for the prevention of conception. However, the most effective method was coitus interruptus, a technique popular among monastics, who took their inspiration from the story of Onan.[42]

Following Dereham's lead, Katherine replied that, 'a woman might meddle with a man and yet conceive no child unless she would for herself,' that is, unless she wished to.[43] Like Dereham, Katherine might have been speaking of contraception. Several methods were available to her if she had the means to procure them. Sponges and tampons had been known at least as long ago as Chaucer's time.[44] Astringent solutions were also used, although they were better known in France than elsewhere in Europe. Herbal preparations included rue, willow and sallow, all of which were 'fruitless' trees thought to correspond to barrenness in women.

On the other hand, Katherine could have been referring to the widely held belief that it was necessary for a woman to enjoy sex in order to conceive.[45] If this was the case, her remark speaks volumes of her feelings for Dereham. At the same time, if Dereham was alluding to this belief, it suggests that his practice was to make sex disagreeable for his partner so that she would not conceive. In that event, Katherine's sexual encounters with Dereham would have been very far from pleasant.

Soon, knowledge of the affair began to spread beyond the confines of Norfolk House. Katherine's uncle, Lord William, thinking the ladies were arguing over Dereham, simply said, 'What mad wenches! Can you not be merry amongst yourselves but you must thus fall out?'[46] He could not understand what all the fuss was about and urged the ladies to stop squabbling and learn to live in harmony together. Lady Bridgewater, Katherine's aunt, was more concerned about how all this 'banqueting by night' might damage Katherine's looks and warned her that 'if she used that sort it would hurt her beauty'.[47] In fact, the banqueting was not confined to the night hours. Katherine and her companions 'would go abroad half a mile from her house having a good company with her', although whether or not Dereham was one of the party is not known.

Such nonchalance was the result of misunderstanding the true nature of the relationship. Thinking it a meaningless dalliance that would soon pass, none of the senior members of the household paid it the attention it deserved. Indeed, of all the people who could have helped Katherine, only one person showed any concern. Alice Wilkes confided once again in Mary Lascelles, thinking the older woman might be able to offer some assistance. However Mary had witnessed similar behaviour in Katherine before, with Henry Mannock. Although Mary had been willing to help her then, Katherine had apparently not learned any lessons from the experience. Now, as she listened to tales of Katherine and Dereham, Mary, who shared the prevailing belief that women were at fault whenever sexual misadventures occurred, was unable to see Katherine as the victim of sexual assault. She had already drawn the conclusion that Katherine was 'light both in living and conditions', that is, wanton or unchaste,[48] and she dismissed Alice's worries, telling her not to concern herself with Katherine.[49]

What Mary did not know, or perhaps she no longer cared, was that Dereham had taken his relationship with Katherine beyond midnight feasts and sexual escapades. They had begun to address each other as husband and wife.[50] According to Katherine, it all came about because of gossip among the servants that the two of them would marry. Dereham claimed that some of his enemies were jealous of this, so he asked Katherine if they could call each other husband and wife, and Katherine agreed.[51]

The reasons for Katherine's compliance are difficult to fathom. Perhaps she was simply doing Dereham a favour, granting him the means to protect himself from his enemies, who could only have been Henry Mannock and his fellow music tutor, Mr Barnes. On the other hand, it is just possible that she thought Dereham was indicating his intent to marry her; but here, she would have known that the decision was not hers to make: her father was still alive at this point, though absent, and it was his prerogative and duty to select a suitable husband for Katherine. The most obvious explanation is that Katherine complied because she felt she had no choice; what Dereham commanded, Katherine granted.

To all appearances, Katherine had consented freely to this change in her relationship with Dereham; yet it is certain that she did not fully understand the implications of what she had done. What was worse, although the situation was known to others in the household, no attempt was made to question the validity of the consent granted by a thirteen-year-old girl to a man more than twice her age. With no one to turn to, Katherine had no guidance whatsoever in a matter that was of the utmost importance. In a society where chastity and virginity were a woman's greatest, and most marketable, assets, Katherine's liaison with Dereham diminished her immensely.

Even this was of little consequence now. By using such terms of address to each other, Katherine and Dereham had entered into a contract of marriage *per verba de futuro*, or a betrothal. However, since they addressed each other as husband and wife publicly and their union had clearly been consummated, it took on the legal quality of a *de praesenti* contract.[52] In other words, whether she was aware of it or not, whether she wished it or not, Katherine was, in the eyes of the law, Francis Dereham's wife.

While the Duchess Agnes was unaware of how far things had gone between her young step-granddaughter and Dereham, she had long believed him to be guilty of dissolute behaviour. When asked where he might be, she would reply, 'I am sure he is sleeping in the gentlewomen's chamber.' When she sent someone to prove it, 'he was found upon one bed or another'.[53] Eventually, she began to suspect that Dereham had turned his attention entirely to Katherine. Worried, she confided in one of her servants, William Ashby, that she 'mistrusted there was love' between Katherine and Dereham.[54] Ashby told her not to worry, saying that he saw 'no such cause'. The aloof Agnes, who seldom had contact with her servants unless they were actually serving her, was reassured by this.

Dereham told Katherine about a little woman in London with a crooked back who was very cunning (skilled) in making flowers. Katherine asked him to see if the woman would make a French fennel for her, saying she that would pay him for it when she had the money.[55] Even so, she was afraid to wear the flower until she could persuade Lady Brereton to say that she had given it to Katherine. The reason for this pretence is not clear. Perhaps Katherine thought the flower would be misinterpreted as a gift from Dereham; since gifts were part of courtship ritual, more would be read into it than Katherine felt it deserved. On the other hand, she might have been afraid of being seen to spend more money than she could afford.

Money borrowed from Dereham allowed Katherine to buy velvet and satin for billyments, or ornaments to adorn a French hood. Clearly, Katherine had acquired a taste for the fashions brought to England by Mary Tudor and Anne Boleyn. Katherine also bought a cap of velvet with a feather and material to make a quilted cap of sarcenet. She gave the material to an embroiderer at Norfolk House called Rose, who made up the cap as he thought best. Rose designed it with friar's knots, at which Dereham said, 'What Wife here be Freer's [Friar's] Knots for Fraunce.' A design that had served as a tribute to the King of France Dereham now claimed for his own.[56] Each time she borrowed money from Dereham, Katherine promised to pay him back once she went to court, although he thought of it as a gift.

The affair carried on through the autumn and winter of 1538 and into the New Year. When the New Year came, Katherine gave Dereham 'a Band and Sleeves for a Shirt', while he gave her a 'Heart's-Ease of Silk for a New Year's-Gift and an Old Shirt of Fine Holland or Cambric'. The shirt had belonged to Lord Thomas Howard until the Duchess Agnes gave it to Dereham.[57] Naturally, everyone in the household exchanged gifts, so nothing of great import should be read into this.

It soon became apparent, though, that Katherine and Dereham were under close surveillance. The rejected Henry Mannock, last seen walking with Katherine in the orchard, was watching the developing affair between her and Dereham with great interest. He approached Mr Ashby and told him what was going on.[58] Dissatisfied with Ashby's lack of response, he collaborated with his colleague, Mr Barnes, to write an anonymous letter to the duchess:

> Your Grace,
> It shall be meet you take good heed to your gentlewomen for if it shall like you half an hour after you shall be a bed to rise suddenly and visit their chamber you shall see that which shall displease you. But if you make any body of counsel you shall be deceived. Make them fewer your secretary.[59]

Mannock left the letter in the duchess's pew at Lambeth Church and retreated to witness the tempest that would surely follow.

Mannock's motives are obscure. Dereham had thought Mannock was jealous of his relationship with Katherine, but given that Mannock had recently married, this explanation seems improbable. Perhaps Dereham had somehow offended him and Mannock was having his revenge; most probably, however, it was nothing more than mischief on Mannock's part. Whatever the case, the letter did not produce the desired effect. Instead, the outcome of his scheme had more of the quality of a French farce than an English sex-scandal. Assuming the duchess would know the identity of the parties involved, Mannock and Barnes had neglected to name them. Unfortunately for Mannock, Agnes had taken the letter as a warning to her to take heed of a relationship between one of her servants, Hastings, and an unnamed partner.[60] Clearly she was aware that some unsavoury activity was going on in her home, but she did not associate it with Katherine and Dereham. Even so, she took the letter as notice that Mother Emet was neglecting her duties and that it was time to show her authority. She 'stormed with her women', letting them know how she had learned of 'their misrule'.

If Duchess Agnes did not know who Mannock was trying to expose, Katherine certainly did. She stole the letter from the gilt coffer into which the duchess had placed it and showed it to Dereham.[61] He copied out the letter, 'and thereupon it was laid in the coffer again'. Dereham immediately suspected that Mannock was behind it and confronted him. A fight broke out, Dereham calling Mannock a knave and saying that Mannock loved neither Katherine nor himself.[62] More dangerously, Katherine's uncle, Lord William, found out about the letter and launched a campaign of harassment against Mannock and his wife, threatening and railing on them 'at their own front door'.[63] Lord William would continue to threaten the couple until his departure for France in January 1541.

Agnes's response was more practical. She watched her servants more closely, and on one occasion she found Dereham embracing Katherine and kissing her. The old lady was so offended that she struck Dereham, beat Katherine and then cuffed Joan Bulmer simply because she happened to be there. Katherine Tylney and Alice Wilkes, who were also present, were presumably out of reach, for they escaped a thumping.[64]

Clearly, the duchess held them all responsible, not just Katherine. Dereham at least had the grace to admit that Agnes blamed himself and Katherine for 'keeping company together, saying he would never be out of Katherine Howard's chamber'.[65] Now, whenever anyone wanted to know Dereham's whereabouts, the duchess would tell them, 'I warrant you if you seek him in Katherine Howard's chamber ye shall find him there.'[66] Her words convey a reluctant resignation as well as anger for the dishonour the couple's behaviour would bring upon her and her house if news of it were ever to spread beyond Norfolk House.

In sending the letter to the Duchess Agnes, Mannock had inadvertently done Katherine a service, for it gave her the means to hold Dereham at bay. That the duchess caught Katherine with Dereham proved a blessing in disguise for, shortly afterwards, the affair came to an end, at least as far as Katherine was concerned. It had lasted only some three months during the autumn and winter of 1538–9, ending just after the Christmas and New Year period.

Despite their addressing each other as husband and wife in the hearing of several members of the household, and having consummated their relationship, Katherine always refused to accept that she was Dereham's wife. Her denial stemmed from the circumstance that Dereham had coerced her throughout and she had not given herself to him freely. Since consent was necessary for a marriage to be valid, Katherine's denial created a grey area that only ecclesiastical law could resolve. Lacking any such resolution, Katherine understood herself to be free to marry elsewhere.

As it was, Katherine and Dereham continued to live and work side by side at Norfolk House, and the tense atmosphere resulting from such close proximity can only be imagined. However, the time when they would both leave Lambeth was fast approaching; when it came, they would go their separate ways for very different reasons.

6

A Lady in Waiting

~

I N THE SUMMER of 1539 a delightful public spectacle was held
on the Thames at Westminster. Described as a great 'triumph', the
colourful water pageant offered Katherine a foretaste of the excite-
ments that court life had to offer; for, even if she had not been
invited, the pageant was clearly visible from across the river at
Norfolk House.

Two barges had been kitted out as though for war, one the
'pope's' barge, the other the king's. Rowing up and down the river,
all guns blazing, they ran three courses against each other in mock
battle. On the fourth course, close combat ensued during which
the king's men overthrew the pope and the cardinals, casting them
unceremoniously into the Thames, which, Wriothesley thought,
'was a goodly pastime'. The king and some of the ladies looked
on from their standpoint on the privy stairs. The whole area was
decorated with canvas set with green boughs and roses so that rose
water sprinkled on to those below and into the river; here, the
ladies and gentlemen who had taken to barges to watch the triumph
were drizzled with the perfumed drops. Two further barges rowed
up and down bearing banners and pennants of the arms of England
and St George and carrying musicians who played on the water.[1]

Yet Henry had other things on his mind than amusements and
entertainment. The once promising list of candidates for his new
wife and queen had gradually reduced until only one viable propos-
ition remained: Anne of Cleves. Her name had been mentioned
as early as December 1537 by Sir John Hutton, who noted that
the 'duke of Cleves has a daughter, but I hear no great praise

neither of her personage nor her beauty'.[2] This less than glowing assessment ensured Anne would be overlooked as the search got under way in earnest.

Now with the failure of talks with the Emperor Charles on one side and François of France on the other, and the rapprochement between those two powers now finalised, it was necessary to look elsewhere. It was time to consider the duchy of Cleves once again.

In fact, the strategic and political importance of Cleves had been acknowledged for some time. In May 1530 Herman Rinck, merchant of the London Steelyard, suggested that Henry could 'strengthen himself by a matrimonial alliance with some prince of these parts in case of war with France, Spain, or Burgundy' and the Duke of Cleves was put forward.[3]

Now, eight years later, an alliance with Cleves remained highly desirable for several reasons besides those pointed out by Rinck. The court of Cleves was not Lutheran, nor did it cling to the old, established Catholic ways. Rather, its religious outlook, similar to Henry's own, was influenced by Erasmus. John, Duke of Cleves, was not beholden to Charles, nor was he overshadowed by him. Finally, and of equal importance, the duke had two unmarried daughters from whom Henry could make his choice.

The elder of these daughters was Anne, who was born on 22 September 1515, the second daughter of John of Cleves and his wife Mary, the only daughter of Duke William of Jülich and Berg. In 1527 Anne's elder sister Sybilla was married to Johann Frederik, the Duke of Saxony, whose position as one of the leaders of the Schmalkaldic League, an alliance of Protestant princes, was another factor that made a Cleves match so desirable. Shortly after the negotiations opened, John of Cleves died, leaving the dukedom to his son, William, who was equally well disposed to an alliance between Henry and the house of Cleves.

As he had demonstrated in his negotiations with France, his wife's personal appearance was as important to Henry as any political alliance she might represent. He was assured by his ambassadors that 'every man praised the beauty' of Anne, 'as well for the face as for the whole body, above all other ladies excellent' and that she 'excelled the Duchess [Christina of Denmark] as the golden sun excelled the silver moon'.[4] However, the English envoys had not seen Anne except for that part of her that was not hidden 'under such a monstrous habit and apparel'. When they asked for a better look at her, the Cleves chancellor was indignant and asked if they would like to see her naked.[5]

Uncertainty surrounding Anne's looks was one reason why the marriage negotiations were beset by delays. Another was Duke William's demands, which were every bit as high in their way as Henry's had been to Charles and François. With matters in danger of screeching to a halt, another envoy was despatched to speed things up, while Hans Holbein was sent to capture Anne's likeness, the Cleves painter apparently being too ill. Holbein returned to England and caught up with Henry, who had embarked on his summer progress, at Grafton.[6]

Gazing at Anne's picture, Henry liked what he saw. As August mellowed into September, he sent ambassadors to persuade Duke William to commission an embassy to England where the marriage treaty between Henry and Anne would be drawn up. There was, however, a major obstacle. In her youth, Anne had been precontracted with the son of the Duke of Lorraine. Envoys were despatched with instructions to do all they could to establish the facts of the case. In the end, Henry was assured that Lady Anne was 'free to marry as she pleases'.[7]

At that point, a new attempt was made to match Henry with Christina of Denmark, initiated by Christina's brother-in-law, Frederick, Count Palatine, who was pressing his wife's interests in Denmark.[8] However, it was to no avail. The marriage treaty between Henry and Anne had been swiftly concluded and arrangements were already being made to bring Henry's fourth wife and queen to England.[9]

The preparations included the appointment of ladies and maidens to serve Queen Anne. Some of those who had served Jane Seymour and who remained at court simply transferred to the new household, but their number would be augmented by new recruits. When the final list of maidens was drawn up, Katherine Howard's name appeared first on the list.[10] As a daughter of the ducal house of Howard, Katherine had every reason to expect to be included in the queen's household. That her name appears at the head of the list of maidens indicates her higher status. Indeed, she had been propelled into first place by very powerful sponsors. Her uncle of Norfolk would certainly have played a part in ensuring that Katherine would be considered for a position, while the influence of her step-grandmother, the Duchess Agnes, should not be under-estimated. That other members of Katherine's family held places at court is another factor. Her sister Margaret was married to Sir Thomas Arundel, who had been appointed receiver to Anne of Cleves. Katherine's half-sister Isabel Legh was the second wife of Sir Edward Baynton, a court veteran, who served as vice-chamberlain to all Henry's wives except Katherine of Aragon.

Yet, no matter which of Katherine's powerful relatives promoted her cause, Henry had the final say. Under normal circumstances, the queen would interview potential maidens in person,[11] observing the manner, disposition and appearance of the applicant. This was not possible in the case of Anne of Cleves, whose English maidens were required to be ready to serve her from the moment she arrived in her new kingdom. The task, then, fell to Henry. Katherine was coached for her meeting with the king, complete with a warning that she should remain silent about her past relationships.

Henry's standards were exacting. He would not accept any lady he thought was not 'meet for the room'.[12] Clearly, he was impressed with Katherine otherwise he would not have employed her; indeed, it was said 'that the King's highness did cast a fantasy to Katherine Howard the first time ever his Grace saw her'.[13]

It would be wrong, however, to think that Katherine had been placed before the king in a deliberate attempt to win his heart or to gain influence for her family by instilling in him the conservative sympathies of the Howards. In the autumn of 1539 Henry was very keen to meet his new bride and was looking forward to beginning a new and happy life with her. Katherine was merely one among several members of the Howard clan to find a position as maiden to the new queen. Katherine Cary, the daughter of Mary Boleyn, also joined the court, as did Mary Norris, a cousin by marriage to the Duke of Norfolk and daughter of Henry Norris, who had been executed in 1536 as one of Anne Boleyn's supposed lovers.

As she eagerly anticipated her new life at court, Katherine found that her transition from student-servant to maiden in the queen's household was not to be entirely smooth. Francis Dereham reacted badly to the news that she was leaving, and was genuinely heartbroken at the prospect of losing her. The court was notorious for its affairs, while her uncle of Norfolk might find a suitor for Katherine and marry her off.

One story has it that Katherine tried to console Dereham. With tears streaming down her cheeks, she said that leaving Norfolk House 'grieved me as much as it did him', assuring him 'that he should never live to say thou hast swerved'.[14] Not only was this untrue, her attitude towards Dereham confirms that she could never have said it.

Dereham initially attempted emotional blackmail. In a bid to make her stay, he threatened that he 'would not tarry long in the [Duchess's] house' if Katherine were to leave. Somewhat unsympathetically, she told him he could do as he liked.[15] She no longer cared what Dereham did, if she had ever done.

With no reason now to stay, Dereham decided he too would leave Lambeth, and he began to look for a means to do so. Duchess Agnes understood him well enough and summed up his position perfectly: 'As long as Katherine Howard was here he desired not to be hence, but ever since she went he is desirous to be gone.'[16]

As Dereham prepared to depart Norfolk House, he left an indenture and obligation of £100 in Katherine's custody saying that, if he never came again, he gave them clearly to her. When Katherine asked where he was going, he replied he would not tell her until his return.[17] In fact Dereham was being deliberately secretive, since he was making plans to go to Ireland.

Dereham had failed to notice Katherine's ambition, or else he had not taken it as seriously as he should have done. For Katherine was certain of what she wanted, which was to go to court. Fiercely ambitious, she wanted more than anything else to be taken into the king's favour. Filled 'with the desire for worldly glory', nothing now was going to stop her.

At court, Katherine was assigned lodgings, provision for a servant, a daily allowance of food at the appropriate table, for herself and her servant, as well as wax candles, stabling for one horse, and an annual stipend of £10.[18] Katherine received her first stipend in December 1539.[19] From this, she set aside £5 or £6 for Francis Dereham to reimburse the money he had lent her to buy clothes and ornaments.[20]

Katherine's training at Horsham and Lambeth was already proving useful; she was more than capable of managing her own household affairs. Although certain accoutrements were provided for her, she was required to supply her own clothes for everyday wear as well as her bedding.[21] The money for these costly items was provided by the Duchess Agnes, who would also give 500 marks to her relative Sir Francis Bryan with a bond for the restitution of the money should Katherine die before her marriage.[22]

Katherine's duty was to obey both the queen and Mrs Stoner, the mother of the maidens, at all times. It was a requirement that her dress and adornments, and also her demeanour, were pleasing. She would receive visitors amiably and escort the queen in her processions. In all, Katherine was expected to be a faithful, dutiful and respectful servant and an ornament in her mistress's court.

This task she would have to balance with another, which was to take advantage of her close proximity to the king to promote the interests of her family. Perhaps she would be more successful in this endeavour than most, if it is true that Henry liked the look of her from the beginning. However, there were dangers at court. It was seen as particularly hazardous to confide secrets to others, while the wise would be wary of flatterers.[23] Lord Husee described the court as being 'full of pride, envy, indignation, and mocking'.[24]

Katherine was among the thirty ladies and maidens, including the king's niece, Lady Margaret Douglas, and the Duchess of Richmond,[25] who had been appointed to await the arrival of Anne of Cleves at Deptford. It was planned that they would be formally presented to their new mistress by the Archbishop of Canterbury and the Dukes of Norfolk and Suffolk 'as her own train and household'. They were then to wait upon Anne until she approached the king's presence.[26] As with most well-laid plans, things soon went awry and Anne found herself stranded at Calais by bad weather. This gave her the opportunity to meet several English courtiers who had been sent out to escort her to England, including Gregory Cromwell, the son of the Lord Privy Seal, Edward Seymour, Earl of Hertford, brother of the late queen, and one Thomas Culpeper the Younger,[27] a gentleman of the Privy Chamber and one of the king's favourites. Anne made the most of her time sitting out the storm by trying to master the English language and learning to play Henry's favourite card games as well as English ways. Then, on 27 December, the weather lifted sufficiently to allow her to cross the Channel.

Because Anne's journey had been delayed, plans for her reception had to be amended. Henry had positioned scouts along Anne's route and they brought him news of her progress. On New Year's Day 1540 he learned that she had arrived at Rochester. Unable to wait any longer, he rode out to meet her. Sir Anthony Browne had been sent on ahead to convey a message to Anne that the king was bringing her a New Year's gift. However, as soon as Sir Anthony saw her, 'he was never more dismayed in all his life to see the lady so far unlike that which was reported'. He said nothing of this to Henry, 'nor durst not'. Watching as the king embraced and kissed Anne, Sir Anthony noticed on the king's 'countenance a discontentment and disliking of her person'. So dismayed was Henry that he 'tarried not to speak with her twenty words'. Instead, he 'deferred sending the presents that he had prepared for her', sending them with Sir Anthony the following morning with a 'cold message'.[28]

Henry then left for Greenwich, leaving Anne to prepare for her official reception the next day. Sitting in their barge, Henry 'very sadly and pensively' said to Sir Anthony, 'I see nothing in this woman as men report of her, and I marvel that wise men would make such report of her as they have done.' This was particularly bad news to Sir Anthony, whose half-brother, the Earl of Southampton, had been one of the 'wise men' who had praised Anne.

Happily, news of the disastrous first encounter had not leaked out so that when, at last, the day Katherine had long awaited arrived, she was as excited as everyone else. On Saturday, 3 January, she left Greenwich Palace in a retinue of ladies and gentlewomen, servants and yeomen, led by the Earl of Rutland,[29] Lady Margaret Douglas and the Duchesses of Richmond and Suffolk.[30] After them came the gentlemen of the households of the Lord Chancellor, the Lord Privy Seal and the Lord Admiral. A tent of rich cloth of gold and various other tents and pavilions had been erected at the foot of Shooters Hill, with 'fires and perfumes for her [Anne] and such Ladies as should receive her Grace'.[31] The route leading to the park gate at Greenwich had been cleared of bushes and firs and was now lined on either side by merchants, aldermen, councillors, esquires, knights, gentlemen pensioners and serving men, all in their velvet finery and glittering chains of gold.

At about noon Anne began her journey towards Greenwich, escorted by one hundred horse of her own German retinue and accompanied by the Dukes of Norfolk and Suffolk; then came Archbishop Cranmer, who was followed by other bishops, lords and knights. Having arrived at the tents, Anne was introduced to the Earl of Rutland, her lord chamberlain, Sir Thomas Denys, her chancellor, and other councillors and officers. An oration in Latin was read by Dr Day, Anne's new almoner, who presented her on the king's behalf to the rest of her servants and offices. Next she was greeted by the premier ladies in the land, at the head of whom were the king's two nieces, Lady Margaret Douglas and the Marchioness of Dorset, followed by the Duchess of Richmond, the Countesses of Rutland and Hertford and sixty-five other ladies all becomingly dressed in French hoods.[32] Anne alighted from the chariot in which she had made her long journey and 'with most goodly demeanour and loving countenance gave to them hearty thanks and kissed them all'. Finally Anne 'with all the ladies entered the tents, and there warmed them a space'.[33]

As only one of the sixty-five ladies attending Anne that day, Katherine Howard, fourteen years old, small in stature and in status, was not mentioned by name and was barely noticed.

7

In the Service of Anne of Cleves

~

HAPPILY FOR KATHERINE, Anne of Cleves turned out to be gracious and kind; Lady Lisle, who had served her at Calais, wrote to her daughter, Anne Bassett, to assure her that the new queen was 'so good and gentle to serve and please'.[1] Katherine and the other ladies were still unaware that the king was unhappy with his new bride. Even at this late hour, Henry was frantically searching for ways to call off the wedding. The precontract with the son of the Duke of Lorraine provided a potential escape route, and the ceremony was delayed for two days while every effort was made to establish whether or not Anne really was free to marry. Unfortunately for Henry, he received assurances from all sides that the precontract had been entered into during the minority of both parties and had never taken effect.[2] Henry sighed that he had a 'great yoke to enter into'.[3]

In fact, the diplomatic situation made it essential that Henry should marry Anne. In November 1539, as the new bride was making her way to England, Charles had travelled through France on his way to Flanders. He had been warmly entertained by François at Fontainebleau, Blois and Amboise.[6] This was greatly troubling to Henry, not least because of a general suspicion that the meetings between François and Charles presaged war against him.[7] In the face of such threat, it was essential not to displease the Duke of Cleves and the German princes. Henry had little choice but to go ahead with the wedding.

Even on the day of the wedding, Henry said to Thomas Cromwell, 'my lord, if it were not to satisfy the world and my realm I would not do that I must do this day for none earthly thing'.⁴ Still, despite the king's desperate attempts to find a reason to back out, the wedding went ahead as planned. So it was that on 6 January 1540 King Henry and Anne of Cleves were married in the queen's closet at Greenwich. The couple heard mass and then went in open procession, the queen 'being in her hair', that is, with her long hair loose to symbolise her maidenly status. She wore a rich coronet embellished with stones and pearls set with rosemary for remembrance and constancy, and a shimmering gown of cloth of silver similarly decorated with stones and pearls. She was accompanied by all her ladies and gentlewomen 'which was a goodly sight to behold'.⁵ The newly-weds then retired to their respective chambers, 'Anne's ladies trailing along behind her'. Since the wedding had taken place at Epiphany, the usual afternoon celebrations were cut short, so Katherine was not to experience the full festivities of a royal wedding. Happily, she and her companions were compensated later in the day with a supper followed by masques and other entertainments.

The following morning, Cromwell entered the privy chamber to find his king 'not so pleasant [cheerful] as I trusted to have done'. He asked Henry 'how ye liked the queen', only to be told, 'surely, my lord, as you know I liked her before not well, but now I like her much worse'. The king then treated Cromwell to a graphic description of his attempts to consummate his marriage, that he had felt Anne's 'belly and breasts' by which he could judge that 'she should be no maid'. This struck him so much to the heart 'that I had neither will nor courage to proceed any further in other matters'.

Even so, Henry remained committed to the marriage. In February he used it as capital in discussions with François. Henry urged the French king to join him in a league with the Dukes of Cleves and Saxony and various German Lutherans against Charles and Rome by which François might 'redubbe [restore] all things past'.⁸ Clearly, Henry continued to consider his marriage useful politically; there was no sign that he wanted to repudiate Anne. However, looks can be deceptive, and Henry's businesslike approach concealed an inner turmoil caused by genuine concerns about the validity of his marriage and Anne's suitability as queen.

For her first few months at court, Katherine's life was absorbed into that of her mistress. On 4 February she attended the queen as she travelled to Westminster for the first time. Leaving Greenwich, the magnificently decorated royal barges gently sailed along the Thames, their route lined with merchants' ships. As they passed by, each ship fired a gun salute to welcome the new queen. Then, when Anne's barge drew parallel to the Tower, another gun salute of 'a thousand chambers of ordinance' thundered. This was Katherine's first great occasion at court. She sat in the barge immediately behind that of the queen, the river slowly carrying her beneath London Bridge and on to Westminster.

Amid her duties, Katherine received visits from family and friends, and sometimes she would cross the river to visit Norfolk House. On one occasion she and the Duchess Agnes were chatting when the topic of Francis Dereham was raised. The duchess was curious to know what had become of him since he left Lambeth, but Katherine did not know; he had never revealed his plans.[9]

Katherine now had no interest in Dereham at all. Surrounded as she was by new people, all of whom were more interesting and younger than Dereham, she was distracted by her duties, her pretty dresses and sparkling jewels; she had formed new friendships and put Dereham quite out of her mind.

Besides, Katherine was being courted. She had caught the attention of Thomas Paston. Aged about twenty-three, and a member of the famous Paston family of Norfolk, he had come to court and was now a member of the privy chamber. However, Katherine appears to have set her cap at one of Paston's companions, her distant cousin, Thomas Culpeper.

Thomas Culpeper was born in Kent, possibly at Bedgebury, which had been brought to the family by his paternal grandmother. His father, Sir Alexander Culpeper of Bedgebury, had married Constance, née Chamberlain, of Capel and Gedding. The couple had at least eight children, including three sons, of whom Thomas was the second, and five daughters. Thomas's elder brother was also called Thomas, a not uncommon occurrence where the elder son was not expected to survive. Their younger brother was John.[10]

While still a boy, Thomas Culpeper entered the court as a page and quickly became adept at navigating the often difficult and slippery world that surrounded the king. As a courtier, Culpeper was accomplished in music, dancing and singing as well as sport and martial pursuits. The king greatly admired these skills, which reminded him of his own youth and the pleasures associated with it. At some point, certainly by 1533, Thomas Culpeper had risen to the privileged position of gentleman of the privy chamber.[11]

The privy chamber was a suite of rooms set apart from the rest of the court as the king's most private space. It was accessed by a private staircase or a small corridor that led from the presence chamber. Here, the gentlemen would attend to the king's most personal needs. One of Culpeper's tasks was to make the king's bed. This included rolling on the mattress to ensure there were no daggers or other lethal objects hidden inside. He also helped the king to dress.[12]

Right of entry to the privy chamber was strictly limited to the gentlemen, the gentlemen ushers and their daily waiters, and grooms and barbers,[13] as well as royal councillors. Everyone else was admitted by invitation only. This gave the gentlemen a measure of power, and they were often petitioned by those seeking to gain access to the king.

Culpeper basked in the glow of royal favour, and he certainly did well out of it,[14] but he took it all as his right rather than an earned privilege. There was an aura of arrogance about him and a tendency towards pretentiousness coupled with burning ambition. This occasionally manifested itself in violence. A dark tale, mentioned in a letter by Richard Hilles, ran that Culpeper had violated the wife of a park-keeper in a woody thicket while three or four of his attendants held her down.[15]

Because Thomas Culpeper's elder brother was also called Thomas, there is some debate as to which of them was involved in this incident. The confusion is understandable, especially as Hilles does not name the alleged culprit. However, there are several indications that the man in question is Thomas Culpeper the Younger. First, the letter asserts that he was executed for adultery with the queen, that is, Katherine Howard. Second, he is described as one of the king's chamberlains, whereas Thomas Culpeper the Elder was in the service of Thomas Cromwell. Finally, the assault was said to have been against a park-keeper's wife and Culpeper the Younger was in charge of several parklands and their maintenance.

At the time, some would have thought that Culpeper had every right to act as he did. Such behaviour found approval in books about courtly love:

> And if you should, by some chance, fall in love with some of their women, be careful to puff them up with lots of praise and then, when you find a convenient place, do not hesitate to embrace them by force. For you can hardly soften the outward inflexibility so far that they will grant you their embraces quietly or permit you to have the solaces you desire unless first you use a little compulsion as a convenient cure for their shyness.[16]

However, the villagers were guided by higher principles. They tried to apprehend Culpeper only for him to kill one of them in his attempt to escape. Undeterred, the villagers overpowered the young man and took him into custody. Despite their heroism, there was to be no justice for the victims as Henry pardoned Culpeper for his crimes.

Just how much of this story is true cannot be ascertained. However, the image of a violent and arrogant Culpeper given to disorderly behaviour is consistent with the character sketch of him written by George Cavendish only a few years after Culpeper's death.[17] Cavendish refers to Culpeper as being 'proud out of measure' and 'drowning in the depth of mine own outrage', while following his own pleasure.

This, then, is the young man with whom Katherine entered

into a relationship during the early months of 1540. Whether it was just friendship between two people who were related and who were living in close proximity within the hothouse environment of the court, or whether it was something more serious, is not recorded. Court gossip had it that they were to marry and one of those who gave credence to the rumour was Francis Dereham, who had recently returned from Ireland. Troubled by what he had heard about Katherine and Culpeper, he confronted her. To his chagrin, Dereham found Katherine every bit as unsympathetic as she had been when leaving for court. She told him not to trouble her, that she had no interest in him and hinted that the report he had heard about her and Culpeper was false.[18]

It is understandable that Dereham should be concerned that Katherine and Culpeper had become close enough to inspire talk about their marriage. As far as he was concerned, Katherine was his wife, or at least his betrothed. Katherine's denial that there was anything between her and Culpeper may have given him cause to hope that he might win her back despite the frostiness of her response. However, what Dereham did not know, although he would soon find out, was that he had a rival more dangerous than Thomas Culpeper, for Katherine had come to the attention of King Henry. Dereham had the good sense to retreat, as did Culpeper.

The contemporary anonymous author of *Chronicle of Henry VIII* offers an entertaining but hugely inaccurate account of the moment at which Henry announced that he intended to make Katherine his new wife and queen.[19] It begins with Henry visiting his son. The king entered the room where the ladies were and called Katherine to him. She approached and knelt before him, but Henry held out his hand and raised her up saying, 'Katharine, from now henceforward I wish you never to do that again, but rather that all these ladies and my whole kingdom should bend the knee to you, for I wish to make you Queen.' Katherine, for her part, said nothing, but simply bowed her head. Henry kissed her and then went on his way.

The *Chronicle* goes on to say that Henry called his council together, announcing, 'Gentlemen, you know I am a widower, and I need company; I wish you to give me your advice.' Here, Henry had already made up his mind that he would marry Katherine, but he wished nevertheless to hear the opinions of his Council. Katherine's uncle, the Duke of Norfolk, was the first to speak up: 'Your Majesty should try to find out whether there is any daughter of a foreign prince, and endeavour to win her.' There were those who shared the duke's view, but others suggested Henry might find a suitable bride in England. Henry, however, would not be persuaded. 'I have seen the lady I wish to take,' he assured them, and they all held their peace, waiting for the king to say who the lady was. 'You know Katharine Howard,' he began, 'she is the one I have chosen.' To this they all replied that, if the king so willed it, 'we shall be contend; what pleases your Majesty pleases us.' It is a charming story, but the reality could not have been more different. Henry, as has been seen, had first met Katherine the previous year when she came to court in search of a position in Anne of Cleves's household and had made quite an impression on him. This had been noticed and news of Katherine's effect on Henry would be reported to the Dowager Duchess of Norfolk.

Who told the duchess of the king's 'fantasy' is not known but, as it turned out, she was not the only person to have heard the news. As the negotiations for the Cleves match were drawing to a conclusion, Archbishop Cranmer and Thomas Cromwell discussed the marriage treaty. At some point mention was made of a certain unnamed lady who had caught Henry's eye. Cranmer suggested that, in view of this, the Cleves marriage should not proceed any further. Instead, he felt it would be more beneficial to Henry if he were to marry 'where he had his fantasy and love'.[20] Cromwell poured scorn on this suggestion. His mind fixed on the political and religious advantages of the marriage, he retorted that there was no suitable woman for the king in the realm. Cranmer, who was more concerned for Henry's personal happiness, replied that he thought it would be strange for the king to marry a woman with whom he could not converse; as a man married to a German wife, Cranmer was in a position to know the potential frustrations involved. Cromwell, however, dismissed the suggestion and the negotiations continued.

Henry did not act on his 'fantasy' – he had no reason to. He was still looking forward to welcoming Anne of Cleves, whom he did not doubt would make a worthy queen and the mother of a new Duke of York. Sadly, upon his first meeting with Anne, Henry knew that he had made a mistake in his choice of bride.

Very few people knew at this stage how unhappy Henry was. Only Sir Anthony Browne, in whom Henry had first confided his dissatisfaction, and one or two others were aware that all was not well. In an attempt to conceal the true situation at home, Cromwell allowed foreign ambassadors to think that Henry was happy with his new wife.[21] Such subterfuge was crucial. In February rumours abounded that François, Charles and the pope were planning to invade England. They had on their side James V of Scotland, who was prepared to 'do against the King, his uncle [Henry], as the Emperor or the French king did'.[22]

Some weeks previously, Henry had sent Ralph Sadler on an embassy to Scotland bearing a letter in which Henry tried to guide James away from friendship with the Emperor Charles and King François, for 'what can he expect of either but fair words? What can he hope to gain by attempting anything at their desires?'

Henry's patronising and cynical approach, which included a suggestion that Henry might recognise James's place in the English succession, was firmly rebuffed. Henry responded to the threat by fortifying his defences. Work to reinforce forts in the Thames estuary, East and West Cowes, Sandgate, Calshot, Portland and Weymouth was soon under way; meanwhile, a new fort at Pendennis was being built, and Henry personally visited the castle and defences at Dover.[23]

In another tactic, the king took advantage of his alliance with his brother-in-law, William of Cleves. Duke William, whose dispute with the emperor over his inheritance of the dukedom of

Gelderland continued, could prove a valuable distraction, keeping Charles occupied with concerns other than an invasion of England. Unfortunately, by March it looked as though they, too, were reaching an agreement.[24]

With the storm clouds of war threatening to break over his head, Henry had little hope of alleviating his troubles in the tender company of a sympathetic wife. He was thoroughly miserable. Confiding in Cromwell, at Candlemas and again before Shrovetide, he made it clear that his 'heart could never consent to meddle with her carnally' even though he would 'lie with her nightly or every second night'. Henry might have shared Anne's bed, but all he did was sleep.

Anne was not so naïve as she might have appeared. Far from being sent to sea with no biscuit, as St Bernardino of Siena would have put it, she was aware from the start that something was not right with her marriage. She even approached Cromwell about it. He told the king that Anne 'had often desired to speak with me, but I durst not'. Henry suggested that Cromwell 'might do much good by going to her and telling her my mind'. Cromwell pleaded a lack of opportunity to go to the queen, although he did find time to speak to the Earl of Rutland, Anne's lord chamberlain, asking him to 'induce her to behave pleasantly' towards the king.[25]

Where Katherine was during this time is not recorded, but there is no reason to think that she was not at court serving her mistress as expected. It is probable, therefore, that she accompanied Anne and Henry at Easter[26] when they went to Hampton Court, returning with them to Westminster on 12 April for the opening of Parliament. At this point, she was as insignificant as she had ever been. Yet, very gradually, the tides were turning.

Henry had all but abandoned his marriage to Anne of Cleves. In his unhappiness, his thoughts returned to the young, vibrant and spirited maiden to whom he had 'cast a fantasy' all those months ago, and he began to court her.

The earliest hint that Katherine had become more to Henry than a servant in his wife's household was so subtle that none but the sharpest of courtiers would even have noticed it. It came in March 1540 when Katherine's cousin, John Legh, was summoned back to England after several years in exile. Legh, the nephew and heir of Sir John Legh of Stockwell, had sided with the supporters of Katherine of Aragon during the king's 'Great Matter'. Unsettled by the religious divisions arising from Henry's increasing desperation to annul the Aragon marriage, Legh went into voluntary exile to avoid being compelled to choose sides. As of November 1538 he was living in Venice, where he had found 'so fair and honest a house', a spacious home overlooking the lagoon.[27]

In religion, Legh was a conservative and a papist, as evinced by his pilgrimage to Jerusalem and, more especially, his meetings with Cardinal Reginald Pole and his agent Michael Throckmorton at St Thomas of Canterbury in Rome.[28] Even so, he still had friends at the English court, men who saw him as wrong-headed, but not malicious. His distant cousin, the evangelical-leaning Thomas Wyatt,[29] thought him excellent company; he invited Legh to visit him in Spain where Wyatt was serving as ambassador.[30] Edmund Harvel similarly found 'no malice in him, but only weakness of reason and imprudence'.[31] Yet his association with Pole was dangerous, for anyone in communication with the cardinal was deemed suspect. As such, Legh was called home in the company of Wyatt, his summons 'compassed in such wise as he shall not stick at it'. With Legh back in England, the king 'may object to him his contemptuous absence at his pleasure'.[32] More to the point, Legh's detachment from Pole and Throckmorton ensured that he would not be allowed to imperil the fortunes of his cousin, Katherine Howard.

Legh's recall from exile was, therefore, the earliest indication, albeit a heavily veiled one, of King Henry's interest in Katherine. The next clue was less subtle. It came on 24 April 1540, when Henry granted Katherine the goods and chattels of William Ledbeter, a Sussex yeoman, and his son, who had been indicted for murder the previous February.[33] The following month, 'twenty-three quilts of quilted sarcenet, bought of Baptist Borowne and

Guilliame Latremoylle, [were] given to Mrs Haward' from the royal wardrobe.³⁴

Since gifts were a recognised part of the ritual of courtship, much might have been read into these awards to a mere maiden of honour. However, at this stage, Katherine's developing relationship with the king was still, largely, a secret. Few beyond the confines of the Privy Council were aware of Henry's dissatisfaction with the queen and that he was already contemplating her replacement.

When May Day arrived, the great celebration of love, the court marked it in the customary fashion with five days of jousts, tourneys and barriers – a martial exercise involving swords and staves, one of the competitors at which was Thomas Culpeper of the privy chamber.³⁵ The festivities, which were presided over by King Henry and Queen Anne, provided Katherine with yet another opportunity to enjoy the entertainments and excitement that life at court offered.

The jousts were a magnificent spectacle that allowed the lords and knights of the court to show off their martial prowess in displays that required great skill. It was also an occasion for dressing up, with challengers and defenders, and even their servants, resplendent in white velvet and sarcenet. Katherine's cousin, the flamboyant and proud Earl of Surrey, was the principal defender, while her uncle, Lord William, followed behind.

Open house was kept at Durham Place, Henry's town house on the Strand, which was richly hanged, and great cupboards of plate were brought out for the occasion. As Henry and Anne feasted they were surrounded by the queen's ladies and all the court, all dining on 'delicious meats and drinks so plenteous as might be, and much melody of minstrelsy'.³⁶

Henry was now deeply in love with Katherine and there is no reason to think that she did not return his affection. Henry found Katherine beautiful, a quality enhanced by her obvious youth. He, like many men whose early manhood was but a cherished memory, was drawn to young people because they reinforced his, perhaps idealistic, vision of his own salad days. Equally importantly, associating with the young rejuvenated him, and Katherine had many years ahead of her in which she could produce a brood of children for the royal nursery, thereby securing the Tudor dynasty for generations to come. As for her character, Katherine had a kindness of heart and a lack of malice that prevented her from remaining angry with anyone for very long, and was generous and caring towards those less fortunate than herself. Of equal appeal was Katherine's freshness and relative innocence about the ways of the court. She was not a seasoned courtier as had been Anne Boleyn and Jane Seymour; and, although she was ambitious, she was unspoiled by a courtier's cynicism and sense of political intrigue. Katherine was musical: she could play the virginals as well as dance and, presumably, sing; all attributes that Henry appreciated and looked for in a wife.

For Katherine's part, Henry could be charming, generous and kind, something to which a young woman, especially one with a difficult past, would readily respond. Perhaps even more to the point, he had taken her into his favour, as she had hoped he would when she first came to court, although perhaps not in the way she might have expected. Marriage to a king was much to be desired, no matter his age or looks.

In another time and place, the situation in which Henry found himself would have posed no problem at all: he would simply have remained married to Anne and kept Katherine as his mistress. For Henry, however, such a solution was unacceptable. What if Katherine should be married elsewhere, perhaps to Master Culpeper. No, as with Anne Boleyn and Jane Seymour, Henry wanted the woman he loved to be his wife, not a mere mistress. He did not want Katherine to belong to another, he wanted her all to himself, and the only way to achieve that was to marry her. This, of course, meant that he had to be free of Anne.

Throughout the spring, Henry's complaints to Cromwell continued with tedious monotony. For her part, Anne had begun 'to wax stubborn and wilful', causing Henry to lament his fate, 'ever verifying' that he had 'never any carnal knowledge with her'.[37] Henry continued to dine in the queen's chambers on occasion. Although appearances were being maintained, Henry was no longer committed to the Cleves match.

The turning point came at Whitsuntide, on 16 May. Henry confided to Cromwell that his 'greatest grief' was that he would 'surely never have any more children for the comfort of this realm' should this state of affairs continue. He added that he thought Anne was not his lawful wife nor had she ever been. Cromwell promised he would do his 'uttermost to comfort and deliver your grace of your affliction', but he did not elaborate.[38]

Although Henry indicated his desire for a divorce to Cromwell in late May 1540,[39] Cromwell did nothing to facilitate it. Instead, he made the blunder of speaking once again to Anne's lord chamberlain and others of her council. As before, his message was to urge Anne to act pleasantly towards the king. However, what had seemed an acceptable and helpful solution at the beginning of the year, when the marriage was just beginning and its difficulties might have been overcome, was imprudent and highly inappropriate in late May, when the marriage was doomed. Even Wriothesley's dire warning, 'For God's sake devise for the relief of the King; for if he remain in this grief and trouble, we shall all one day smart for it,' could not prompt Cromwell to action.[40]

As it was, a way out of Henry's predicament had already shown itself. Shortly after New Year it had become clear that relations between François and Charles were not as cordial as initially thought. When the emperor left France in late January, the people 'were very joyous and assured'.[41] Then, in March, a planned journey to the Low Countries by Anne de Montmorency, the constable of France, was abandoned, giving the English to suppose that 'the final resolution between Francis and the Emperor is not so near as was said'.[42]

Consequently, Henry suspended his war preparations and turned his attention to reviving relations with Flanders.[43] April brought rumours that affairs between François and Charles had now grown so cold that it was thought 'war is more likely than a continuance of this fervent amity'.[44] Although this was emphatically denied by François,[45] Henry decided to make use of these developments to broker an agreement with either the French king or the emperor.

In short, the political situation that had made the Cleves marriage so necessary had calmed to the point that, by June 1540, it looked as though Henry might safely repudiate Queen Anne. Moreover, Henry had no need of Cromwell's services in order to secure his annulment. There was no reason why Henry should not take matters into his own hands.

It was no coincidence that, about this time, Thomas Culpeper was granted the reversions of several manors and estates. This was said to be 'in consideration of his true and faithful service',[46] but it was also an expression of gratitude on Henry's part as well as compensation to Culpeper for giving up Katherine.

Meanwhile, Anne of Cleves was upset by her husband's attentions to one of her maidens and she complained to Karl Harst, her brother's ambassador, about it. Harst tried to reassure her, saying that it was nothing but a passing fancy. A day or two later, Harst found Anne in much better spirits; the reason for this was obvious: Katherine had been sent away from court.[47]

Shortly after Katherine's departure, Anne was removed to Richmond on the pretext, so Marillac heard,[48] of an outbreak of plague in the town. This was patently untrue because, as the ambassador rightly notes, had there been 'any suspicion' of disease, Henry 'would not stay for any affair however great, as [he is] the most timid person that could be in such a case'. Nevertheless, the king promised Anne that he would join her in two days' time. This was another lie. Henry had already planned a progress and the route did not go in the direction of Richmond.

Soon, citizens in London began to notice Henry crossing the river in a little boat, sometimes during the day, other times at midnight. As Richard Hilles observed, this was seen as a sign that the king was having an adulterous affair, for he was 'much taken' with another young lady.[49] Nobody, at this point, expected the king to divorce the queen.

Hilles thought that Henry was going to Bishop Stephen Gardiner's sumptuous episcopal palace on Clink Street in Southwark, where he and Katherine were treated to 'feastings and entertainments'. He was unaware that Henry also had a house in Southwark, as did Katherine, Countess of Bridgewater, where the couple could just as easily have been entertained.[50] In reality, Henry was visiting Katherine at Norfolk House.[51]

Here, in the home where Katherine had grown to womanhood, Duchess Agnes was able to assure Henry that her step-granddaughter was chaste, and that there would be no impediments to their marriage. The duchess did not lie to Henry; as far as she knew, Katherine's sexual experiences were limited to a few stolen kisses and embraces with Henry Mannock and Francis Dereham, for which she had been duly punished.

The prospect of another Howard queen on the throne presented an opportunity not to be missed for Katherine's family, who would find advancement and prosperity during her reign. They assisted Katherine as she made the difficult transition from servant to queen, supplying her with new clothes, shoes and jewellery.[52] Although Katherine received a stipend as a maiden of honour, much of it was spent on essentials, while some of it was set aside to repay her debts to Dereham. Also, funds from the revenues Henry had given her might not have come in yet, so any financial help would be welcome.

Katherine needed advice as to how to behave with the king. Unfortunately, while her education had tended towards a court position, Katherine had no idea of the procedures of being a queen on a practical level. The only example of queenship she had witnessed at close hand, that of Anne of Cleves, had been atypical. Through no fault of her own, Anne had not been a success in her career. Duchess Agnes, however, was a court veteran and in a good position to help Katherine in this respect. As such, the duchess fulfilled her obligations to a young woman for whose upbringing and advancement she had been responsible. Later, all this would be given a sinister twist when Katherine's world came crashing down.

The real reason for Katherine's removal to Lambeth and Anne of Cleves's sojourn at Richmond was to get the two women out of the way while the investigation into the Cleves marriage was in progress.[53] It would not do for Henry to keep Anne in close proximity while the validity of her marriage was in doubt. He had learned a valuable lesson from his struggle to annul his marriage to Katherine of Aragon. Nor would it be a good idea to flaunt his intended bride before his present marriage had been dissolved.

Notwithstanding his attentiveness to such niceties, the king's forthcoming nuptials continued to be a source of gossip. Among the most injurious was that between Archbishop Cranmer's servant, Thomas Wakefield, and the chief legal draughtsman brought in to assist with the annulment, Dr Richard Gwent. Wakefield raised the perfectly legitimate question of the possibility of affinity between Katherine and the king. This resulted from the close relations each of them shared with Anne Boleyn: Katherine as first cousin, Henry as former husband,[54] as well as their mutual descent from Edward I.

Gwent assured Wakefield that such an affinity was dispensable, but then the conversation became more salacious. The two men noted that the king had banqueted with Katherine for the past two nights, and that there was probably more to these entertainments than mere feasting. So far, the gossip was imprudent and distasteful, especially considering the dignity and status of those involved. However, now it took on a more dangerous turn. They speculated that Cromwell had been sent to the Tower because he did not consent to the annulment. Furthermore, the two men ventured that the Howard match was the work of Bishop Gardiner. At this point Cranmer was alerted to what was being said. The archbishop rushed in and ordered them to hold their peace. Then, erring on the side of caution, he wrote a full report of the gossip for the other members of the Privy Council. As a result, all those working on the annulment were called upon to make depositions.

In the end, Wakefield and Gwent escaped with no other punishment than shock and embarrassment.

Wakefield and Gwent had placed Cranmer in a difficult position, but he received help from an unexpected source. Katherine sent the archbishop a note assuring him 'that you should not care [be concerned] for your business, for you should be in better case than ever you were'. This welcome reassurance originated with Henry acting through the as yet politically innocent Katherine. The king was acknowledging the man who had tried to stop the Cleves marriage all those months ago, and expressing his gratitude.

The process of annulling the Cleves marriage was initiated on 2 July. As a preliminary, Henry introduced a bill reducing marriage impediments.[55] The bill stated that marriages contracted and consummated after 1 July 1540 would be deemed valid and indissoluble no matter what unconsummated betrothals had been entered into by either party in the past.

The bill for reducing marriage impediments was simply a safeguard for Henry. Should the annulment of the Cleves marriage be questioned, it gave him the means to prove that he was divorced from Anne.[56] This was one of the main reasons why it was so necessary to establish beyond doubt that the Cleves marriage had not been consummated. The bill also provided a dispensation to allow Katherine and Henry to marry despite the close degrees of consanguinity that existed between them. Since Katherine was related to two of the women with whom Henry had had relations, Mary and Anne Boleyn, the bill provided dispensation for these affinities too. As things now stood, all impediments to the proposed marriage between Katherine and Henry had been removed.

The bill was then passed to Archbishop Cranmer, Cuthbert Tunstall, Bishop of Durham, and Stephen Gardiner, Bishop of Winchester. They were required to examine it and, if necessary, make corrections. That it passed the following day indicates their satisfaction with it, and it became law on 5 July.

Next, the Lords and Commons sought Henry's permission to appoint a joint convocation of clergy to examine his marriage to Anne of Cleves.[57] Several depositions were exhibited,[58] of which two were of particular importance to Katherine because of their bearing on Henry's right to remarry. The first was from Dr Butts, who deposed that Henry had spoken to him of his inability to consummate his marriage. Henry was anxious to emphasise that he had experienced *duas pollutions nocturnas in somno*, two wet dreams, and so 'thought himself able to do the act with other [women] but not with her [Anne]'.[59] This is an important point because, if Henry were impotent, he would not be allowed to remarry as he would be unable to satisfy his wife's conjugal rights. The deposition showed that his impotence was specific to Anne, indicating that the problem lay with the marriage, not with him.

The second deposition was that of Queen Anne's senior ladies, Catherine Edgecomb, Jane Rochford and Eleanor Rutland. In a statement that was presented jointly, the ladies recalled that they had wondered why there were no signs that their mistress was pregnant. Although they 'wished her Grace with child', Anne assured them that she was not. Lady Edgecomb asked, 'How it is possible for your Grace to know that, and lie every night with the King?' Anne was firm: 'I know it well,' she said, 'I am not.' At this, Lady Edgecomb suggested that perhaps Anne was 'a maid still'. Anne laughed. Lady Rochford then joined in: 'By our Lady, madam, I think your Grace is a maid still, indeed.' 'How can I be a maid,' Anne wanted to know, 'and sleep every night with the King?' Lady Rochford then told her that 'there must be more than that . . . or else I had a leve the King lay further.' 'Why,' said Anne, 'when he comes to bed he kisses me, and taketh me by the hand, and byddeth me, Good night, sweet heart; and in the morning kisses me, and byddeth me, Farewell, darling. Is this not enough?' Lady Rutland assured the queen that this was most certainly not enough: 'Madam, there must be more than this, or it will be long ere we have a Duke of York, which all this realm most desireth.' 'Nay,' said Anne, 'is this not enough? I am content with this, for I know no more.'[60]

The conversation reported by Anne's ladies almost certainly never took place, but was invented for the purpose of giving the false impression that the queen was ignorant of the facts of life. This, in turn, provided further proof that her marriage to the king had never been consummated; and since the marriage had never been consummated, it had, in fact, never existed. Henry was free to take a new wife. The Cleves marriage was declared null on 9 July, and both partners were declared free to marry elsewhere.[61]

Throughout the annulment process Anne had acted with quiet dignity. She had co-operated with the investigation and accepted her demotion, which she knew to be the king's will. She was rewarded properties in Essex, Suffolk and Sussex, and Bletchingly Manor and Richmond Palace were provided for her use for life. However, Anne felt a deep sense of grief that would never leave her, and she harboured a silent hope that, once day, she and Henry would be reunited.

As the most recent royal marriage was being dissolved, rumours abounded as to who the king would marry next. According to the ambassador Richard Pate's letter to the Duke of Norfolk, the gossip in Bruges had it that Henry would marry either the Duchess of Denmark or 'an English Duke's daughter';[62] meaning Mary Howard, the widow of the Duke of Richmond.[63] Norfolk must have smiled at this. It would not be a duke's daughter whom Henry would lead down the aisle, but a duke's niece – his own niece – and the preparations were well in hand.

Still only in her sixteenth year, Katherine's life was filled with excitement and anticipation as she took her first steps into a future none could have envisaged for her. It was at this point that she received an unwelcome reminder of her past in the form of a letter from an old friend.[64] Joan Bulmer had heard of Katherine's good fortune and wanted to congratulate her:

> If I could wish unto you all the honour, wealth, and good fortune you could desire, you would neither lack health, wealth, long life, nor yet prosperity. Nevertheless, seeing I cannot as I would express this unto you, I would with these my most heartly salutations pight [let] you to know, that whereas it hath been shown unto me that God of his high goodness hath put unto the knowledge of the

king a contract of matrimony that the queen [Anne of Cleves] hath made with another before she came into England and thereupon there will be a lawful divorce had between them; and as it is thought that the king of his goodness will put you in the same honour that she was in, which no doubt you be worthy to have.

Joan was back living with her husband, Sir William Bulmer, at York. Their marriage was an unhappy one and Joan felt isolated and lonely, and she wanted Katherine to know how miserable she was in her current state. Then, having flattered her friend, Joan suggested that she, in her goodness, could remedy Joan's situation by offering her a position in the new royal household:

Most heartily desiring you to have in your remembrance the unfeigned love that my heart hath always borne towards you, which for the same kindness found in you again hath desired always your presence, if it might be so, above all other creatures, and the chance of fortune hath brought me, on the contrary, into the utmost misery of the world and most wretched life. Seeing no ways, then, I can express in writing, knowing no remedy out of it, without you of your goodness will find the means to get me to London, which will be very hard to do; but if you write unto my husband and command him to bring me up, which I think he dare not disobey, for it might be, I would fain be with you before you were in your honour; and in the mean season I beseech you to save some room [an assigned position or post] for me, what you shall think fit yourself, for the nearer I were to you the gladder I would be of it, what pains soever I did take.

There follows more flattery, with Joan estimating herself unworthy to be in Katherine's presence, now that her friend had risen so high:

I would write more unto you, but I dare not be so bold, for considering the great honour you are toward, it did not become me to put myself in [your] presence; but the remembrance of the perfect honesty that I have always found to be in you, and the report of sir George Stafford, which hath assured me that the same thing remains in you still, hath encouraged me to this.

So far, Joan's letter is a standard plea from a forlorn friend seeking the help of a more fortunate one. As such, it is typical of the sort those looking for a placement in a new royal household might send. But there is more to this letter than meets the eye. As Joan approaches the final paragraph, the tenor of her letter changes dramatically:

> Whereupon I beseech you not to be forgetful of this my request; for if you do not help me, I am not like to have worldly joys. Desiring you, if you can, to let me have some answer of this for the satisfying of my mind; for I know the queen of Britain will not forget her secretary, and favour you will show.

Joan ends by describing herself as Katherine's secretary. In this context, a secretary is a confidante or someone privy to another's secrets. Joan is appealing to the close friendship the two women once shared, but she is also implicitly warning Katherine that she knows everything about her encounter with Henry Mannock and, worse still, her relationship with Francis Dereham. This letter could be seen as a veiled attempt at blackmail.

Joan's letter, dated 12 July, would have reached Katherine some four or five days later. She had found out about the change in Katherine's circumstances from Sir George Stafford,[65] one of the Duchess Agnes's men.

Joan was not the only one of the duchess's servants to see a glittering future in Katherine's service. Another was her tailor, Roger Cotes, who said that if Katherine 'were advanced he expected a good living'.[66] Later, Agnes would be questioned as to whom she had told about the king's favour towards Katherine.[67]

Joan Bulmer was among the earliest to know that Katherine was to become the fifth wife of Henry VIII, but her privileged position was not to last long. Shortly after Katherine received her friend's letter, the French ambassador, Marillac, wrote to François of a rumour that 'this King will marry a lady of great beauty, daughter of Norfolk's deceased brother'.[68] He added: 'If I were permitted to write what I hear in diverse places, I would say with many others this marriage has already taken place and consummated; but as this is kept secret I dare not yet say for certain that it is true.' Marillac is less cautious in his letter to Montmorency, written on the same day. He tells the constable that the cause of the sudden settlement with Anne of Cleves is that the king has already consummated marriage with 'this last lady, a relative of the duke of Norfolk, and it is feared she is already *enceinte*'. Marillac, however, is unable to affirm this because 'these things are kept secret'.[69] Meanwhile, Henry was distributing new robes and other apparel to members of his staff, including Katherine's brothers, Charles and George, as well as Thomas Culpeper.[70]

The news of Henry's divorce and his impending remarriage quickly spread to other parts of Europe. The Portuguese ambassador, Manuell Cyrne, wrote: 'some [say] that the King would marry an English lady, niece of the duke of Norfolk, daughter of his brother, and that she is already with child'.[71]

Speculation was rife that Katherine was already Henry's mistress. The belief that Katherine was pregnant at the time of her marriage would persist; the papal nuncio Giovanni Poggio was still repeating the gossip as fact in mid-August.[72] Poggio took a cynical view of the new marriage, saying that Henry was 'pleased with his new wife' — so far anyway — while 'the other, the sister of Cleves, has retired in peace'. He noted, ominously, that Anne was still alive.[73] However, Henry was almost certainly adopting the same restraint he had exercised during his courtship of Anne Boleyn and Jane Seymour. As such, it is highly doubtful that their relationship was fully consummated at this stage because it was essential to avoid uncertainty surrounding the legitimacy of any children Katherine might give him. As it was, with the Cleves marriage finally dissolved, the way was now clear for the king to marry his 'jewel of womanhood'. Katherine Howard was about to become the fifth wife and queen of King Henry VIII.

8

A New Howard Queen

~

What a man is the king! How many wives will he have?[1]

HENRY VIII HAD acquired Oatlands Palace, a country residence at Weybridge in Surrey, in 1537, and since then he
had transformed it from a modest manor house into a beautiful
palace. It was the perfect setting for a summer wedding. Its moated
buildings of stone and brick were arranged around three courtyards
overlooked by an octagonal tower. The grounds boasted a pleas-
ance, a deer park and an orchard, while fountains watered lush
green gardens. It was here on 28 July 1540 that Katherine Howard
and King Henry VIII came together in a small private chapel in
a ceremony presided over by Bishop Edmund Bonner, and
Katherine promised to be faithful and to surrender herself to the
will of her husband. How appropriate, then, that she would choose
as her personal device *non autre volonté que la sienne*: 'no other
will than his'.[2]

The summer of 1540 was hot and dry. No rain fell between
June and the first week of October.[3] Those of a superstitious
bent might have made much of reports from France, where it
was said to have rained blood for seven hours;[4] nature weeping
tears of blood for the lost Cromwell, whose brutal and horrific
execution took place on the day that Katherine became queen.

The tragic demise of a faithful servant was of little consequence
to the new couple. Despite the sanguineous omens that heralded
it, Katherine and Henry entered into married life full of optimism,

and the happy beginning to their relationship pointed to a blissful future together.

The wedding itself was a modest affair and no descriptions of it have been found. Henry, at the age of forty-nine and embarking on his fifth marriage, felt that he could dispense with sumptuous ritual and the abandoned celebration that went with it. He preferred quiet weddings; his only elaborate ceremonies had been for foreign brides. For the fifteen-year-old Katherine, too, perhaps the quiet formality of a simple and private wedding appealed. After all, the fewer witnesses there were, the less chance that someone might answer positively to the demand that 'if anyone knew any impediment thereto he should declare it'.[5]

While the marriage was quietly consummated, perhaps in the ornate pearl bed that the king had recently acquired,[6] uncertainty prevailed as to whether or not it had yet taken place, so understated had the wedding been, and others were unsure that the Cleves marriage had ended. Marillac, relating the latest news about Henry and the court, noted that the king:

> being lately with a small company at Hampton Court, ten miles hence, supped at Richmond with the Queen that was [Anne of Cleves], so merrily that some thought he meant to reinstate her, but others think it was done to get her consent to the dissolution of the marriage and make her subscribe what she had said thereupon, which is not only what they wanted but also what she thinks they expected.[7]

In fact, Henry had paid a visit to Anne on 6 August. He wanted to assure himself that his 'sister' was happy and well, and that she approved of her domestic arrangements. He would also have wanted to prepare her for the imminent announcement that he had remarried and that Katherine was to be presented to the court as the new queen. For, two days later, on Sunday, 8 August 1540, 'was the Lady Katherine Howard, niece to the duke of Norfolk, and daughter to the lord Edmond Howard, showed openly as Queen at Hampton Court'.[8] As queen, Katherine was included in prayers said in church for the royal family,[9] and children would be named after her.[10]

Katherine, brought up to serve, formerly employed in the mundane tasks of a maiden of honour, now had a large household to cater for her every need. Many of her members of staff had transferred to her service from Anne of Cleves's household. They were familiar to Katherine for this reason, but also because some of them were family or friends, such as Sir Edward Baynton, vice-chamberlain, and his second wife, her half-sister, Isabel; her cousin Mary Howard, Duchess of Richmond, daughter of the Duke of Norfolk; and Margaret, Lady Howard, the wife of Lord William Howard and Katherine's aunt.

Serving in Katherine's privy chamber were Malyn Tylney, Marget Morton, and two other ladies known only as Friswith and Lufkyn.[11] Among the new queen's maidens of honour was Lady Lucy,[12] the niece of William FitzWilliam, Earl of Southampton and lord privy seal, her appointment an example of people in high places helping with the careers of family members. Anne Bassett was a court veteran, having served Jane Seymour and Anne of Cleves. The mother of the maidens was Mrs Stoner, who had supervised Katherine when she was a maiden of honour to Anne of Cleves.

One significant omission from Katherine's household was Joan Bulmer, her friend and former bedfellow. Joan's petition for a position had been unsuccessful. This was because Joan's husband, ordered by the Privy Council to take her back, had refused to allow her to go to court.

The most noteworthy of Katherine's attendants, however, is Jane, Lady Rochford. Born in 1504–5, Jane was some twenty years older than her new mistress. One of her earliest appearances at court was in the part of Constancy in the Château Vert pageant of Shrove Tuesday, 1522. Ten years later, she took part in the entertainments held for King François at Calais, where the court had gone to seek his support for Henry's marriage to Anne Boleyn.

Well established at court, Lady Jane would go on to serve four of King Henry's queens. She married George Boleyn at some point between late 1524 and early 1525, making her Katherine's cousin by marriage, but she and Katherine were also related through Jane's paternal grandmother, Alice Lovel, who had been married to Katherine's uncle, Edward Howard.[13] Following her husband's execution in 1536 for alleged treason, adultery and incest with his sister, Anne Boleyn, Jane, who never remarried, fell upon difficult circumstances. Dependent on her jointure settlement, she sought the help of Thomas Cromwell. He, seasoned in aiding widows, won a fair settlement for her and helped her to find a new position at court, and so Jane became lady of the bedchamber to the new queen, Jane Seymour.

Now independently wealthy as a result of jointure settlements and the successful haggling over property rights, Lady Jane retired to Blickling following the death of Queen Jane. However, for a lady for whom the glamour and excitement of the court had become a way of life, retirement to the country was only ever going to be short-term. In the happy position of being free to choose her own destiny, Jane returned to court to serve Anne of Cleves as lady of the privy chamber. Following the annulment of the Cleves marriage, she remained at court, where she was appointed to serve Katherine Howard. Lady Jane, however, had not been the first choice for the post of lady of Queen Katherine's privy chamber: the position had originally been held by one of Katherine's sisters. Later, when speaking of the dismissal of Katherine's household after her fall, Marillac remarked that the queen's sister had been found to be innocent of any involvement with her alleged crimes and set free. Since Margaret Howard was living with her husband Sir Thomas Arundel in Dorset,[14] Marillac could only have been referring to Mary, who had 'not long since been turned out of her sister's chamber to be replaced by Lady Rochford'.[15]

Katherine's ladies would find their mistress quite demanding. Dorothy Josselin, who later joined the queen's household, complained that 'the Queen's work troubles me so much and yet I fear I shall scant content her grace'.[16] Chapuys, more concisely, described Katherine as 'imperious and commanding'.[17] While

Katherine had been taught to serve, and had gained experience in service, she was not yet used to being served.

Within days of Katherine's debut as queen, the royal couple embarked on a short honeymoon. Sadly, the only details the ambassadors were able to glean were that the pair took just a small company with them as they went on a hunting expedition.

Most of the lords took advantage of this short holiday to withdraw to their own houses and attend to private business.[18] However, no sooner had Katherine and Henry returned to court than they left for the summer progress. This was to last for the rest of the summer and into the autumn. Their route, which had been planned as far back as 6 July,[19] took them from Windsor to Reading, Ewelme, Notley, Buckingham, Grafton, Ampthill, Dunstable, St Albans and More Park.[20] The king and queen were due back in London on 20 October.

Most of the business transacted during this time was routine, although one item concerned Katherine directly. On 29 August, as the court was settling in at Grafton, news arrived of a certain priest of Windsor who had been imprisoned for 'speaking unfitting words of the Queen's grace'.[21] What the priest said or what had induced him to speak in such a manner is not recorded; ominously, the word 'prison' can still be seen in the badly mutilated Minute of the Privy Council. The priest had perhaps heard sensational gossip about Katherine's past, although it is doubtful that he would have had access to information regarding either Mannock or Dereham. Rather, he simply made disparaging remarks about a woman who, having been courted by one man, Culpeper, could so quickly transfer her love to another. This was a typical example of the double standards applied to the sexes, for Henry had done exactly the same in switching wives so rapidly.

While at Grafton, the court was visited by the French ambassador, Charles de Marillac, who saw Queen Katherine, although he was not introduced formally to her. In a pen portrait of the new queen,[22] he described her as 'a young lady of moderate beauty, but very graceful'. She was 'petite and slender' in stature, while her bearing was 'modest' and her face 'sweet and *délibéré*', meaning she appeared thoughtful, reflective. This indicates an unexpected introverted side to her character. Perhaps Katherine was shy in the face of so much close scrutiny, or she may simply have been tired, temporarily worn out by endless parties and the unaccustomed travelling. It was obvious to Marillac that Henry was so much in love with Katherine 'that he could not treat her well enough, and he made such demonstrations of affection, and caressed her more than he did' his other wives.

As though to endorse the ambassador's words, the anonymous Spanish chronicler claimed that 'the king had no wife who made him spend so much money on dresses and jewels as she did, who every day had some fresh caprice'.[23]

It was the queen's prerogative to decide how she and her ladies would dress.[24] As he noted Katherine's taste in fashion, Marillac remarked, perhaps with a touch of Gallic pride, that she wore French styles, as did the other ladies of the court. Katherine, therefore, favoured the highly flattering French fashions, with the pretty hoods that showed off a woman's hair and accentuated the contours of her face to the best advantage. This had been the preferred style in England since its introduction by Mary Tudor, the French Queen, and it was continued by Anne Boleyn, who took fashion to new heights. Following a brief respite during which Jane Seymour re-introduced the heavier and less becoming English dress, a tradition continued by Anne of Cleves, the French styles came firmly back into vogue as ladies followed Queen Katherine's example.

Katherine had her own coat of arms badge with marriage augmentations. It was not the badge of the crowned rose bearing the motto '*Rutilans rosa sine spina*' (the blushing rose without a thorn), which was once thought to apply to Katherine but in fact applied to Henry.[25] Rather, Katherine's arms feature, first quarter: an 'azure fleur-de-lis or in pale, between two flaunches ermine each enlarged with rose gules'; second quarter: 'England with a label of three points argent', taken from Katherine's descent from Thomas de Brotherton, the fifth son of Edward I; third quarter:

'Howard with the Flodden augmentation'; fourth quarter: 'azure two lions passant or within a ordure of four fleurs-de-lis dimidiated of the same'. The quarters were contained within a 'floriate wreath of pale blue glass interrupted at intervals by ruby ribbon, the background being amethyst glass'.[26]

Life for Katherine was now an endless round of hunts, banquets and entertainments laid on by a husband eager to please and indulge his new young wife.

On 8 September Katherine and Henry moved into Ampthill, in Bedfordshire, where they would stay for the rest of the month. One of Henry's favourite residences, Ampthill Castle had begun renovation work in 1534 in preparation for a visit Henry had planned to make with Anne Boleyn. New windows had been placed in the king's chamber and a new kitchen wing had been built. The Great Hall and the east and south wings were retiled. The brickwork was pointed in 1539, while the gutters, drains and privies were repaired the following year.[27]

The honeymoon atmosphere continued at Ampthill as it had at Grafton; Marillac, relaying news from his London residence, wrote that the king and no doubt Katherine too went 'with a small company, hunting'.[28] During this time, Henry had become ill, but he quickly recovered.[29]

It was while staying at Ampthill that Katherine's magnificent jewels were brought to her.[30] Items in her treasure chest included an upper habiliment or headdress of goldsmith's work enamelled and garnished with seven fair diamonds, seven fair rubies and seven fair pearls, and seven other similar items. This was jewellery rich in symbolism. As a token of Henry's love, diamonds meant durability, incorruptibility and sincerity; rubies symbolised royalty, Katherine's new status, as well as beauty and passion; pearls were for purity, the meaning of Katherine's name.

The same combination of jewels appears in other pieces. A carcanet, that is, a collar or necklace, made of goldsmith's work, was set with six very fair table diamonds and five very fair rubies; two fair pearls were set between the stones, totalling thirty-four pearls in all. There was a square containing twenty-seven table diamonds and twenty-six clusters of pearls, six to a cluster. Two other squares included goldsmith's work which was 'put into broken gold by the Queen', indicating that Katherine took an active interest in the design of her jewellery. She also designed a partlet, an item of clothing worn over the décolletage, containing sixteen diamonds, ten of which were 'set in a cipher by the Queen'. Two laces contained twenty-seven fair table diamonds and 158 fair pearls. Seventeen girdles were made of gold or goldsmith's work. There was a 'fair brooch of gold enamelled with white having a border of antique boys about the same, with a very fair square diamond held by a man whose coat and boots are enamelled with blue, and a king, crowned, with a sceptre in his hand at the one end thereof, and five persons more standing behind the same'. This brooch was inscribed by the king, his words engraved above the heads of the figures. There was a 'tablet of gold with a border of antique about the same having ten emeralds, and upon the one side thereof is an antique man standing in red, and upon the other side an antique man riding upon a lion, having also one pearl hanging at the same'. Katherine carried a small bag drawn closed at the top: a 'purse of gold enamelled red, containing eight diamonds set in goldsmith's work, with also hinges and button of wire gold'. Katherine would receive other gifts of jewellery in the months to come.

In addition to this stunning collection of jewels, Katherine received a clock in the shape of a book of 'gold enamelled'. On each side of the clock were three diamonds, one of which had a little man standing on it. Four turquoises and three rubies provided decoration, while a small gold chain enamelled in blue finished off the piece. Another clock was set into a golden pomander. This was 'enamelled with divers colours and garnished with twelve small rubies and a chain of gold containing eight pieces of gold of one fashion enamelled black and garnished with sixteen small rubies and sixteen small turquoises, twenty-four small pieces of gold and thirty-two pearls in links of gold in the same chain'.

As if all this were not enough, Katherine received several books, all highly elaborate and richly decorated with precious stones.[31] One was made of gold enamelled with black, garnished with twenty-seven rubies and finished with a gold chain containing forty-three pearls. Another was enamelled in green, white and blue, decorated with a fair sapphire on each side and eight rubies. A further book was gold enamelled with black, white and red, and garnished with eight small rubies. The back of this book was made of glass and it bore the initials H.I., indicating that it had once belonged to Henry and Jane Seymour. Yet another book of gold was decorated with twelve diamonds and forty rubies.

These books were meant for decoration rather than for reading. Katherine might have kept them with her jewellery, mirrors or other personal items. She would also wear small jewelled books such as these at her girdle, where they would catch the light as she walked. The jewels were cared for by Anne Herbert, who delivered them to Mrs Tyrwhitt, one of the queen's ladies of the privy chamber, at Ampthill.[32]

The occasion at which Katherine wore her jewels occurred about mid-way through her residency at Ampthill, and Katherine and the king were not the only ones to enjoy themselves. On 18 September Sir Edward Baynton and several others were 'advertised of the King's pleasure concerning as well the sober and temperate order that his Highness would have them to use in his Highness' chamber, and the Queen's, of presence, as also the behaviour of themselves towards the King's Privy Council, gentlemen of the privy chamber and all other his Highness's servants in every degree'.[33] That the Privy Council specifically mentioned 'sober and temperate order' suggests that Baynton and his cronies had become drunk and disorderly, perhaps letting themselves get carried away with the celebratory mood that had prevailed since the royal marriage. Shortly afterwards, William Dufair, 'one of the king's players on musical instruments' received an annuity of £38 while at Ampthill on 20 September.[34]

The king was taking every opportunity to show off his jewel of womanhood. Ambassadors and other visitors sent back news of the delightful new queen to their respective masters. Excited tittle-tattle had it that Katherine was with child; Francesco Contarini, the Venetian ambassador, took it a step further, insisting that 'Queen Katherine is said for certain to be pregnant.'

Soon, the little court moved on once more. Leaving Ampthill on 30 September, they arrived at Dunstable on 1 October, staying for two days before going to More Park in Hertfordshire. More Park, or the Manor of the More, had been acquired in 1522 by Cardinal Wolsey as Abbot of St Albans. He embellished the manor, adding new wings, a new range and an outer walled courtyard to the southern side of the moat. He also built lodgings on three sides, corner towers and a new gatehouse. On the north side, he added a second rectangular moat which enclosed a formal garden intersected by a timbered walkway. Other moated gardens extended to the south-west, all of which were interconnected by leats, or watercourses. Here, the Treaty of the More had been signed in 1525 and Katherine of Aragon had spent the winter of 1531–2, exiled from the court as her husband attempted to annul their marriage. The Manor of the More boasted fine royal apartments, with separate public and private chambers for the king and queen. These were connected in the centre of the north range, and were decorated with extravagant plasterwork and gilt.[35]

While they were staying at the More, Henry decided to show his generosity to Katherine's immediate family. Her brother Charles received an annual grant of £100 in tail male, meaning he would be allowed to bequeath this grant to his male heirs only. Similarly, another brother, George, received 100 marks annually on the same condition. He would later be granted various manors in Wiltshire, complete with the advowsons of rectories and certain lands in tenure, all of which had belonged to the dissolved monastery of Wilton. Katherine's stepsister Isabel Baynton and her children received 100 marks yearly in fee simple; that is, the grant was hers for ever, with no stipulation as to whom she could bequeath it.

The queen's sister Margaret, the wife of Sir Thomas Arundel, and her children received a similar award to that of Lady Baynton.[36]

Katherine received further gifts from Henry: two pairs of beads decorated with crosses, pillars and tassels (in other words, rosaries); and a gold brooch with thirty-five small diamonds and eighteen rubies set with the figures of 'three persons and two horses in the same being the story of Noah'. Lastly, three of the seventeen girdles Katherine would eventually own were given to her now, all three being of gold or goldsmith's work.

Although the king and queen were expected to go to London at the close of their progress, they went instead to Windsor, driven by news of plague in the city. They had settled in by 20 October 1540. Henry's fear of illness was notorious, but the plague frightened him most of all. He issued orders that no persons were to enter his house until they had been 'eight or ten days out of any suspected place'.

Among those who visited the court at this time were Lord William Howard and his wife, Margaret. Katherine asked where Dereham was, and Lady Margaret answered, 'Madam, he is here with my lord.' Katherine then explained that 'My lady of Norfolk hath desired me to be good to him, and so I will.'[37] That Dereham was visiting the court did not worry Katherine unduly.

The royal couple's self-exile from their capital incurred no hardship. Originally a Norman fortress, Windsor Castle had been used for royal apartments by Henry I, who was able to hold court there by 1110. Fifty years later, his grandson, Henry II, had replaced the timber structures with state apartments built of luxurious stone. When forced to strengthen the castle's defences during the rebellion instigated by his sons, he used heath stone from nearby glacial deposits, which was hard and difficult to work. The domestic arrangements became increasingly lavish as Henry III and then Edward III each made their mark on the castle. Edward, who would go on to found the Order of the Garter, demolished Henry III's buildings, establishing the Chapel of St George on the site as a fitting home for the new order. It was to Edward's royal residence that Katherine and Henry withdrew in the autumn of 1540; in this safe, magnificent and well-appointed retreat from plague and the unwanted attentions of ambassadors, the royal newly-weds could enjoy their extended honeymoon in perfect peace.

9

Royal Children

~

THE NEW QUEEN has 'completely acquired the King's grace'.[1] So said Charles de Marillac who, both frustrated and amused by Henry's reluctance to apply himself to business, had quickly grasped that the royal bridegroom had much more entertaining matters on his mind than the affairs of kingship.

Henry was keen to spend as much time as possible with Katherine. A somewhat diminished Privy Council did, however, continue to meet that autumn. Much of the business had to do with raising taxes, the money to be used against the ongoing threat of war. Otherwise, foreign ambassadors, as Marillac had already found out, were often left alone to kick their heels.

Henry was not the only one to be captivated by his new wife. In October Marguerite d'Angoulême, Queen of Navarre and sister of King François, had requested a picture of Henry 'with the Queen's Grace, my Lord Prince, my Lady Mary and Lady Elizabeth', a family portrait. Marguerite had previously befriended Anne Boleyn while she was in France, and the queen's request might have been prompted by curiosity about Anne's much younger cousin. However, exchanges of portraits and other gifts were not unusual among Europe's royal families; they were valuable diplomatic tools as well as tokens of friendship between princes.[2] The ambassador Wallop duly wrote to the Duke of Norfolk asking him to speak to Henry about it.[3] Just over a week later, Marguerite again sent her greetings. This time she wanted to know whether Her Grace was with child yet. She also reminded Wallop about the picture of the royal family that she had asked for.[4] When this was still not forthcoming, Marguerite wrote once more, with increasing impatience, for the requested picture.[5]

Sadly, this painting so eagerly sought by Marguerite appears never to have been executed; or if it was, it has since gone missing. This is to be deeply regretted, as it would have provided the earliest, and perhaps the only indisputably authentic likeness of Queen Katherine Howard.

While Katherine was possibly not 'esteemed the most beautiful of all the women of her time', as the Greek traveller and attaché Nucius of Corcyra insists,[6] a Holbein miniature of the queen shows her to have been blessed with a well-proportioned and full figure. Her heavy-lidded hazel eyes are framed by well-shaped dark eyebrows, while her auburn hair is shown off to good effect by her French hood, complete with a long black veil and upper habiliment encrusted with jewels and pearls. Her complexion is translucent. The hint of an emerging double chin and the wide Howard nose complete what is overall an attractive face. She wears a gown of cloth of gold with a wide jewelled band at the neckline over a white chemisette and deep furred sleeves. Her jewellery also includes several rings and a long necklace of pearls and rubies from which is suspended a pendant of gold adorned by a large ruby and what could be an emerald or, perhaps, a diamond.[7]

Another portrait believed to be of Katherine, although highly stylised, can be found in the Great East Window of King's College Chapel, Cambridge. The window was commissioned in 1515, with the initial work done by Bernard Flower, the king's glazier. Flower died in 1517 with only four of the planned eighteen windows in the chapel completed. After an unexplained delay, the contract to complete the remaining windows was granted to Galyon Hone, who began work in 1526. He was due to finish the work in 1531, but the initials H K (Henry and Katherine) indicate that he did not complete the east window until after 1540. The windows had been designed long before Katherine became queen – indeed, before she was even born. It is clear, however, that the design for the Solomon and Sheba window was modified after Katherine's accession. The image of Henry as Solomon belongs to a later date than the initial designs allow. Therefore, there is every possibility that Katherine's features were captured for the Old Testament queen.[8]

The pleasures and excitement of having a beautiful new queen were working wonders for Henry. The last time Frederick, the Count Palatine, had seen Henry was before his marriage to Anne of Cleves. The king, at that point, had still managed to cut a handsome figure. Now, having viewed a recent portrait, Frederick thought he saw a change for the worse in the king and wondered if 'Henry were not waxen fat'.[9] Indeed not, assured Richard Pate, adding that Henry was 'as merry and lusty, lauded be God, as ever you were, and well enseamed'. Since 'enseamed' refers to a hawk cleansed of superfluous fat, Pate, with more discretion than honesty, was implying that Henry was trim. At this Frederick mused, 'then is this painter . . . not his craft's master, that offered me in this town his picture to buy, whereby it appeared that his majesty, since my being in England, was become much more corpulent'.

Frederick might not have been the most diplomatic of men, but he did have a point. Henry was fast approaching a waist measurement of fifty-four inches, which was only slightly less than his chest measurement of fifty-seven inches. Moreover, the king was all too aware of his decline. Only four years previously, he had confided to Cromwell that 'he felt himself already growing old' and he despaired of having any child by the queen, Jane Seymour. Now, two queens later, Henry was a new man. Marriage to Katherine had restored to him a cherished youth he had thought long lost.

Since Katherine had come into Henry's life, there was nothing but talk of 'rejoicings and amusements'. Henry had never been 'in such good spirits or in so good a humour as he is at present'. Ambassador Marillac described the 'new rule of life' Henry had adopted. 'He rises in the morning between five and six; at seven he hears mass; and afterwards he rides till dinner, which is at ten a.m.' Henry loved being in the country, 'and changing places so often, he finds himself in much better health than in winter, when he was residing in London'. Possibly, Henry was trying to keep up with the energetic young Katherine. Sadly, Marillac does not describe the queen's routine, but a tiny hint of it comes from Katherine herself: at six o'clock, Master Hennage would bring her knowledge of the king.[10]

So happy were Katherine and Henry away from London, their days filled with hunting, their evenings passed in music and dancing, that the king was reluctant to return. Instead, he prolonged his honeymoon and allowed those who had business with him to visit, provided they observed every precaution against the plague.

However, even Katherine's beauty and charm could not entirely chase matters of state from Henry's mind and, as of mid-November, the king began to feel the weight of pressing affairs. Several weeks earlier, Philip Melanchthon, the German theologian and reformer, had expressed his dismay at the 'atrocious crimes' being committed in England: 'the divorce with the lady of Juliers is already made and another married.'[11] Henry increasingly worried that the German diets would think that 'he only observed the law of marriage at his pleasure, and innovated nothing in religion but what served his ambition and avarice'. Henry was anxious to 'purge himself' with the Emperor Charles and the German princes, feeling the need to give his reasons for repudiating Anne of Cleves and marrying Katherine Howard. Particularly, he wanted to prove that 'nothing has been innovated here upon the doctrines of the primitive Church'. To that end, he sent the rigidly conservative Stephen Gardiner, Bishop of Winchester, on embassy to the emperor. His task was to persuade Charles that, in religious matters, Henry was far from insincere and self-serving. Winchester was to be accompanied by a large entourage of over one hundred horsemen, all handsomely dressed in grey velvet and wearing great gold chains. This display of opulence was designed to demonstrate to Charles that the power and dignity of the Catholic Church was being protected.[12] Moreover, Winchester could point out that Queen Katherine, as a member of the predominantly Catholic Howard family, was inclined towards religious conservatism rather than reformation.

Ambassador Marillac, thinking entirely in political terms, believed that the Bishop of Winchester had been selected to lead the delegation to Charles because he had been 'one of the principal authors' of the Howard match.[13] This was true to the extent that Gardiner had helped prepare the legal case for the annulment of the Cleves marriage.[14] Marillac's comment is a contributing factor to the persistent belief that Katherine Howard had deliberately been placed at court to be used as a pawn by her conservative family and supporters during the religious and political squabbles that resulted in the destruction of Cromwell and the rise of the Howards. This view does not take into account that Henry had been the one to notice Katherine, had turned to her when the unsuitability of Anne of Cleves became clear, courted her, won her and had then taken her as his bride and queen. He had done this without pressure from anyone or anything except his own desires. Henry had been attracted by Katherine's physical beauty. He had admired her musical talents and was charmed by her sparkling personality. He saw her as maidenly and capable of producing more children, preferably sons. She possessed all the qualities he looked for in a wife and queen, as was revealed during the search for his fourth consort. To put it another way, Katherine, although she had received help from her family in the form of advice, new clothes and a quiet corner in which to entertain her suitor, had captured Henry's heart entirely on her own merit.

In matters of religion, although Katherine's personal religious leanings are not easily discerned, there is no reason to think that she was not as good a Catholic as any other. At the very least she observed the rituals of her faith, as evinced by her collection of rosaries. She also owned several religious books, mainly mass-books.[15] Of course, the books of a queen are far from ordinary: one was covered with purple velvet and closed with copper clasps; a smaller mass-book, bound in leather, reflected the growing fashion for leather as a binding, but it was also practical and sturdy enough to be handled frequently. Katherine owned a New Testament too, which was covered in purple velvet with silver and gilt decoration and clasps. Finally, she had a small French book covered with crimson velvet with two clasps of gold, which bore the scripture *Ihesus fiat voluntas tua*, 'Jesus, thy will be done'.

Katherine also possessed several books conjointly with Henry. Bearing the initials K and H, they comprised a collection of works by the Church Fathers: Ambrose, Augustine, Jerome, John Chrysostom and Gregory the Great. As with the queen's own highly decorated books, these fine volumes were printed and bound for display rather than for reading. In this case, they were intended to grace Henry's new palace of Nonsuch in Surrey.

One final book should be mentioned. Following the untimely death of Queen Jane Seymour from complications following the birth of Prince Edward, concerned midwives and physicians looked for any new books that could provide them with up-to-date information on childbirth and its dangers to the mother and the child. Several years previously, Eucharius Rösslin's *De Partu Hominis* was published in Germany, with subsequent editions appearing periodically in various other European countries. In 1540 it was translated into English by Richard Jonas as *The Byrth of Mankynde*. Although originally intended to be dedicated to Anne of Cleves, the first edition is inscribed 'Unto the most gracious and in all goodness most excellent virtuous Lady Queen Katherine wife and most dearly beloved spouse unto the most mighty sapient Christen prince King Henry the VIII. Richard Jonas wisheth perpetual joy and felicity.'[16] The book deals with all matters concerning pregnancy and birth, from menstruation, fertility and conception to labour and the health of the new mother and her new-born infant, by way of humoral theory and anatomy. It was a highly appropriate book to dedicate to the young Queen Katherine, whose principal job it was to add to the royal nursery.

Katherine and Henry, accompanied by their small retinue of Privy Councillors, moved on from Windsor and made their leisurely way to Woking Palace, which had once belonged to Henry's grandmother, Margaret Beaufort, arriving on 23 November. Henry had gradually transformed the original manor house into a royal hunting lodge complete with great hall, privy court, king's hall, queen's gallery and apartments, king's apartments, great kitchens modelled on those at Hampton Court, and two chapels, all enclosed within a double moat. There were lodgings for courtiers and visitors, stables, even a corn mill and a fulling-mill. The grounds were a paradise of bowling greens, orchards, fishponds and extensive parklands, which included a deer park. Even as winter drew on, the luxurious palace was a fine place to be.

It was amid the tranquil beauty of Woking that Katherine received an unexpected visit. Katherine Tylney, her kinswoman and companion from Norfolk House, arrived in the company of Francis Dereham,[17] come to request a place in Katherine's household. Unlike another of her companions from the old days, Joan Bulmer, Tylney's petition was successful and, on 29 November, Katherine engaged her as a chamberer. Dereham, whose influence may or may not have swayed Queen Katherine's decision, stayed with the court overnight and departed the following day.[18]

A few days after this, the new queen received a most illustrious guest. Upon her marriage to Henry VIII, Katherine had acquired three stepchildren. Mary, aged twenty-four, whose education had been directed according to her future status as queen, was the daughter of Katherine of Aragon. Elizabeth, the intellectual and spirited daughter of Anne Boleyn, was approaching seven. Finally, there was Edward, the intelligent and precocious son of Jane Seymour, who was now almost three years old. Because each of them lived in their own households, they were not all introduced to Katherine straight away. The first to meet her was Mary, and relations between the two ladies did not get off to the best start.

The anonymous author of the largely unreliable *Chronicle of Henry VIII* had it that Katherine, as soon as she became queen, did not 'make so much account of Madam Mary as the good Queen Jane had done'. Such behaviour was attributed to Katherine's being 'a mere child', rather than any lack of love for Mary.

Katherine, the chronicler continues, was put out because 'all the ladies paid as much court to Madam Mary as they did to the Queen'. As a result, Katherine, 'although she was so young, got angry with them and told the king of it'. Henry's solution was to 'order his daughter away from court, sending her to live in her own establishment, and to take the Prince Edward with her'. This Mary did, 'and during the Queen's life returned no more to court'.[19]

As is often the case with this chronicle, a small measure of truth is mixed with a heavy dose of fantasy. While the whole story is not known for certain, much of what had happened between Katherine and Mary can be reconstructed from a paragraph in a letter written by Mary's greatest champion, the imperial ambassador, Eustache Chapuys.[20]

Mary had been shocked to learn that two of her maids were to be taken away from her. Not knowing why, she turned to Chapuys, a man who had steadfastly supported her mother through the difficult last years of her life and perhaps the only person she felt she could fully trust, and he looked into the matter for her. He found out that the attempt to deprive Mary of her maids had 'proceeded entirely from this new Queen, who was rather offended at her not treating her with the same respect as the two preceding ones'. Armed with this information, Mary managed to find 'some means of conciliation' with Katherine and straightened out the matter, with the result that 'for the present, at least, her two maids will not be dismissed from her service'.

What had actually happened? Clearly, Mary had caused some offence by word or deed and had been taken to task over it. The injured party was Katherine, but Henry was also angry on Katherine's behalf and he threatened to take away Mary's maids.

He had used this form of punishment against his daughter before. In October 1533, when Mary refused to acknowledge Anne Boleyn or her daughter, Henry reduced her household and her yearly allowance. In February 1541 he would remove another of her maids, an affair that would end in tragedy: Ambassador Chapuys would report Lady Mary's distress and sadness 'at the death of one of her damsels, who has actually died of grief at her having been removed from her service by the King's order'.[21]

The range of Mary's putative offence is almost limitless. She was the proud daughter of a proud queen and a reigning king. She was born a princess, while Katherine, although she carried royal blood in her veins, was not. Mary knew and understood kingship, or, more precisely, queenship, in a way that Katherine never could. This perspective meant that Mary viewed her own mother, Katherine of Aragon, as queen even after Henry had annulled their marriage. Those same firmly held principles meant that Mary could never accept Anne Boleyn as queen because the 'real' queen, her own mother, still lived.[22] On the other hand, Jane Seymour and Anne of Cleves had been acceptable to Mary because neither of them had become queen while their predecessor was still living. As such, Mary was able to recognise their queenly status. In Katherine's case, she could not. For Mary, Katherine was not queen and never would be while Anne of Cleves, Henry's true wife and queen, was still alive.

Mary was in a difficult situation and her inability to make friends with Katherine is entirely understandable. Mary, despite her age, was still unmarried. The much younger Katherine was not only a wife, but she had every chance of becoming a mother; and her eldest son would be the long-awaited new Duke of York. Finally, there is a personal element to consider. The two women were polar opposites. Katherine was effervescent and fun-loving. Mary was sedate and pious. Katherine, as Anne Boleyn's cousin and a member of a family that Mary had every reason to dislike, would always be resented no matter how kind or accommodating she might try to be.

On Katherine's part, she might have been sensitive to an unusually high degree to anything that might be interpreted as a slight. Perhaps there was more than a touch of Howard pride involved. Mary's refusal to accept her, combined with gossip about Anne of Cleves and the pressure to produce a child as soon as possible, could well have undermined the young queen's self-confidence.

In the end, and contrary to the assertions of the Spanish chronicler, the differences between Katherine and Mary were quickly resolved. Mary would later come to live permanently at court with the blessing both of her father and Queen Katherine.

The royal couple remained at Woking until 7 December when they moved on to Oatlands. No sooner had they settled in than Katherine received a letter from Archbishop Lee of York, whom she had been pressing throughout the autumn of 1540 for an advowson for Mr Lowe, one of her chaplains. The archbishop promised he would grant the next one to Mr Lowe, but Katherine wanted preferment for one of her chaplains now. She made a further attempt, this time on behalf of Dr Henry Mallett. Having sent several letters, she eventually received a reply. The archbishop pointed out to the queen that he had 'never granted advowson saving at the King's command, but one, which I have many times sore repented'. Going on, he explained that 'Those who labour for such advowsons espy out where any man having promotion is like to die, and having obtained the advowson of his promotion they "harken and gape every day when he will die"; and this uncharitableness is so discrepant to the order of priesthood that I am loath to make such grants.' He assured her, 'as he did before', that he had promised the next promotion of £40 or thereabouts, to her chaplain, Mr Lowe.[23] As Katherine settled into life at Oatlands, she could be satisfied that she had at least tried to fulfil one of her primary duties as queen: patronage.

Oatlands, which had provided the idyllic setting for her tranquil summer wedding, its parklands softened in the golden autumn light, now became the perfect honeymoon venue. The king and queen would remain there in blissful seclusion for a further eleven days. During this time, Henry gave Katherine two more rosaries, similar in style to those he had already given her.[24] Since the king was so deeply in love with his wife, such lavish gifts were to be expected. Like any ardent lover, Henry continued to court Katherine even after she was his. He would present her with yet another gift after they arrived back at Hampton Court on 18 December,[25] this time a 'rope of fair large pearl containing a hundred pearls'.[26]

For Katherine, a king's jewel for womanhood, life had changed beyond all measure and expectation. Maiden to a queen at the dawn of the year, she was now queen herself. Courted by the most eligible beaux in the king's entourage, she had ended up with the most eligible man in the land. Having grown up sharing a bed in the crowded household of her step-grandmother, Katherine now slept in a luxurious bed of her own; and when she was visited during the night, it was not by a man who gave little thought to her pleasure and comfort, but by a gentle and loving husband. The wheel turns with the seasons.

10

The First Christmas

~

T HE TUDOR CHRISTMAS was a contrast of solemn religious
observance and festal merriment. Much more than one day of
celebration, Christmas was in itself a season in which the birth
of Christ was celebrated alongside the feast days of several saints,
including St Stephen and St John the Apostle. Childermas or the
feast of the Holy Innocents was celebrated on 28 December and
commemorated the murder of the male infants of Bethlehem by
Herod. The season culminated on Twelfth Night or Epiphany,
which commemorated the visit of the Magi to the Christ child as
well as Jesus's baptism.

The four weeks of Advent were marked by fasting. No meat,
but only fish was eaten at this time, a practice that served several
purposes, both secular and sacred. Eschewing meat allowed people
to fulfil their religious duties of abstinence and self-abnegation; on
a more practical level, it helped conserve the meat supply and
assisted the fishing industry. On Christmas Eve, the fast was even
more strict than usual, with meat, eggs and cheese all prohibited.

The fasting laws were vigorously enforced by King Henry, and
he was careful to observe them himself. Katherine would follow
her husband's example, either by choice or expediency. Even so,
it was no hardship. For someone of Katherine's status, fasting simply
meant putting aside the large pies and roasts for a while and eating
soups, stews and fish. If this should prove too much, special dispensation could be obtained, especially by the sick and pregnant
women.

As 1540 drew to a close, Ambassador Marillac reported that

Katherine was *grosse*.¹ While this could mean that the queen had grown stout, this word more usually describes pregnancy. Once again, gossip had it that Katherine was with child. As if to confound matters, another rumour arose that insisted that Henry was planning to repudiate Katherine and take back Anne of Cleves. As before, it was inspired by Henry's kindness to his former wife, to whom he had sent many presents. Marillac knew better. He had witnessed the public caresses that Henry bestowed upon Katherine and was able to say 'that I think the rumour to be just talk'.²

Once the asceticism of Advent and Christmas Eve was over, the court abandoned itself to banqueting and entertainments, interludes, games and disguisings, all overseen by the Lord of Misrule. It was an enchanting time. Mumming or masquing was popular, in which people donned costumes and masks, often with symbolic or allegorical themes. Households welcomed players and jesters, and even acrobats, into their homes, while shouts of 'wassail' and 'drink-hail' could be heard above the clamour of merrymaking. By now the celebrations included Christmas carols, which had made their first recorded appearance in the household books of Henry's mother, Elizabeth of York,³ and were danced and sung by the revellers.

The palace was decorated with holly, ivy and mistletoe; there was also the traditional kissing bough, comprising hoops of greenery hung from the ceiling and lit with candles from which a sprig of mistletoe was suspended. Kissing under the mistletoe was long established, having been brought to England by the Vikings.

The dishes Katherine enjoyed now that the fasting was over included the traditional Christmas pie, made with beef, lamb, chicken and goose held together with suet and flavoured with fruit and spices. It formed part of the main meal alongside the boar's head, decorated with garlands and served with an apple in its mouth. As queen, Katherine was entitled to eat swan, the meat of which was served in a pie decorated by the bird's own head, neck and feathers. Peacocks were served in the same way, although the often unpalatable meat was sometimes replaced by that of a goose.

These dishes were accompanied by forcemeat or stuffing made of meat mixed with sage, thyme and marjoram. The stuffing served to disguise the taste of badly cooked meat, but it also held the bird together during roasting and made the meat go further. Sweet dishes included furmenty, which was hulled wheat boiled in milk and seasoned with cinnamon and sugar, and plum porridge, a thick soup containing raisins, currants and spices and flavoured with brandy or wine. The traditional drink was wassail, ale brewed with apples and spices, served in a large bowl, decorated with ribbons, which was passed from person to person as wassail songs were sung.

New Year's Day was the traditional day of gift-giving. If Henry followed his father's example, he would receive his gifts in his chamber as soon as he had put on his shoes. Heralded by the sound of trumpets, servants bearing presents would enter, those from the queen coming first. The process was then repeated, with the queen being given her presents in her own chambers.[4]

Katherine's presents from Henry were magnificent, and included an upper habiliment set with eight diamonds and seven rubies, a square containing thirty-three diamonds and sixty rubies with an edge of pearl, a 'Jesus' or crucifix of gold containing thirty-two diamonds and enhanced with three pearls drops, a girdle of gold-smith's work and a chain of gold. How different from two years ago, when she had received a silken heart's-ease and an old shirt from Dereham!

Sadly, Katherine's gifts to Henry are not recorded, but she did give a cross 'with the pillar reserved' to Lady Margaret Douglas.[5] At the same time, Lady Mary presented her father with a gift, and Henry sent one to her 'both from himself and from his queen'.[6] Katherine and Henry also sent presents to Anne of Cleves, 'rich clothes, silver plate and jewels, thought to be worth some six or seven ecus'.[7] Anne, meanwhile, had sent her new brother 'two fine, large horses caparisoned in mauve velvet, with trappings and so forth to match'.[8]

Thus far the festivities had carried on very much as they always had. However, this year would see royal Christmas customs upended by a most extraordinary event. On the second day of the New Year, and upon Henry's express order, Anne was invited to Hampton Court.[9] Making her way from Richmond, she promptly arrived having been 'conducted very honourably by several gentlemen',[10] one of whom was Lord William Howard, the queen's uncle, whom she had met on the way. Lord William 'could not well, for courtesy's sake, refuse to accompany her to the gates' of Hampton Court.

Anne went immediately to the quarters that had been prepared for her, and here she was received by several ladies, first among them Katherine, Duchess of Suffolk, and Anne, Countess of Hertford. They accompanied Anne to her chambers before conducting her to the queen's apartments. Here, Anne's progress was paused. The situation was unique, and royal protocol did not cover occasions such as this. With their roles now reversed, Katherine was being instructed on the correct etiquette to use when receiving Anne, and as Chancellor Audeley and the Earl of Sussex coached her, the queen's former mistress waited patiently outside.

Finally the doors opened. Anne entered and approached the queen 'with as much reverence and punctilious ceremony as if she herself were the most insignificant damsel about Court'. She remained on her knees as she addressed Katherine, despite the queen's 'prayers and entreaties'. Katherine received Anne 'with all courtesy and favour, and showing all *humanité* [kindness]'.

At this point, Henry entered the room. He bowed low to Anne then embraced and kissed her before all three took their seats at the supper table. Katherine and Henry sat in their usual places, while Anne was seated 'lower than the Princess Mary is accustomed to be',[11] that is, she occupied 'a seat near the bottom of the table, all the time keeping as good mien and countenance, and looking as unconcerned as if there had been nothing between them'. However, this was not to slight Anne; king, queen and 'sister' were merely following protocol. After supper Katherine, Anne and Henry conversed together 'in a most gracious manner' before the king retired to his apartments.

Although the king had withdrawn, that did not mean the evening was at an end. Katherine and Anne took to the floor, first dancing together and then separately, their partners selected from among the king's gentlemen.

Music for this and other occasions throughout the festivities was provided by the king's trumpeters, sackbuts and drumslades as well as Katherine's minstrels, Thomas Evans, William More and Andrew Newman.[12] Marillac noticed that 'the said lady of Cleves made no demonstration of being unhappy that the other occupies her place'. Rather, Katherine and Anne spent the rest of the evening, '*beurrent l'une à l'autre*' (getting plastered), and enjoying themselves so much that 'the former queen showed no sign of being jealous'.[13]

Katherine and Henry dined with Anne the following day amid 'conversation, amusement and mirth'. As he had done previously, the king again withdrew, leaving the two ladies to dance together once more. This time, the dancing was interrupted when one of the king's 'confidential chamberlains' entered bearing the gift of a ring and two small dogs for Katherine. The delighted queen, in her kindness, passed the gifts to Anne. Later that day, Anne retired to her apartments. Emerging two hours later, she returned home to Richmond with the same company who had escorted her to Hampton Court.

It had been a delightful interlude, and there was none of the awkwardness that might have marred the celebrations. Katherine had thoroughly enjoyed herself, as had Anne. In fact, Anne had been so graciously received by the queen and, especially, her former husband that the tale-wrights, swinging back into action, insisted that the king wanted to take her back. Once again the ambassador Marillac felt it necessary to refute such silly stories. He noted that it was contradicted by the *grands caresses* that Henry continued to give Katherine and offered the observation that 'this king would rather keep two [queens] than to leave this one, who is so much in his favour'.[14] Chapuys, too, was aware of the latest gossip. Anne of Cleves 'has been recalled' to Richmond, he noted, although this was not quite true, as Anne had simply returned home at the end of her holiday. This, together with the fact that Katherine is 'not yet in the family way', had inspired some to think that reconciliation between Anne and Henry was a possibility. Should that be the case, however, Chapuys pledged that he would 'seize every opportunity of indirectly thwarting it'.[15]

While Katherine was presiding over the Christmas and New Year festivities, a dispute erupted between Thomas Smith, clerk of the queen's household, and William Gray, 'sometime servant to the late Lord Cromwell'.[16] The men had been writing invectives against each other, the altercation being opened, in print at least, by Smith, who scorned 'that false traitor Thomas Cromwell'. Gray rebuked Smith for reviling the dead and accusing him of being popish. Smith retaliated with a stanza on 'seditious persons', and, angry at being named popish, he vowed to seek redress 'before the higher powers'. Gray came back in a similar vein, ending his stanza with prayers for Henry VIII, Queen Katherine and Prince Edward.

With the quarrel threatening to spiral out of hand, it came to the attention of the Privy Council. Not only Smith and Gray, but the printers Richard Bankes and Richard Grafton were called to explain themselves. Bankes denied any part in the matter, which was patently untrue,[17] but he appears to have been believed and no more is heard of him. Grafton had printed part of the invectives, but he was also caught in possession of an epistle, written in English by Melanchthon, which was contrary to the Six Articles, an Act which consolidated Catholic doctrines and reflected Henry's own religious beliefs and aspirations. Grafton was 'committed to the porter's ward' overnight, while Smith and Gray were commanded to appear before the Privy Council at seven the following morning. Considering that Smith was a royal servant, and he had said he would appeal to 'higher powers', Henry would certainly have been alerted to the situation, as would Katherine. However, neither of them made any effort to support Smith, who was left to his fate.

The following day he, Gray and Grafton were committed to the Fleet Prison 'there to remain during the King's pleasure'.

Her indifference on this occasion did not mean that Katherine was unwilling to become involved in politics. For instance, at her uncle of Norfolk's bidding, she was instrumental in obtaining the appointment of her uncle, Lord William, as ambassador to France.[18] Norfolk had wanted to promote Lord William as the replacement for John Wallop for the past year, but his plan had been thwarted by Cromwell.[19] Now that Katherine was queen, her family took every advantage of her influence with Henry.

Not only was Katherine a woman of considerable power, she also now became very wealthy. At a meeting at Hampton Court in mid-January, her jointure was settled, conferring upon her the castles, lordships and manors that had formed part of the jointure of the late Queen Jane. Covering a wide geographical area, these properties consisted of manors in Essex, Cambridgeshire, Norfolk, Suffolk, Northamptonshire, Gloucestershire, Wiltshire and Huntingdonshire. They included the castle, lordship and manor of Fotheringhay, with its associations with the house of York, and Great and Little Walsingham, the place of pilgrimage; there were forests, chases and parks, advowsons and patronage, such as that of the appropriately named St Katherine near the Tower of London as well as the mansion and castle of Baynard's Castle on the north bank of the Thames. At the same time, Katherine received properties formerly belonging to the executed Henry, Marquis of Exeter, Thomas Cromwell and Sir Walter Hungerford. Some of the properties had belonged to Margaret, Countess of Salisbury, who now languished in the Tower awaiting an uncertain future, and Hugh, the attainted former Abbot of Reading. In addition, Katherine was granted the goods and chattels of all the men and tenants in those properties, as well as those of fugitives and felons. She benefited from 'fines, forfeitures, amerciaments, returns of writs, waifs and strays, deodands, treasure trove and divers other perquisites'. She was given power to appoint her own clerks of the market, free warren and other privileges.[20] All this was to ensure that Katherine could support herself and her household in due dignity should she outlive her husband, not a doubtful scenario given their respective ages. That Katherine's possessions and privileges were to be held for life would make her appear more eligible should she decide to place herself on the marriage market. Meanwhile, the Earl of Southampton could report that 'His Majesty and the Queen, with my lord Prince, are in good health.'[21]

Life took on a more sedate pace now for Katherine, contrasting markedly with the excitement of her first few months as queen. However, an event was about to occur that was to have far-reaching consequences. As with most such events, it began inconspicuously, giving little sign that things were about to change in the most dramatic way.

In February Henry planned to visit his coastal defences, particularly Dover, to inspect them and to oversee repairs. As preparations for the visit got under way, he became ill. Forced to cancel his excursion, he stayed put at Hampton Court, where he was attended by physicians and worried over by courtiers.

Although he had been unwell the previous September, he had quickly recovered; now his health failed him again. At first it was thought that Henry had a slight tertian fever. This, in Ambassador Marillac's opinion, would have been of great benefit to the king, since he was very stout.[22] Soon, however, the true cause of the infirmity revealed itself.

This was an ulcer on Henry's left leg which, because 'he is very stout and marvellously excessive in his drinking and eating', often troubled him. The sore, normally 'kept open to maintain his health, had suddenly closed to his great alarm'. This had happened once before, in the late spring of 1538, when the 'King has had stopped one of the fistulas of his legs, and for 10 or 12 days the humours which had no outlet were like to have stifled him, so that he was sometime without speaking, black in the face, and in great danger.'[23] So great was the danger, in fact, that the court began to divide so 'that one party is for the young prince, and the other for Madame Mary'.

Happily, with careful treatment, the king made a full recovery once again, and was 'now so well that no one ever expected it'. His condition was severe but it was easily treated and the Privy Council recorded that 'the King's Majesty had been somewhat diseased with a tertian [fever] but thanks be to God recovered again to his health'.[24]

Nevertheless, Henry's infirmity had left his spirits low; he became despondent and irascible. Courtiers and ministers found him 'of a different opinion in the morning than dinner'. Henry had his complaints too. His subjects murmured about his religious reforms. He had 'an unhappy people to govern', although he would soon make them 'so poor that they would not have the boldness nor the power to oppose him'. Nor did ministers escape the king's wrath. Most of the Privy Council, he said, 'under pretence of serving him, were only temporising and dissembling for their own profit'. Henry assured them, however, that he 'knew the good servants from the flatterers, and if God lent him health, he would take care that their projects should not succeed'. He even reproached them for the death of Cromwell, saying that 'upon light pretexts, by false accusations, they made him put to death the most faithful servant he ever had'. As though anyone could make Henry do anything he did not want to do.

A very dull Shrovetide came and went, with none of the festivities that usually marked the occasion. Katherine's chaplain, Dr Mallett, preached before the king and queen on Passion Sunday, 9 March.[25] Shut away at Hampton Court, 'with so little company that his court resembled more a private family than a king's train', Henry received no visitors; musicians and ambassadors alike were sent away.[26]

Despite his best efforts to maintain a healthy lifestyle, Henry had been unable to turn back the clock and recapture his lost youth for very long. Although he lusted for life and his queen, he faltered under the weight of almost fifty years, increasingly failing health and the results of injury. The spirit, so very willing, was thwarted by flesh that was just too weak. Unwilling to allow his jewel to see him in such a reduced, vulnerable condition, the proud king closed his doors to her. In the subdued, near silent corridors and chambers of Hampton Court, Katherine found herself alone.

King Henry, 'feigning indisposition, was ten or twelve days without seeing his queen or allowing her to come to his room',[27] so said Eustache Chapuys. In his assertion that Henry had feigned indisposition, he was quite wrong. Henry really had been ill, although not as seriously as was originally thought.

Still, feverish illnesses often leave depression in their wake. As Marillac had noticed,[28] Henry was particularly affected, as might be any ageing man with a young wife. It was this more than anything else that Henry wanted to hide from Katherine, but he had other matters on his mind too. Marillac reported that, during the king's illness, 'there was no talk of anything else, except the finishing of the bulwarks at Calais and Guînes',[29] a matter that had concerned Henry for some time. As it was, Henry's mood eventually lifted and the court became a more cheerful place. By the third week in March, the crisis appeared to be over, and the king was well enough to move to Greenwich, where he planned to spend Easter with his queen and court.

In a life that had become a series of happy occasions, feasts and celebration, still another joyous event awaited Katherine as she and Henry made their way to Greenwich. Since this was her first entry into London as queen, a traditional water pageant was prepared for her. Unusually, the royal couple travelled together in the king's barge, the *Lion*. They were escorted by the Lord Mayor, the aldermen and all the crafts of the city dressed in their finery. It was a splendid and colourful scene, with the barges, all 'goodly hanged and set with banners', lining the route between the Tower and London Bridge. As Katherine and her king drew level with the Tower, 'there was a great shot of guns'.[30]

Katherine was welcomed and acclaimed in full accordance with her right as queen. When her reception was finished, she turned her attention to one of the great duties that were required of her. Queens regnant are bound by virtue of their coronation oath to uphold the laws of justice; not so queens consort. Katherine, from this 'triumphal march', took the opportunity 'and courage to beg and entreat the King for the release of Master Wyatt, a prisoner in the said Tower'.[31]

Thomas Wyatt, together with Sir Ralph Sadler, had been arrested at Hampton Court on the evening of 17 January, an 'unexpected and important event'.[32] The following morning, their hands bound, the two men were 'conducted with 24 archers to the Tower'. For gentlemen to be forced to walk through the streets of London like common criminals was bad enough, but 'what is worse', said Chapuys, Wyatt's house had 'been searched, and the King's seals have been placed on the chest and cupboards'.[33]

Marillac was at a loss to understand why Wyatt and Sadler had been arrested, and was frustrated that it would be 'difficult to learn the true cause of their taking, for, by a law made at last Parliament, they condemn people without hearing them'.[34] Worryingly, the ambassador added that 'when a man is prisoner in the Tower none dare meddle with his affairs, unless to speak ill of him, for fear of being suspected of the same crime'.

For Sadler, the ordeal was a short one. He was back in attendance at the Privy Council two days later. As to Wyatt, Ambassador Chapuys made an attempt to gain more information. As far as he could learn 'no substantial charge has yet been brought against Master Huyet [Wyatt] . . . with the exception of words, which elsewhere than here would not have been noticed.' While nothing could be proved against Wyatt, 'these people are so suspicious that they are apt to qualify as mortal sin any innocent doing and saying that may at the time thwart their political plans'.[35] Even so, it had been words, 'spoken but in familiar secret talk, nothing affirming', that had condemned Sir Thomas More.[36]

Thomas Wyatt's story was to have a happier ending than that of More. Henry was disposed towards leniency, and he was further swayed by Katherine's gentle supplication on behalf of the poet. The royal pardon was duly granted, although there were conditions. The first was that Wyatt 'should confess the guilt for which he had been arrested'. That was reasonable enough, but the second condition was harsh. He 'was to resume conjugal relations with his wife, from whom he had been separated for upwards of fifteen years'. The irony of this demand cannot have been lost on the luckless Wyatt, who had witnessed at uncomfortably close quarters the king's own marital adventures.

Next, Katherine directed her husband's attention to John Wallop, whom her uncle, Lord William Howard, had replaced as ambassador to France. Wallop, whose Catholicism was well known, was suspected of treasonous activity or, as far as Ambassador Chapuys could find out, of 'having said something in favour of Pope Paul'.[37] In fact, he was accused of holding treasonous correspondence with Richard Pate and was arrested upon his return to England. He was detained at the house of the Earl of Southampton, the lord privy seal, before being brought to the Privy Council where Henry graciously permitted him to present his defence. As in Wyatt's case, Henry was inclined to be merciful, while Katherine's pleading for Wallop's pardon provided a sympathetic and very public platform upon which he could demonstrate his magnanimity.

More can be read into Katherine's actions than merely the fulfilment of her queenly duty or providing an opportunity for Henry to make himself appear even more lovable to his subjects. Although Thomas Wyatt was Katherine's distant relative, as an evangelical he was in opposition to her when it came to matters of religion. Katherine, therefore, was tacitly making a statement of religious neutrality by placing Wyatt before Wallop in her intercession.[38]

Royal duties having been fulfilled, the king and queen continued their journey, 'and all the ships to Greenwich shot off guns as they passed by, which was a goodly sight to behold'.[39] The beautiful palace of Greenwich was of deep significance for King Henry. His father, Henry VII, had rebuilt the paradise that had been created by Marguerite d'Anjou, who had named it Placentia or the Palace of Pleasaunce. Greenwich was Henry VIII's birthplace and he had married his first queen, another Katherine, there. It had then witnessed the birth of his two daughters, Mary in 1516 and Elizabeth in 1533. Now, a new Queen Katherine was about to add her own chapter to the long history of Greenwich. Driven by the vicissitudes of fortune, the wheel had turned full circle. The palace had been her first home at court when she had been only one of a handful of maidens of honour to the new queen, Anne of Cleves; an obscure Howard girl fired with ambition. Now she returned in triumph, and the gun salutes and the honours that had once heralded her mistress now proclaimed the arrival of Katherine, the new Queen of England.

11

Dear Master Culpeper

~

AT THE BEGINNING of Holy Week 1541, Ambassador Marillac wrote to Montmorency with exciting news.[1] Rumours were circulating at the English court that Queen Katherine was with child. This was wonderful news. It was the queen's primary function to provide Henry with more children. Naturally, the preference would be for a boy, but at this stage the fact that she could produce children at all was a good sign, especially considering Henry's age and condition.

Henry, who had just returned from a tour of his properties in Kent, was delighted at the prospect of becoming a father again. He announced that, if this dream should turn out to be true, he intended 'to have Katherine crowned at Whitsuntide'. Entertaining high hopes he would soon have his longed-for Duke of York, he ordered arrangements to be made. In the chambers, 'all the embroiderers that can be found are employed in making decorations and tapestries, and copes and ornaments taken from churches are not spared'. Meanwhile, in the tilt-yard of Greenwich, 'the young lords and gentlemen of the court are exercising every day so to improve their skills for the jousts and tourneys that will take place then'.

Suddenly no further mention is made of the pregnancy. Perhaps Katherine had been mistaken and she had never been pregnant, or perhaps she had lost the child. Whatever the case, plans for the festivities were quietly dropped. Katherine and Henry took part in the solemn observances of Holy Week. On Maundy Thursday, 14 April, they carried out their traditional royal duties by distributing specially minted Maundy money to the poor. Another of Katherine's duties was to wash the feet of the recipients and hand out food and clothing.[2]

With her religious obligations fulfilled, Queen Katherine returned to her privy apartments and sent a servant to the king's privy chamber. He was instructed to meet a gentleman and escort him back to the queen. This, then, is how the relationship between Katherine Howard and Thomas Culpeper recommenced.

It had been almost a year since Culpeper had stepped aside, having become aware that the lady he was courting had attracted the attention of the king. Since that time, Culpeper, his favour with the king ever increasing, had been granted several properties and estates. Some of these, like those granted to Katherine, had formerly belonged to Master Secretary Cromwell.[3] Another grant consisted of manors seized from the dissolved monastery in Winchcombe. Adding to these, the king granted him the manor, rectory and advowson of the vicarage of Endford in Wiltshire, which had once been the property of the monastery of St Swithin at Winchester.[4]

Men as successful, and as wealthy, as Thomas Culpeper were surrounded by an entourage of servants and hangers-on, who were devoted to their master and who jealously watched over his interests. This sometimes led to rivalry and hostility with the servants of other men, resulting in outbreaks of violence. On one occasion, William Brice of Southwark, a tailor and servant to Thomas Culpeper, found himself before the Privy Council. He was examined concerning an affray that had occurred in Southwark between servants of Culpeper, Thomas Paston and another gentleman of the privy chamber.[5] As a result of Brice's testimony, Culpeper's servant, John Hurley, and Paston's men, John Cousyns and John Hubbard, were brought before the Privy Council, together with another, unnamed, serving man. They were charged with 'making a riotous and unlawful assemble and affray in Southwark'. For this, they 'being both by their own confession and also other sufficient witness', were found to be 'faulty and culpable of the same'. This earned them a spell in the Fleet Prison.[6] Meanwhile, other men on Paston's staff, Morgan Welles and John Blacknell, were held on their own recognisance until 29 April.[7]

What had sparked the affray is not known. That it took place at Southwark suggests that the young men had spent the evening in the local stews and taverns. Having had too much to drink and with their tongues loosened, they had said more than they should about each other's master. Once in a while the drunken talk would turn to even more inappropriate subjects. Easier to say than to confine, gossip eventually reached Katherine's lady of the bedchamber, Jane, Lady Rochford, that Thomas Paston did 'bear her favour'.[8] This was the same Thomas Paston who had been Culpeper's rival for Katherine's affections in the spring of the previous year. Clearly, he still carried a torch for her. Perhaps, then, the violent scenes at Southwark that had brought the men before the council had been caused by a quarrel over whose master best deserved Katherine's favour.[9]

There were those who had no doubts about which of them Katherine should prefer. The delightfully imaginative author of the *Chronicle of Henry VIII*[10] relates the unhappy story of Thomas Culpeper and his lost love. The young man, so 'much grieved' when Katherine married Henry, 'fell very ill but did not dare to speak of the cause'. Each time he went to the palace and saw Katherine, 'he did nothing but sigh, and by his eyes let the Queen know what trouble he was suffering'. After some time, Katherine noticed Culpeper's plight, 'until the devil tempted her; and as Culpeper was a gentleman and young, and the King was old', she remembered the love she had formerly borne him. She 'let him know by signs that he might cheer up'. Culpeper, gladdened by Katherine's promise, 'determined to write a letter to the Queen'. While they danced one day, he slipped the letter into her hand. Katherine concealed it until she reached her chamber, where she opened it and read it. Katherine then wrote a reply to Culpeper in which she told him 'to have patience, and she would find a way to comply with his wishes'. The day after, as the two danced together again, Katherine passed her letter to Culpeper, who 'was overjoyed beyond measure'.

As charming as this story is, the reality, as so often, is rather different. Katherine did meet Thomas Culpeper after her marriage, but the circumstances were far less romantic than those related by the Spanish chronicler.

The story, as related by Thomas Culpeper in his own words,[11] began when Katherine's servant, Henry Webb,[12] brought him to the entrance between her privy chamber and the chamber of presence. Here, she 'gave him by her own hands a fair cap of velvet garnished with a brooch and three dozen pairs of aglets and a chain'. She then said to him, 'put this under your cloak that nobody see it'. Culpeper replied, 'alas, madam, why did not you this when you were a maid?' Katherine said nothing and the two parted.

A short while later, they met again; this time, Katherine was clearly put out. Piqued at Culpeper's response to her gift, she asked him, 'is this all the thanks you give me for the cap, if I had known you would have spoken these words you should never have had it'. Katherine was angry because Culpeper's response made it clear that he had wrongly taken it as a love token. At the most, she would have expected him to thank her, not to remind her of their past relationship. That she told him to hide the cap under his cloak shows that she feared that others might misconstrue its purpose, as Culpeper had done, and spread dangerous gossip about his apparent favour with the queen. Katherine herself had been very wary of letting others catch her with items that might be interpreted as courting gifts, as the business of the French fennel clearly showed.

However Katherine was incapable of remaining angry with anyone for very long. As with Henry Mannock before him, she soon forgave Culpeper his transgression. Shortly after their second meeting, Culpeper became ill. That Katherine sent him 'at diverse times flesh or the fish dinner by Morris the page', suggests that his illness lasted for at least two days. After that, the meetings ceased and Katherine, if not Culpeper, promptly forgot about them. The time frame of these events can roughly be determined from Culpeper's statement. They were initiated on Maundy Thursday, 14 April, and continued only while the court remained at Greenwich. Since the court left that palace on 27 May, it is evident that the three recorded incidences of contact between Katherine and Culpeper took place during a period of just over six weeks. By any standards, these encounters were sporadic to say the least and can hardly be taken as indication that Katherine was betraying Henry.

What had prompted Katherine to arrange the reunion with Culpeper? Although he remembered their meetings vividly and could recount them in some detail, Culpeper never said why the queen had sent for him in the first place. The answer can be found in a letter written by Katherine to Culpeper at the time.[13]

Master Culpeper, I heartily recommend me unto you, praying you to send me word how that you do. It was showed me that you were sick, the which thing troubled me very much till such time that I hear from you, praying you to send me word how that you do. For I never longed so much for [a] thing as I do to see you and to speak with you, the which I trust shall be shortly now, the which does comfort me very much when I think of it, and when I think again that you shall depart from me again it makes my heart to die to think what fortune I have that I cannot be always in your company, yet my trust is always in you that you will be as you have promised me and in that hope I trust upon still, praying then that you will come when my Lady Rochford is here, for then I shall be best at leisure to be at your commandment. Thanking you for that you have promised me to be so good unto that poor fellow my man which is one of the griefs that I do feel to depart from him, for then I do know no-one that I dare trust to send to you and therefore, I pray you take him to be with you that I may sometimes hear from you one thing. I pray you to give me a horse for my man for I had much ado to get one and therefore I pray send me one by him and in so doing I am as I said afore and thus I take my leave of you, trusting to see you shortly again and I would you

was with me now that you might see what pain I take in writing
to you.

Yours as long as life endures, Katheryn

One thing I had forgotten and that is to instruct my man to tarry
here with me still, for he says whatsoever you behove[14] him he
will do it and[15]

Intriguingly, Katherine breaks off at this point. It is possible that
she added the postscript after she had summoned her messenger;
then, he or she having arrived before she had finished, Katherine
ended the letter anyway because she had said all that she wanted
to say. Differences in handwriting and the colour of the ink show
that this letter is written in two hands. The first eight words (in
bold) are in the hand of an amanuensis. Katherine then took over
and finished the letter herself.

What, then, was Katherine trying to say to Culpeper? Lady
Rochford once remarked that Katherine 'trusted Culpeper above
her own brother',[16] that is, Charles Howard, who, like Culpeper,
was a gentleman of the privy chamber. But Lady Jane did not
elaborate upon in what regard Katherine trusted Culpeper. The
answer lies in his position in the royal household. Culpeper was
one of the king's favourites and was known to have 'succeeded
Master Nourriz, who was in like favour with his master'.[17] Henry
Norris had occupied the senior position in the privy chamber until
he was implicated in the downfall of Anne Boleyn and executed.
Culpeper had intimate access to the king and was well placed to
provide Katherine with information about her husband's health
and his ever fluctuating moods. More importantly, Culpeper could
warn her of any indication that Henry was angry, perhaps because
she was not yet with child; he could also listen out for any gossip
about her, and report on speculation that her husband was considering repudiating her in favour of Anne of Cleves. Throughout
Katherine's queenship, this topic would surface time and again, to
her consternation and grief.[18]

Katherine, therefore, cultivated Culpeper's friendship. He was, in many ways, a good choice. Their previous relationship made him well-disposed towards her, he was related to her, albeit distantly, and was one of her husband's favourites; more importantly, he was in the king's confidence. For Culpeper, too, the arrangement had its uses. Considering that his master was ageing and increasingly infirm, it was prudent to look to the future. Although Prince Edward was a Seymour, and his family would play a major part in the regency, Katherine, as dowager queen, would still be in a powerful position. She was someone whose favour was worth cultivating.

This is not to say that Katherine lived in a state of apprehension. There were many happy occasions in her life, one of which occurred in the early summer of 1541. 'At the request of the Princess Mary, but chiefly at the intercession of the queen herself', plans were made for a royal family reunion, and Katherine was deeply involved.[19] She commissioned the royal close barge, complete with twenty-six men, and a second barge carrying a further twenty men to follow on behind. The floors of both barges were strewn with rushes, a symbol of welcome, and rosemary, for its pleasing, refreshing perfume.[20]

Katherine's first stop was Chelsea, where she oversaw preparations for the arrival of her stepdaughter, Lady Elizabeth, the following day. She then travelled to her town house of Barnard's Castle, leaving Chelsea free for Elizabeth and her household, who took the queen's barge from Suffolk Place in Southwark. Katherine returned the following day to Chelsea, and she and Elizabeth journeyed together to Prince Edward's residence at Waltham Holy Cross in Essex. It might have been on this occasion that Katherine gave Elizabeth the gift of a brooch.[21]

While Katherine had been busy taking care of Lady Elizabeth, Henry had gone on ahead and was waiting with Lady Mary for the arrival of Katherine and Elizabeth. In this delightful setting, with its charming family scene, Katherine met her stepson, Prince Edward, for the first time.

It was only a short family holiday, lasting from 5 to 12 May. It had been organised as a private get-together before Henry and

Katherine turned their attention to preparations for the summer progress. This was due to begin in July, but there was much to organise first, and both the queen and the king would be occupied with the many necessary arrangements.

The holiday had, nevertheless, gone very well. Katherine and Mary had managed to put their differences behind them. Under Katherine's tender influence, Henry began to think that, perhaps, his family might find the happiness that had been sorely lacking in recent years. He 'granted the Princess [Mary] full permission to reside at Court', and Queen Katherine 'countenanced it with a good grace'.[22]

Shortly after they returned to Greenwich, Katherine remained behind while Henry travelled to Westminster. He was occupied with contention between his officers and the citizens of Southwark, as well as the mayor and citizens of London.[23] Other events kept the king busy, such as correspondence from Katherine's uncle, Lord William, dealing with matters in France.[24] However, he was back at Greenwich on 21 May.

On his arrival Henry found that Katherine had lost some of her sparkle. Ambassador Chapuys reported that Katherine, 'being some days ago rather sad and thoughtful, and the king wishing to know the cause, she declared to him that it was all owing to some rumour or other afloat that he (the king) was about to take back Anne de Clèves as his wife'.[25] Once again, Chapuys was using his imagination where informed news from a good contact would have been more appropriate. He stated that Henry had told Katherine that 'she was wrong to believe such things [of him] or attach faith to reports of the kind,' adding that 'even if he had to marry again, he would never retake Mme de Clèves.' As before, there was nothing to indicate that Henry wanted to put aside Katherine. Rather, Chapuys's comments reflect his own concerns, inspired by gossip that 'for fear of king Francis making war upon him, at the solicitation and with the help of the duke of Clèves, as well as of the king of Scotland, this king might possibly some time or other effect his reconciliation with Anne'..

There was another reason, however, for the dark mood that fell upon Katherine. She had not yet been crowned, which could have made her feel insecure; certainly, as it was, her status contrasted markedly with Katherine of Aragon and Anne Boleyn before her. With the former, a coronation was simply the natural thing to do. She was, after all, the king's wife and would be, if things turned out as they should, the mother of several children, royal princes and princesses to secure the Tudor dynasty on the throne for years to come. In Anne Boleyn's case, there had been a strong political necessity to crown her. From Henry's point of view, he wanted to show that his former marriage, the supposedly sham, illegal marriage he had endured for so many years, was no more. Anne's coronation had firmly established her as the king's true wife and queen and it pressed the demand that she should be recognised as such at home and internationally. Jane Seymour, too, would have been crowned had she lived, her reward for fulfilling her royal function. With Katherine, Henry had not felt the need to establish her politically, nor had she yet fulfilled her royal duty which, as Marillac pointed out, would have sealed her queenship with a coronation. Katherine was vulnerable.

In fact, the relationship Henry shared with Katherine was strong and loving, despite the difference in their ages. Katherine was ambitious, certainly, but this was not necessarily a negative trait. Most importantly, Katherine did not argue with Henry as had Anne Boleyn, whose strength of character exasperated him at times and whose quick wit dazzled him. Instead, whether by design or inclination, Katherine had pledged to submit to the king's will, and it was a pledge she meant to fulfil.

Henry continued to treat Katherine well. His manly pride had caused him to shelter her from his vicious temper as he wallowed in self-pity following his illness. However, he had shown her genuine, passionate love, and had treated her with respect. This was in marked contrast to the treatment she had received from the other men in her life, Henry Mannock and Francis Dereham.

Following his recent scare, Henry had persuaded himself that he had completely recovered his health. Fortified with a renewed strength and energy, invigorated by his beautiful young wife, his thoughts turned to something that had always been close to his heart: military adventure. It was at about this time that Henry began to toy with the idea of once again making war on France.[26] However, there were two precautions that he had to take before he could set out on this undertaking. One was to subdue the northern counties, where Catholic rebellion and conspiracy remained an ever present threat; the other was to secure his border with Scotland.

The north of England was notorious for its uprisings. Most recently, rebels had taken the opportunity of the Spring Fair at Pontefract to instigate a revolt. Led by Sir John Neville, this disturbance had not attracted the support it might have done, and was quickly crushed. However, the fact that it had occurred at all served as a stark reminder to Henry of the dangers of neglecting his aggrieved subjects in the northern counties.

He had intended to visit the north a few years previously in the wake of the Pilgrimage of Grace but time went by and other matters intervened. As the months turned into years, it took this new uprising to instil in Henry a fresh sense of urgency. As soon as he 'heard of this last conspiracy in the Northern counties, he announced his intention to go thither in person and visit the districts where the rising had taken place. Having lately had news that the affair might grow worse still unless he was personally on the spot, he has now decided to undertake the journey.'[27] The progress to the North Country would allow Henry the chance to deal with any lingering unrest in his realm. It was essential, if Henry were to wage war on France, to ensure that his subjects would not take the opportunity for another uprising.

The second imperative was to secure the northern border of the kingdom. Henry remembered all too well what had happened in 1513, when no sooner had he left the country than the Scots invaded. The solution lay in relations with his nephew, King James V of Scotland.

Following a failed attempt at strengthening links between England and Scotland by diplomatic means the previous year, Henry renewed his communication with James. He began by appealing to James's kingly pride. Because James had refused to follow Henry's reformation policies, he was, in Henry's opinion, in danger of being manipulated by the clergy. Unaware that James was cultivating the favour of the clergy to suit his own agenda, Henry urged him to 'see that no distinction is made between kirkmen and others'.[28] Although James alleged that 'kirkmen are altogether exempt from the temporal power', Henry deeply regretted that the Scots king 'should, to the detriment of his own honour, consent to set up a new kingdom within his realm'.

There was no reasoning with Henry, whose underlying tactic was to ensure James's neutrality in the event of his next French war. He pressed James to declare for true religion and to break with the Catholic powers in Europe, which would naturally require James to disregard Scotland's Auld Alliance with France. Henry then invited James to meet him at York in September, where the two kings could consolidate their friendship and discuss new developments in mainland Europe. The objectives of the summer progress were now in place.

However, there was another important aspect to the summer progress of 1541. Henry would be travelling in the company of his new queen, Katherine Howard. The Howards were of great political significance in the north of England, where they had been a powerful presence for several decades.

Katherine's great-grandfather, John Howard, first Howard Duke of Norfolk, had been a loyal friend and supporter of the house of York and of Richard III in particular. He had taken part in several campaigns during the Wars of the Roses and had died beside King Richard at Bosworth.

The second Duke of Norfolk, Katherine's grandfather, had been Vice-Warden of the East and Middle Marches towards Scotland. As the king's lieutenant in the north, Howard had carried out administrative duties, subdued discord and engaged in military expeditions, leading the English to victory against the Scots at Flodden in 1513. Here, he had been joined by his sons Thomas and Edmund, respectively Queen Katherine's uncle and father. Equally significant, in view of Henry's plans for the summer progress, was that Howard had assisted in the negotiations between Henry VII and James IV of Scotland for the latter's marriage to the Princess Margaret Tudor. After lengthy negotiations, Howard escorted the young bride to her new home in Edinburgh, where he gave her away in her father's name. Margaret, Henry VIII's sister, was the mother of King James V, whom Henry planned to meet at York.

Katherine's uncle, the third Duke of Norfolk, had accompanied his father on several military campaigns in the north; he had also carried out many administrative and diplomatic missions. His most famous, or infamous, association with the northern counties had been during the Pilgrimage of Grace in the autumn of 1536.

This great rebellion, which had presented one of the most serious threats to the realm, had been inspired by several causes. There was the enclosure of lands that had, until that time, been worked by the peasantry. This had brought poverty and made thieves and beggars of many. Then new laws had been introduced to make begging a capital offence. The people, with nowhere else to turn, went to the monasteries for alms. However Henry's reforms soon deprived them of even that option. The dissolution and plunder of the monasteries did more than destroy a way of life that had endured for centuries. As the great religious houses disappeared, so did the security of employment, the comfort of spiritual and medical care and the hope brought to the people through charity and education. All this took place against a back-drop of decline among the northern baronial families, many of whom sympathised with the insurgents. The Pilgrims had demanded the restoration of the monasteries, the reinstatement of the abolished holy days and an end to taxation; they wanted the Princess Mary to be made legitimate; lastly, they had called for the death of Cromwell.

Norfolk had gathered an army of some 8,000, but faced a rebel force of some 40,000. Wisely, he preferred diplomacy as the best means to defuse the situation and encourage the rebel army to disperse. As negotiations continued, Henry prevaricated and the matter dragged on until the Pilgrims, with winter approaching, gradually dispersed and the Pilgrimage of Grace came to an end.

However, the rift Norfolk had observed among the Pilgrims ensured that any armistice would be only temporary. Before long, news arrived of a fresh outbreak of disturbances in the region. This time there was no chance of diplomacy. Carrying Henry's instructions to 'cause such dreadful execution to be done upon a good number of the inhabitants of every town village and hamlet that have offended in this rebellion', the duke wreaked the royal revenge on the people 'without pity or respect . . . remembering that it shall be much better that these traitors should perish in their wilful, unkind and traitorous follies than that so slender punishment should be done to them as the dread thereof should not be a warning to others'.[29] Norfolk then presided over the executions of two of the leaders, Sir Robert Constable in Hull and Robert Aske in York. Hanged in chains, their deaths were slow and agonising.

Norfolk had carried out the king's terrible retribution on the northern rebels. He had acted not out of conviction that they deserved their punishment, but in order to refute persistent whispers in certain quarters that he secretly sympathised with their cause. He left behind him a trail of dissolved religious houses, including the great abbeys at Sawley and Hexham, and a devastated region where hope had died alongside a desperate people. Henceforth, the name of Howard would carry a different meaning in the North Country.

Katherine would be the balm of consolation to the very people her uncle had subdued at such a great cost. She would be the kind face of the Howards and the arbiter of royal mercy as she interceded on behalf of felons and former rebels. In this, she would be assisted by Lady Mary. The Pilgrims' demand that she be returned to legitimacy had not been fulfilled, but her visit to those areas where she was held in high regard would show her to be in the king's favour; Mary's presence in the royal entourage would provide reassurance and be a calming influence.

That Katherine accompanied Henry on this progress is the best indication that the news that had circulated in April had been wrong and that she was not pregnant. Had she been, Henry would have postponed the journey to the north once again, as he had done four years earlier when Queen Jane was pregnant. Henry had feared that Jane, left at home while he travelled to such dangerous parts of his realm, might hear 'sudden and displeasant rumours and brutes that might by foolish or light persons be blown abroad'.[30] Then, 'being a woman', she would take 'such impression as might engender no little danger or displeasure to that therewith she is now pregnant'. Henry had been concerned that Jane would worry for her absent lord, thereby endangering her unborn child; there is every reason to believe that he would have been equally cautious with Katherine.

There was one important task to get out of the way before the court embarked on the progress. Shortly after the return of Katherine and Henry to Greenwich, a horrific deed took place. On 27 May 1541 Margaret Pole, Countess of Salisbury, a lady in her late sixties, was taken from her chamber in the Tower of London at seven in the morning and led to 'the midst of the space in front of the Tower'.[31] King Henry's decision to execute the countess had been sudden, even impulsive. During her two years in the Tower, Lady Margaret had been treated relatively well. She had been provided with the privileges proper to her rank, and supplied with clothing made for her by Queen Katherine's own tailor, John Scott. Now, barely two months after that act of kindness, she was to be executed.

The countess did not even know why she was to die. As Chapuys notes: 'when the sentence of death was made known to her, she found the thing very strange, not knowing of what crime she was accused, nor how she had been sentenced.'

Margaret had been arrested on the unsubstantiated belief that she had conspired with her sons, Cardinal Pole and Lord Montagu. In fact, her real 'crime' was to be too closely related to the English royal family, thereby posing a threat, as Henry saw it, to the Tudor dynasty. Several factors contributed to Henry's decision to execute Margaret. One was that she was implicated in the affair of Sir Thomas Wyatt and Sir John Wallop, who had been suspected of treasonous involvement with Margaret's son, Cardinal Reginald Pole. Another was the recent uprising in the north. Led by Sir John Neville, whose family shared Yorkist blood with Margaret, it had largely been driven by hostility towards Henry. Finally, there was the fear that Cardinal Pole might attempt to rescue his mother from the Tower. On a more practical level, Marillac had heard that there was a desire to clear the Tower, and that 'before St John's tide they reckon to empty the Tower of the prisoners now there for treason'.[32] The purpose of this was to make way for fresh traitors arrested following the recent uprising as well as those who continued to show signs of defiance.

The countess's execution had not been anticipated, so no scaffold had been erected for her 'nor anything except a small block'. Now, watched by the Lord Mayor of London 'and about 150 persons more', Margaret commended her soul to God before asking those present 'to pray for the King, the Queen, the Prince [Edward] and the Princess [Mary], to all of whom she wished to be particularly commended'. Her prayers finished, 'she was told to make haste and place her neck on the block, which she did. But as the ordinary executor of justice was absent doing his work in the north, a wretched and blundering youth (garçonneau) was chosen, who literally hacked her head and shoulders to pieces in the most pitiful manner.'[33] It was a tragic, shocking scene, and a terrible illustration of how easily execution by means of beheading with an axe can go disastrously wrong.

As the countess was sent to her death, Katherine and Henry took up residence at Westminster, while the household went on to Eltham.[34] A month later, two of the queen's brothers, Charles and George Howard, were awarded the lucrative licence to import 1,000 tuns of Gascony wine and Toulouse woad.[35] The benefits for her family flowing from the king's love for Katherine knew no bounds.

12

The Summer Progress

~

THE ROYAL PROGRESS to the north of England was the largest such undertaking of King Henry's reign. It was befitting, then, that he and Katherine should make the journey in the most spectacular fashion. The royal entourage included carefully selected members of the council: the Dukes of Norfolk and Suffolk, the Earls of Southampton and Sussex, Lord Admiral Russell, Bishop Tunstall, Sir Robert Cheyney, Sir John Gage, Sir Anthony Browne, Sir Anthony Wingfield, Sir Thomas Wriothesley and Sir Richard Riche. Not all of these men would serve at each council meeting, but all would be at the king's command throughout the progress.

Most of these men were Catholic, while others held ambivalent or neutral religious views, or else merely aligned their propensities with those of the king. This is not to say that Henry deliberately surrounded himself with religious conservatives. Rather, his choices were dictated by his favour towards the Howards and their allies as well as his own personal preferences.

A small caretaker council was left behind in London. This included Archbishop Cranmer, Chancellor Audeley, the Earl of Hartford, Ralph Sadler, Lord Andrew Windsor, Sir William Paulet St John and Robert Southwell. While most of these men were reform-leaning, others were ambivalent or orthodox in their religious outlook. There was no absolute divide between those with whom Henry surrounded himself and those he left behind.

Since it was Henry's intent 'to repair to the North in pompous array', he and Queen Katherine were to be accompanied by 4,000 or 5,000 horse, for which 'several lords and gentlemen have been summoned'.[1] This was in contrast to the usual number of 1,000. Many of these gentlemen were from Kent, and were those the king trusted most. The fifty gentlemen of the horse were each to have a tent and war equipment, as were several other young lords. In all, over 200 tents were packed, artillery was sent by sea 'to within 10 miles of York' and great horses were also taken. It was, said Marillac, 'as if it were a question of war'.[2]

In a way, it was. Memories were long in the rebellious north, and the images of dead Pilgrims were ever present in people's minds. Families still lived with the hardship caused by the loss of fathers, husbands and sons. The ruined monasteries were a constant reminder of all they had lost. However, the heavy military presence, the armies of courtiers and the obvious show of majesty served another purpose: Henry wanted to make an impression in a part of the country to which he was a stranger. Few of his subjects knew him except by name and reputation. Moreover, it appeared to the people of the north 'that there is no currency among them in consequence of the King having seized the rentals, not only of the abbeys and monasteries in those provinces, but likewise those of the principal lords in the land, like Northumberland and various others, by which means all the money which formerly circulated in the Northern counties now comes here to this City of London'.[3] Henry, therefore, wanted to show the people of the north that 'a good portion of the money spent will remain in the country'.

The progress, upon which so much rested, finally got under way on 30 June after more than three months of planning.[4] Even so, it encountered problems almost straight away. Katherine and Henry had been expected at Lincoln in mid-July, but their progress was slowed considerably by the weather. By 18 July they had reached as far as Grafton, Northamptonshire, having passed through Enfield, St Albans, Dunstable and Ampthill, all of which Katherine had visited before.

Marillac notes that the weather was 'unseasonable cold and stormy'. Heavy and incessant rains had flooded the already marshy roads, making it difficult for the carts to get through. Crops were damaged and the incidence of contagious diseases had increased, adding to the misery. In addition, Katherine became ill; that she was not, for once, thought to be pregnant suggests that she had succumbed to one of the ailments mentioned by the French ambassador. Although there was talk of breaking the progress, the great efforts of Katherine's uncle of Norfolk and the Duke of Suffolk, who had gone on ahead to oversee preparations for later stages, made this unlikely.[5]

By 21 July, Katherine had recovered. While still at Grafton, the council with the King wrote to the council in London with news that 'the King and Queen, and all the train, are merry and in health'.[6] On the following day, she and Henry moved on to Northampton, where they stayed for two days before going on to Pipewell.

The abbey at Pipewell had been dissolved in 1538 despite the efforts of Sir William Parr, the brother of the future queen. Here, on 25 July, Henry 'made answer' to Thomas Bellenden, the Scottish ambassador, who had been sent by James with some complaints about safe conducts and the delivery of rebels.[7] The court would remain here until 28 July, when it set off once more, this time for Lyddington.

Set amid the sprawling countryside of Rutland, the village of Lyddington boasted a magnificent manor house,[8] which had been in the possession of the Bishops of Lincoln since the time of King John, who had granted them a licence to enclose a park. Here, the court stayed for almost a week, plenty of time to settle in and recuperate from the rigours of the journey so far.

The stay at Lyddington saw business as usual for King Henry and the members of the Privy Council who were travelling with the court. However, Katherine had business of her own. One night she gave one of her chamberers, Marget Morton, a sealed letter for Jane, Lady Rochford. At daybreak Marget returned to Lady Rochford's chamber for her reply, which came with a request for the queen to keep its contents secret.[9]

The next stop was Collyweston, once the home of Henry's

grandmother, Lady Margaret Beaufort, Duchess of Richmond. Following her death, Collyweston House had been used by Henry's illegitimate son, Henry Fitzroy, Duke of Richmond, who died in 1536. Still crown property, King Henry continued to use the house, and he and Katherine stayed there for four days before moving on to Grimsthorpe.

Formerly the seat of William Willoughby, eleventh Baron d'Eresby, Grimsthorpe House was now the home of his daughter, Katherine, and her husband, the king's boon companion, Charles Brandon, Duke of Suffolk. Charles and other Privy Councillors had been tasked to 'entertain their master and provide for his amusement' during the progress.[10] In a letter written on 3 July to the Earl of Southampton, the duke asked for a 'fat stag' to be sent in time for the royal visit.[11] Suffolk expected the king and queen to arrive on 5 August and, as it turned out, they entered Grimsthorpe exactly on time.

Katherine was reunited with the Duchess of Suffolk, a lady with whom she had much in common. The two women were not too dissimilar in age, the duchess being twenty-two years old, and Katherine sixteen. Both had been educated with a view to marrying well and running a household and estate. It is fair to say, however, that the Duchess of Suffolk fared better than did Katherine in this respect, having been brought up very close to the court. Both had gone on to marry men considerably older than themselves: the duchess had married Brandon at the age of fourteen; Katherine was a year older when she became Henry's fifth queen. Finally, both were adored by their husbands and, although Katherine had not yet fulfilled her duty in adding to the royal nursery, the duchess's example in this regard was a good one: she had given birth to two fine sons, Henry and Charles.[12]

Katherine and Henry spent three nights with the Suffolks. On 8 August they once again took to the road, reaching Sleaford in time to spend the night. Here, final preparations were made for the magnificent entry into Lincoln.

The dignitaries of Lincoln had been keeping watch.[13] Soon, the

news they had been waiting for arrived: the royal party had reached
Temple Bruer, seven miles away, and had stopped to have dinner.
The Archdeacon of Lincoln and other members of the clergy rode
out to meet the king and queen. After hearing a proclamation in
Latin, the king was presented with the gift of a victual. Henry and
Katherine then made their way to Lincoln Minster,[14] the route
lined with the civic authorities led by the Mayor of Lincoln, to
prepare for the next stage of their visit.

The king 'came riding and entered into his tent, which was
pitched at the farthest end of the liberty of Lincoln, the Queen's
grace with him in his own tent'. Here, Katherine and Henry
changed their clothes. Henry, who had been wearing green
velvet, put on a suit of cloth of gold, while Katherine changed
from her crimson velvet into a shimmering gown of cloth of
silver.[15]

With all the preparations complete, Katherine and Henry
mounted their horses, the heralds put on their coats, 'and the
gentlemen pensioners, with all other of the King's most royal train,
did ride in order honourably, according to the ancient order'.

The royal procession was led by Lord Hastings, who carried the
sword. King Henry followed, his horse of estate being led by
the master of the horse. The six children of honour came next,
one behind the other, all mounted on great coursers. The Earl of
Rutland followed the children ahead of his mistress, Queen
Katherine. She was followed by her horse of estate, after which
came the ladies 'in good order'. The captain of the guard led the
guard, and they were followed by the 'commoners as they fell to
the train'.

Then, before the procession had come very far, Mr Myssleden,
sergeant at law and recorder of Lincoln, accompanied by the
gentlemen of the county, the mayor and his brethren and other
commoners, waited at the entry of the liberty. When the king
approached, they knelt and cried out twice, 'Jesus save your grace!'
The recorder knelt twice more before drawing near to the king
to read a proclamation in English as the other dignitaries remained

kneeling. When he had finished, he kissed the proclamation and delivered it to the king along with the gift of a victual. Henry passed the proclamation to the Duke of Norfolk, Katherine's uncle, who had joined the progress at Lincoln.

The mayor now presented the sword and mace of the city to Henry and he and the gentlemen of the county led the procession into the city. The air rang with the sound of bells as the train entered Lincoln. At the gates the mayor and his men drew aside, while Henry and Katherine made their way towards the minster. The Bishop of Lincoln awaited them, while the whole choir with the cross stood along both sides of the body of the church. King Henry alighted at the west end of the minster where carpets and stools with cushions of cloth of gold had been set out. Crucifixes had also been laid out, one each for the king and queen.

The great Henry and the tiny, delicate Katherine knelt side by side. The bishop came forward, in full regalia, and censed the king and offered him the crucifix to kiss. He then did the same for Katherine. He censed them again and led the royal couple into the church, 'the King and the Queen's grace going under the Canopy to the Sacrament' where they prayed while the choir sang the *Te Deum*. The service over, the king and queen retired to their lodgings for the night, as did the rest of their entourage.

The entrance of King Henry and Queen Katherine into Lincoln had been nothing short of spectacular. The people of the city, as they had all over Lincolnshire, came out to see their king and to make 'humble submission . . . confessing their offence, and thanking the king for his pardon'. Henry had won over the people of the county, and he had accepted vast sums of money from them: £20 from the people of Stamford, £40 from Lincoln, Boston gave him £50, Lynsey £300, while Kestren and the church of Lincoln gave £50.[16]

For her part, Katherine brought to Henry's attention the case of a certain Helen Page, otherwise known as Clerk. A spinster of Kedby in Lynsey, Helen was guilty of certain unspecified felonies committed between 12 September of the previous year and the present day, 10 August.[17] Katherine requested pardon on Helen's behalf, an appeal her doting husband was only too happy to grant.

As night fell, Katherine went to visit Lady Rochford in her chamber, where she stayed until the early hours. The following afternoon, Henry rode out to view the castle and the city. Whether Katherine accompanied him is not recorded. That evening, Katherine, taking only Katherine Tylney with her, went to Lady Rochford's chamber again, staying until the early hours as she had done before. What passed between mistress and servant was a mystery.

The stay at Lincoln afforded the French ambassador, Marillac, the leisure to write to his master about the events of the progress so far. In particular, he described King Henry's hunting technique, which was, 'wherever there are deer numerous, to enclose two or three hundred and then send in many greyhounds to kill them, that he may share them among the gentlemen of the country and of his Court'.

As to royal etiquette, whenever 'the king passes any town that he has not visited during his reign, and, considering that this was his first visit to the north, there are many such towns, he has no other ceremony than to see the streets decorated and the inhabitants to go before him on little geldings in their ordinary clothes.' There, Henry, 'mounted on a great horse, with all the most notable lords of England in front, two and two, and sixty or eighty archers with drawn bows behind' goes, followed by Queen Katherine, Lady Mary and some other ladies as they make their way to the lodgings prepared for them.[18]

From Lincoln, Katherine and Henry moved on to Gainsborough, staying at the hall owned by Thomas, third Baron Burgh.[19] A place steeped in history, one of the earliest mentions of a manor at Gainsborough dates from the reign of King Stephen in the twelfth century. Having inherited the manor from his mother, Elizabeth, in 1455, Lord Burgh began to transform it, with the main part of the building being completed in the 1460s. The timber-framed great hall and the magnificent brickwork kitchen were built first, followed shortly after by the east range. The west range dates from slightly later than 1470, while additions were made during the 1480s. The manor boasted orchards, hunting grounds and a mart yard.[20] Legend has it that Katherine and Henry lodged in the upper bedchamber in the tower. However, Henry's obesity and his ulcerated leg made the narrow staircase difficult for him to negotiate; he, therefore, kept a room on the ground floor, while Katherine took the tower bedchamber.

After a night at Scrooby Manor in Nottinghamshire, on 18 August Katherine and Henry crossed into Yorkshire. This county, like the one they had just left, had risen up against the king several times. The most recent uprising had been the Pilgrimage of Grace, followed by the short-lived uprising the previous spring. The county now repentant, the gentlemen came 'by bailiwicks and stewardships, to the number of 5,000 or 6,000 horse' to meet their king and queen. 'Those who in the rebellion remained faithful were ranked apart, and graciously welcomed by the King and praised for their fidelity.' As for the others, those who had conspired against the king, 'among whom appeared the archbishop of York, were a little further off on their knees'. Then, one of their number, Sir Robert Bowes,[21] speaking for them all, 'made a long harangue confessing their treason in marching against their Sovereign and his Council'. They thanked Henry 'for pardoning so great an offence and begging that if any relics of indignation remained he would dismiss them'. At this point, they delivered several 'bulky submissions in writing' and Henry gave them 'a benign answer', no doubt inspired as much by their capitulation as by the £900 they offered him. They then 'arose and accompanied the King to his lodging'. The gentlemen, after 'staying a day or two about the Court, were commanded to retire home'.[22]

The first stop in Yorkshire was Hatfield in the East Riding. The court stayed at the hunting lodge, where Henry took full advantage of the facilities. Marillac writes of 'boats on the water and arbalests and bows on land'. Some 200 stags and does were killed in one day, with a similar number taken the day after. 'In the King's presence were taken in the water a great quantity of young swans, two boats' full of river birds, and as much of great pikes and other fish; so that, within the same enclosure, they took at one time both flesh and fish.' Henry was very pleased and he urged Marillac to inform King François of the slaughter, adding that afterwards, 'supping in his tent, this King [Henry] pointed out 200 or 300 stags as near the company as if they had been domestic cattle or those enclosed in parks'.

The court remained at Hatfield for six nights. On one occasion, the eagle-eyed Marget Morton noticed Katherine looking out of the window at Thomas Culpeper.[23] She thought nothing of it at the time, but when Katherine ordered that no servant was to come to her chamber unless called, Marget's curiosity was piqued.

The court moved on to Pontefract on 24 August. Here, Henry accepted the submission of yet more insurgents who declared 'that they and their posterity will henceforth pray for the preservation of his Majesty, Queen Katharine, and Prince Edward'.[24]

As her husband impressed his limitless power over the lives and souls of his subjects in the volatile north, relations between Katherine and Lady Mary continued to warm. Katherine presented Mary with a clock very similar to one of her own, though without the chain.[25] Unfortunately, happy occasions such as are suggested by the exchanges of gifts were to become significantly fewer. For it was at Pontefract that Katherine was faced with a significant new crisis in her life. Only one day after entering the town, she found herself playing host to a most unwelcome new arrival, Francis Dereham.

13

Sinister Stirrings

~

T HE MAGNIFICENT CASTLE at Pontefract, known as the Key
to the North, would be Katherine's home for the next twelve
days. It had sheltered many kings and queens since it was first built
in the years following the Norman Conquest and was a favourite
of Richard III, who used it as an official residence, both before
and after his accession. However, its association with royalty had
not always been a happy one. It served as a prison for Thomas,
Earl of Lancaster, first prince of the blood and cousin to King
Edward II. Thomas, who disapproved of Piers Gaveston, the king's
favourite, was captured and imprisoned in his own castle of
Pontefract and later executed. Richard II was also held there only
to die under mysterious circumstances. James I of Scotland was
another prisoner, while Charles, duc d'Orléans, was held at the
castle after his capture at Agincourt in 1415. The castle, beautiful
though it was, cast a long, dark shadow. It is almost fitting, then,
that Francis Dereham should make his appearance while Katherine
was in residence at Pontefract.

Dereham had come for a specific purpose: he wanted a position
in Katherine's household. Ever since Katherine had left the service
of the Duchess Agnes, Dereham had kicked his heels, uncertain
what to do, unable to settle to anything. He had travelled to Ireland,
and was believed by some to have engaged in piracy. Since his
return, he would occasionally be found lingering on the fringes
of the court, making himself useful to people such as Katherine
Tylney, whom he had escorted to Woking the previous November
when she was seeking a position in Katherine's household. He

renewed his association with Lord William Howard, who had 'been a great maintainer of Dereham since the Queen's marriage'.[1] However, he never wandered far from the dowager duchess, his kinswoman and former employer.

Recently, during the course of a conversation with the duchess at Norfolk House, Dereham had revealed a dangerous secret. He recalled the letter that Mannock and Barnes had written to the duchess some three years before, warning her about the naughty behaviour of the ladies in the maidens' chamber. Agnes had assumed the letter referred to a certain Hastings and another party.[2] Now Dereham enlightened her as to the real subject of the letter: himself and Katherine. The duchess was angry; her own step-granddaughter, for whose welfare she was responsible, had dared to defy her. Dereham, who had exploited his position of trust in her household with such despicable acts, had betrayed the faith she had placed in him. The duchess was furious: 'for that bill Dereham and she had fell out, about the beginning of the King's progress, and she commanded him out of her gates.'[3]

Banished from Norfolk House, Dereham's plight moved Lady Bridgewater and Lady Howard to pity. They approached Agnes 'to speak to the Queen for Dereham'.[4] Now, here he was, looking for a position. It was 25 August. Two days later Katherine, reluctantly, took him into her service.[5]

Dereham's job description is vague; he had no official title, and Katherine used him for the 'sending of errands and writing of letters when her secretary was out of the way'. His duties entitled him to enter her privy chamber.[6]

While life had suddenly become awkward for Katherine, Henry applied himself to the business of the progress. In response to comments Henry had made via Thomas Bellenden some weeks previously, his nephew James V said he had taken 'singular comfort' from this correspondence, but felt that certain points Henry had made 'require consultation'; he thought 'it expedient to send some of his Council to 'amoif [lessen] things which might hurt the conservation of peace'.[7] Henry, for his part, urged James to 'accelerate the councillors' coming', considering that he awaited 'his resolution so far from the parts where he is accustomed to lie, and that the time of year will soon make travelling tedious for the ladies'.[8]

Henry was anxious to get the meeting with King James under way, so that he could assure himself of James's neutrality in the event of his planned war with France. Unbeknown to Henry, James was in consultation with his French allies about his uncle's overtures. He was awaiting news from David Beaton, the Archbishop of St Andrews, whom he had sent on embassy to France.[9] Having promised Beaton that he would not go into England until he heard from him, James was biding his time.

Henry, on the other hand, wrote to the council in London with orders to 'make out under the Great Seal . . . four safeconducts for the king of Scots and three councillors'.[10] Meanwhile, Marillac noted that 'provisions of wine came daily from London', which he took to be 'a sure sign that they expect the King of Scotland'.[11] In the end, the uncertainty surrounding the meeting of the two kings did not worry Henry, largely because he was unaware of what was going on behind the scenes. It simply did not occur to him that his nephew would refuse to meet him.

At Pontefract, the close relations between Queen Katherine and Lady Rochford carried on as before and again Katherine commanded that none of her ladies should enter her bedchamber unless called. This time Marget Morton, accompanied by Mistress Lufkyn, tried to find out what was happening in the queen's apartments after dark. Their insolence merely earned them their mistress's wrath.

However, Katherine faced a more serious problem than inquisitive and mischievous maids. Francis Dereham had begun causing trouble in the household and was already making enemies. To his friend and former colleague at Norfolk House, Robert Damport, he would brag 'since his coming to the court that many men despised him because they perceived that the queen favoured him'. Dereham's arrogance knew no bounds. On one occasion, 'Mr Johns being gentleman usher with the queen fell out with the said Dereham for sitting at dinner or supper with the queen's Council after all others were risen.' Mr Johns had 'sent out to him the said Dereham to find [out] whether he were of the queen's Council'. Dereham sent the messenger back, saying, 'go to Mr Johns and tell him I was of the queen's Council before he knew her and shall be when she hath forgotten him'.[12]

Dereham's answer was a masterpiece of sarcasm and wit, but it won him no favours. News of his behaviour reached Katherine, who felt the need to warn him to take care what he said.[13] For Dereham, however, warnings were not enough. His silence would cost the queen dear, and she once sent him 3l. for his hose. On another occasion Dereham accepted 10l. from Katherine in her private apartments, taking full advantage of his right of entry there.[14]

As the summer drew to a close, the caretaker council in London became concerned that the court had been away for longer than planned. On 2 September they wrote to their colleagues with the king to ask for news as well as to enquire after the 'good health of the King's Majesty, the Queen's Grace and the whole train'. They added that they 'had lever [rather] learn by your letters, than by common bruits and rumours, which be sunderly spread here'.[15]

Two days after this, the court was on the move again to Cawood, Wressel, Leconfield and Hull, where they stayed at the manor house that Henry had acquired in 1539. Since that time he had employed John Rogers, master mason, to convert the house into a comfortable royal residence, complete with spiral staircases and an unusual T-shaped staircase. Rogers was also working on the town's defences in readiness for a possible attack by the Emperor Charles or King François, and Henry had come to inspect these.[16] Apparently satisfied with Rogers's progress, Henry and Katherine left the town after two nights. Retracing their steps, they made their way back to Leconfield in order to prepare for their entrance into York.

Work on the new royal lodgings that Henry had ordered for York beside the suppressed Benedictine Abbey of St Mary was now complete. The former abbot's mansion became the headquarters of the Council of the North, and in order that all memory of its previous use should be swept away, it was renamed the King's Manor.

Throughout the summer, some 1,500 workmen had been labouring day and night to erect the long, narrow building between the abbot's house and the river,[17] to paint it and to erect tents and pavilions in the grounds. Henry had brought rich tapestries from London to furnish the new building and lend it the appearance of a home from home. He had also sent for gold and silver plate and vestments, not only for himself but for all his archers, pages and gentlemen of the household, as well as 'marvellous provision of victuals from all parts'.[18]

Ambassador Marillac knew that all this lavish preparation signalled 'some extraordinary triumph'; he also knew that the triumph would not be the meeting of the two kings. He was fully aware that James would never come 'so far into the country to make court to this king'. Were James to do so, he would be acting 'against the will of his prelates, who may thereupon fear that he wishes to confiscate the goods of the Church, being incited by the example of his neighbours and constrained by the scantiness of his revenue'.[19]

Instead, Marillac considered the possibility that these sumptuous arrangements were intended for the 'coronation of this Queen, which is spoken of in order to put the people of this county of York in some hope of having a Duke should this lady have a son'. Was Marillac repeating old gossip that Katherine might be pregnant, or was this yet another rumour? Certainly, rumours that Katherine was pregnant were cultivated for political purposes, the significance of which was not lost on the French ambassador. Katherine's first son would indeed be created Duke of York. This, in turn, would encourage the people of the unstable north to support Henry and his policies.[20]

The court entered York on 16 September and took up residence in the luxurious lodgings Henry had organised. Here it was to remain, apart from one brief excursion to Sheriff Hutton, some ten miles north of the city.[21] Meanwhile, as the royal party awaited news from Scotland, Henry issued a royal proclamation, which read:

> whosoever dwelling in these parts found himself grieved for lack of justice ministered unto him either by the King's Majesty's Council now in this city of York resident, or by any other which His Majesty hath put in trust heretofore for that purpose, and could justly prove to have been done unto him, the same party should have free access to His Majesty his Council attendant upon his person to declare his said grief, and thereupon should have right at the hand of his Majesty with favourable audience during his Grace's abode in these parts.[22]

It was a fine proclamation, designed to press the royal authority in an unruly area. Henry wanted to show the people of the north that their concerns would be addressed and that their king, now that they had humbly submitted to his will, had their best interests at heart.

As to his meeting with James V, whatever Henry's thoughts about the likelihood of its ever taking place, he had apparently given up on it by 25 September. On that day, the court departed from York and began the slow journey south.[23]

The route taken by the royal train on their return journey was very much the reverse of the one they had followed on the northbound stages of the progress. In addition, they spent one night at Holme Hall at Holme on Spalding Moor, the family seat of Sir Robert Constable, who had been attainted and executed for his part in the Pilgrimage of Grace.

Having left Holme, Katherine and Henry spent a night at Leconfield, then returned to Hull, where they arrived on 1 October. At a Privy Council meeting held there three days later, privileges were granted to the town and instructions laid down for the inhabitants, no doubt in readiness for a possible attack. Finally, there were further discussions about the town's all-important fortifications.[24]

Thornton came next, followed by Kettleby, Bishops Norton,

Katherine Howard was young and ambitious: 'All that knew me, and kept my company, knew how glad and desirous I was to come to the court'

Henry VIII married Katherine for love, but he expected her to give him more sons

Agnes, Dowager Duchess of Norfolk, gave Katherine a home and educated her. She appointed another woman to look after her ladies, so had no idea how Katherine was being exploited by the men of her household

Thomas Howard, Duke of Norfolk, Katherine's uncle. He would abandon his niece in her hour of need

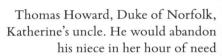

Anne Boleyn, Katherine's cousin, was the first Queen of England ever to be executed; none could have imagined that she would not be the last

Anne of Cleves, whom Katherine served as a maiden of honour. Within months Katherine replaced her as queen

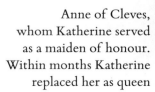

Queen Katherine Howard took her role as queen seriously. She exercised patronage, interceded on behalf of felons, fulfilled her religious obligations and was kind. She would have been as good a queen as any of Henry's wives

Henry VIII adored Katherine, calling her his jewel for womanhood

Lady Mary, Katherine's elder stepdaughter. Relations between the two women were difficult at first, but they quickly improved

Lady Elizabeth, Katherine's younger stepdaughter. Katherine gave Elizabeth a brooch when they were both at Chelsea during a royal family reunion

Prince Edward, Katherine's stepson, was Henry's son and heir. Katherine met Edward for the first time during a family holiday in the early summer of 1541

Greenwich Palace was Katherine's first home at court. It was also the scene of her private meeting with Thomas Culpeper at Easter 1541

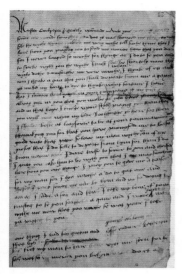

Katherine's letter to Culpeper is not a love letter, as is often thought. Instead, Katherine was cultivating his friendship, since he occupied a high position in Henry's household

A replica based on contemporary sources of Katherine's gown of cloth of silver, which she wore as she made her entrance into Lincoln

Pontefract Castle, Yorkshire. While Katherine was staying here, Francis Dereham asked her for a position in her household. His behaviour was far from discreet, making life very difficult for Katherine, who was also secretly meeting Culpeper at night

Thomas Cranmer, Archbishop of Canterbury, put what he had learned of Katherine's past in a letter which he left in Henry's pew. He later questioned Katherine and tried to establish the true nature of her relationship with Dereham

The Haunted Gallery at Hampton Court. After her arrest, Katherine is said to have broken free of her guards as she made a desperate attempt to reach Henry

William Fitzwilliam, Earl of Southampton, interrogated John Lascelles and his sister, Mary, about Katherine's past

Thomas Wriothesley questioned Henry Mannock and Francis Dereham about their relationships with Katherine

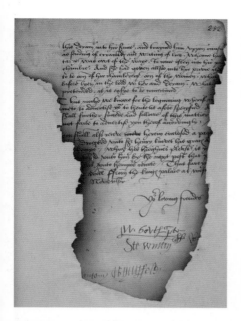

Letter from the Privy Council to William Paget, ambassador in France, detailing Katherine's supposed infidelities

Chancellor Thomas Audeley was one of the councillors who questioned Katherine at Syon House. He was acutely aware that she had not been given the opportunity to defend herself

Charles Brandon, Duke of Suffolk, was one of the judges at the trials of Katherine's 'accomplices'. He later led the delegation to Syon House to hear Katherine's defence and to escort her to the Tower

Stephen Gardiner, Bishop of Winchester, one of the councillors involved in Katherine's case

Site of the landing stage at Syon House. In a distressing scene, Katherine was violently bundled into the barge that was to take her on her last journey to the Tower

London Bridge, beneath which Katherine passed on her final journey. It was still adorned with the severed heads of Culpeper and Dereham (*below right*)

Katherine Howard was buried without ceremony beneath the altar of the Chapel Royal of St Peter ad Vincula in the Tower of London. This memorial plaque, bearing her name and coat of arms, was laid in 1876

Ingleby, Nocton, Sleaford, Collyweston and Fotheringhay, which was part of Katherine's jointure.

After a night at Higham Ferrers, on 21 October the court arrived at Willington Manor in Bedfordshire. In a way, this short visit to Willington Manor was a sort of homecoming for Katherine since the manor had been associated with her Mowbray ancestors since the thirteenth century and had been inherited by her uncle, the third Duke of Norfolk, who had sold it to its current owner, Sir John Gostwick, in 1529.[25]

After leaving Willington, Katherine returned to more familiar ground. The first stop was Ampthill, where the court stayed for two nights before moving on to Hampton Court. There, the members of the council who had been left behind in London were joined by those who had travelled with the king for the first time since the end of June. The progress, however, was not finished yet. On 25 October the court set off once again, this time to stay at Chenies, which belonged to the lord admiral, Sir John Russell. Having acquired the manor in 1526 on his marriage to Anne Jerningham, he made it into a family home. Now, he acted as host to the king and queen, as well as to the council, which met there on 25 October.

It was while she was staying at Chenies that Katherine was reunited with an old colleague from her days at Horsham and Lambeth. Alice Wilkes, who had been so concerned about Katherine's treatment at the hands of Henry Mannock, had left the Duchess of Norfolk's service and found employment with Lord William Howard.[26] She had then met Anthony Restwold, who was a servant to Lord Maltravers, the deputy of Calais, whom she married. Now Katherine, 'at her first being at Chenies, my Lord Admiral's house', sent for Alice 'to come to her chamber first by Dereham and then by Katherine Tylney'. The queen showed every indication of being delighted to see Alice again. She 'kissed her and welcomed her and she ordered her to lie with her chamberers, and after sent to her by the lady of Rochford an upper and nether habiliment of goldsmith's work for the French hood and a tablet of gold'.[27]

However, was Katherine's delight genuine? Everywhere she looked there was danger. She had felt obliged to take Katherine Tylney into her household because of what Tylney knew of her past, while Francis Dereham's boastful and careless talk threatened to expose secrets about her time at Norfolk House. Now Alice Wilkes, who knew just as much about the queen as Dereham and Tylney, had turned up. Katherine's expensive gifts were not necessarily tokens of affection for an old friend but, rather, the price of Alice's silence. Under such an atmosphere of menace, Katherine's increasing sense of disquiet can only be imagined. Yet, as though all this were not bad enough, events were now taking place in London that would have disastrous consequences for Katherine. It had all begun innocently enough, or so it seemed, a young man paying a visit to his newly married sister, but would end in horrific bloodshed.

John Lascelles had trained at Furnivall's Inn, one of the ten inns of Chancery established the previous century. Studies naturally focused on law, but Furnivall's offered instruction in music and dancing, as well as other pursuits deemed necessary for the aspiring courtier.[28]

That the Inns of Court were among the principal breeding grounds for new religious ideas should be no surprise. The Church–State controversy that had reached a critical point in the 1530s converged at the confluence of civil and canon law. Lascelles might have been converted at Furnivall's, but it is equally possible that he was already inclined towards the new learning, as Reformist doctrines were called. The Worksop area of Nottinghamshire where he grew up had long been awash with such ideas.

At some point, Lascelles entered the service of Thomas Cromwell, almost certainly having been introduced at court by his cousins, Humphrey and John Hercy. His assignment, initially, was to carry messages and orders to Cromwell's co-religionists, leading members of the Nottingham gentry, and return to his master with their replies and reports. His success in this task and the zeal with which he carried it out led Cromwell to promote him to a situation closer to the centre. Then, in 1539, Lascelles was appointed as a sewer of the Outer Chamber. This was part of a strategy to balance the numbers of courtiers and councillors who had been won over to the conservative party at court.

Following the fall of Cromwell, Lascelles left court for a time. Upon his return, on 15 September 1540, he met up with three colleagues, Jonson, Maxey and Smithwick. He confided to them his fears for 'God's holy word' following the demise of their master, for which he held the Duke of Norfolk and Bishop Gardiner responsible.[29] Maxey told them that he had heard Norfolk avow that he 'was not ashamed to say that he had never read the Scriptures nor ever would'; moreover, the duke had declared that 'it was merry in England before this new learning came up'. Lascelles advised Smithwick not to be 'too rash or quick in maintaining the Scriptures, for if we would let them alone and suffer a little time, they would overthrow themselves, standing manifestly against God and their Prince'.

Lascelles then recited what the Duke of Norfolk had said to various people. On one occasion, the duke was said to have rebuked a man in the Exchequer for marrying a nun. The man had replied that he knew 'no nuns nor religious folk in this realm, nor no such bondage, seeing God and the King have made them free'. To which the duke had answered, 'By God's body sacred, it will never out of my heart as long as I live.' Technically, this was treasonous, since it could be construed as violating the 1534 Act of Supremacy.[30] The following day, Smithwick reported the duke to Sir Nicholas Hare, whom he considered a trustworthy man because of his former closeness to Cromwell. Unfortunately for Smithwick, Sir Nicholas, although he had no love for Norfolk, did not want to become entangled in a dispute with him. He advised Smithwick to take his case to the king's council. By this time, however, Norfolk was bathing in the reflected glory of his niece and no action was taken against him. Lascelles and his friends were forced to bide their time.

A perfect opportunity to attack Norfolk and the conservatives came during the summer of 1541. The court had just left on its extended progress to the north. John Lascelles had not been selected to accompany the king, so he spent at least part of the summer visiting his sister, Mary.

Last seen in the service of the Duchess Agnes, Mary had married a man named Hall and settled in Sussex. As she and her brother fell into conversation, the subject of Queen Katherine came up. Lascelles suggested that, 'because she was of the Queen's old acquaintance', Mary should 'sue to be her woman'. Mary, however, was not enthusiastic. She said that she 'would not do so', although she was 'very sorry for the Queen'. When Lascelles asked her why, Mary explained that Katherine was a woman of loose morals. When pressed further, Mary remarked on Francis Dereham, a servant in my Lady of Norfolk's house, who had lain in his 'doublet and hose abed between the sheets and that one of the maidens that did lie with her [Katherine] said that he and she should lie elsewhere for fear that she know what matrimony means because there was such puffing and blowing between them that she wist not what it meant'. Mary then mentioned Henry Mannock, who claimed to have seen Katherine's private parts.[31]

For John Lascelles this news was a double-edged sword. On the one hand, his sister's revelation seemed like a gift from God. It presented him with the chance to inflict major damage on the conservative cause by initiating the downfall of the Catholic Queen Katherine, who might then be replaced with someone more sympathetic to the reformers. It was the perfect opportunity to avenge Cromwell and put the reformation back on a firm footing. On the other hand, he was well aware that possession of such knowledge was extremely dangerous. Should he pass on his sister's remarks and they were found to be false or were rejected for any reason, he would be in grave peril for slandering the queen. Conversely, should he conceal what he knew, and the information came out anyway, Lascelles would be guilty of misprision of treason, that is, failure to denounce treason known to him. This was a serious offence carrying a penalty of life imprisonment and the confiscation of all property. He had twenty-four hours in which to decide what he would do.[32] In the end, whatever his personal and religious motives might have been, Lascelles had little choice but to disclose what he knew. Nevertheless, he would have to be cautious.

In a way, circumstances were on Lascelles's side. Many of the councillors Henry had taken with him to the north were conservative. Those who had been left behind in London were reformers or ambivalent. Among these, one in particular would know best what to do: Archbishop Cranmer. Indeed, the archbishop was the only one among them who would dare to give such bad news to the king. Lascelles approached him and related the story he had pieced together from the snippets of information gleaned during his conversations with Mary.

Now it was Cranmer who faced a dilemma. He was aware that, as a Howard and a Catholic, Katherine posed a threat to the reformist party. With the backing of her powerful family and their allies, she might even become the figurehead for a new phase of persecution against his co-religionists. Then again, Katherine had shown kindness to Cranmer in the past and she had protected him when it looked as though he might go the way of Cromwell. Still, no matter how sensitive he might be to the matter on a personal level, he knew that, like Lascelles, he was duty-bound to act. Therefore, 'considering the weight and importance of the matter, being marvellously perplexed therewith', the archbishop consulted his colleagues on the caretaker council as to the best way to deal with it. They, in their turn, 'weighed the matter and deeply pondered the gravity thereof', and 'resolved finally [that] the said Archbishop of Canterbury should reveal the same to the King's Majesty'. Even so, 'because the matter was such as he both sorrowfully lamented and also could not find it in his heart' to tell the king what he had learned 'by word of mouth', Cranmer decided to declare 'the information thereof to his Highness in writing'.[33] Having carefully prepared his letter, Cranmer anxiously awaited the return of the king and Queen Katherine.

14

'It is no more the time to dance'

~

A s CRANMER, LASCELLES and everyone else who was aware of what was about to break braced themselves, a still more devastating event occurred. Prince Edward had fallen seriously ill. It was 29 October, and Katherine and Henry were at Windsor. The young prince was 'ill with a quatrain fever',[1] which was considered to be 'an unusual malady for a child of three to four years, who is not of a melancholic complexion'. The anxious father 'summoned all the physicians of the country to advise', and, following long consultation, they agreed that the fever would put the child in danger. Marillac, who was informed by one of those physicians, was also told that 'apart from this accident, the Prince was so fat and unhealthy', that he was not expected to live.

This was shattering news. Edward's illness brought into sharp focus the delicate state of the succession. Edward was the only legitimate male heir to the Tudor dynasty. What if he should die? It had been Henry's hope that Katherine would fulfil her duty as queen and provide more sons for the royal nursery, but so far she had failed. Was her failure her fault or Henry's?

The king's fertility record is available for all to see in the history of his previous wives' pregnancies. Katherine of Aragon had suffered several miscarriages and stillbirths. She had given birth to sons, but none had lived longer than a few weeks. Only one daughter, Lady Mary, had survived into adulthood. It was a dismal record for one as vigorous and virile as Henry.[2]

With Anne Boleyn, the situation was not much better. Anne had given birth to a strong and healthy daughter, Elizabeth. She had suffered one miscarriage in January 1536, which was referred to by Chapuys as a spontaneous 'abortion which seemed to be a male child which she had not borne 3½ months'.[3]

Anne had also remarked on Henry's sexual ability, saying that he was unable to satisfy a woman. The implication was that Henry was impotent, but was this a true assessment of Henry's prowess, or merely an act of spite on Anne's part? The understanding that a woman must enjoy sex in order to conceive cast aspersions upon her husband's virility and potency should she fail to fall pregnant. However, Henry had successfully fathered a son and heir, Prince Edward, by Jane Seymour. He also had an illegitimate son, Henry Fitzroy, by his then mistress, Elizabeth Blount. It is highly probable that he was also the father of Henry Carey, the son of another mistress, Mary Boleyn.

With Anne of Cleves, Henry had been unable to perform the act, but this was because he had been unable to accept her as his true wife. The root of the problem was not the unloveliness, or otherwise, of her face or her figure. Instead, it was due to Henry's fervent belief that she belonged to another man, the Duke of Lorraine's son, with whom she had entered into a precontract, and because he felt that she was not a virgin. Although assured that the precontract had never taken effect, Henry could never bring himself to know Anne carnally.

Things were entirely different when Henry married Katherine Howard. She had no previous contract, or so Henry thought, and Katherine would be entirely his own. She was young, fresh and alluring. With her, Henry could look forward to having 'some more store of fruit and succession to the comfort of his realm'.[4] The future could not have looked brighter.

Yet, there were those who doubted that everything really was as rosy as it appeared: 'But who can tell (for the grossness and indisposition of the King's body) whether he ever knew her or not? Surely there concur some conjectures whereby it may be surmised he did not know her, or at least it might so chance.'[5]

The truth of the matter can be discerned from the way Henry

treated his new wife. He was very attentive towards Katherine. He showered her with gifts. Courtiers and ambassadors noticed that he caressed her more often than he had his previous wives. He could not keep his hands away from her. Notwithstanding his failing health, Henry was enjoying sexual relations with Katherine from the moment they married. The ageing king acted like a giddy schoolboy carried away on the ecstasy of his first love. It was clear to all who saw them together that Henry was very much in love with Katherine. It is almost impossible to imagine that their marriage was not consummated.

Could it be that the problem lay with Katherine? Failures in conception and childbirth were always blamed on the woman. Any wife deemed incapable of producing sons was seen as unable to fulfil her marital duty; in a queen, this was serious indeed. In Henry's view, it was enough to make him question the validity of the marriage, as he had done with Katherine of Aragon. Her lack of success in providing heirs led him to conclude that their union did not have divine approval, and he began to look for reasons why that should be so.

In Katherine Howard's case, it is possible that she had been physically damaged by her violent encounters with Dereham. Also the much older and considerably more experienced Dereham might have passed on some infection to her that had affected her fertility.

On the other hand, pure dread at the prospect of being repudiated could have led to conception problems for Katherine. At various times throughout her marriage, she had heard talk that her husband was contemplating taking back Anne of Cleves. At least once Henry felt he had to reassure her that this was not the case, but Katherine had taken the gossip to heart and it had frightened her.

Moreover, Katherine was under immense pressure to produce sons to grace the royal nursery. Even the book on pregnancy and childbirth, which had been hastily dedicated to Queen Katherine, could be seen as a nudge for her to get on with it.

To each of these elements was added yet another: stress caused by the constant threat posed by those who knew dangerous secrets about her past. It all conspired to make life very difficult for the young queen. Now there was a new factor to cope with: Prince Edward's illness reminded Katherine of her failure to give Henry another son to secure the fragile Tudor succession.

A vigil was kept for Edward's recovery, and prayers begged God to spare the child. As it was, the boy was soon out of danger, though he was still unwell. In his frail state, it was thought best that he should be sent to the country to recover.

The young prince was safe. It was an outcome to be thankful for, and thankful Henry was; not only for the safety of his son and the succession, but also because he had Katherine, his beloved queen, by his side. On All Hallows Day, he went to hear mass in the beautiful Chapel Royal. Here, in the quiet of this most peaceful place, Henry received his maker and 'gave most humble and hearty thanks for the good life he led and trusted to lead' with Katherine.[6]

After the recent scare, the king was beginning to look to the future again. No doubt, that included the birth of a new son. He asked his chaplain, John Longland, Bishop of Lincoln, 'to make like prayer and give thanks with him' the following day, All Souls Day.

Henry had every right to be grateful that he had found Katherine, and he had every reason to love her as he did. Throughout the summer progress, Katherine had presented a perfect image of queenship. Majestic, graceful and beautiful, she had carried out her royal duties impeccably. Her poise and dignity marked the progress as the highlight of her reign so far. Katherine's past performance held the promise of a happy and successful future; in short, Katherine possessed all the qualities of a fine queen consort. This makes what happened next all the more tragic.

On the morrow, Henry returned to his closet in the Chapel Royal and was surprised to find that a letter had been placed in his pew. He picked it up, opened it and read Cranmer's devastating account of the accusations against Queen Katherine and how they had come to be made.

Oddly, Henry remained calm. His reaction was one of perplexity. His love for his wife and his 'constant opinion of her honesty' led him to suppose the calumny 'to be rather a forged matter than of truth'.

Even so, an accusation had been made; it could not be ignored. Henry called together a few select members of his council: William Fitzwilliam, Earl of Southampton and lord privy seal; John Russell, the lord admiral; Sir Anthony Browne and Sir Thomas Wriothesley. Some of these men had been away on their own estates in the country; now they rushed to London at the king's command. They and others of the Privy Council would question witnesses and gather evidence against Queen Katherine in the coming weeks.

The Privy Council, as it emerged after the fall of Cromwell, had become increasingly divided, with conservatives, such as the Duke of Norfolk and Bishop Gardiner, on one side, and reformers, such as Archbishop Cranmer and Lord Audeley, on the other. While this could so easily open the doors to personality clashes and factionalism, Henry kept a rein on his councillors by adopting a policy of balancing out these elements and by appointing two principal secretaries, so that no one man would dominate the council. Although day-to-day affairs could and were carried on under its own authority, the Privy Council was never allowed to act according to its own agenda. The king 'was himself the centre from which every measure emanated; and his Ministers had nothing more to do, than to receive his commands and obey them'.[7] This was especially true in the case of the fall of Queen Katherine. The proceedings against the queen could not have taken place except by Henry's direct orders and sanction. While the ruin of Queen Katherine was of great interest and benefit to the reformers, this was the result of the process, not the cause; there was no reformist conspiracy behind Katherine's downfall.

It had always been Henry's practice to collect all the evidence in a case, to weigh it carefully and draw his own conclusion before issuing orders as to how to proceed. Indeed, Henry saw it as an accomplishment of his duty to God and the world 'first to search, examine and inquire where should rest the culp, blame, default, and occasion of so many evils, to the intent that, the cause once removed and extirpated, the effects of the same may also be disappointed'.[8] He applied exactly this principle to the accusations against Queen Katherine.

In a meeting, which took place in conditions of the utmost secrecy, Henry disclosed to his councillors what had been reported of the queen. He added that 'he could not believe it to be true', yet he 'could not be satisfied till the certainty thereof were known'. An inquiry was established, but Henry warned his councillors that he 'would not in anywise that in the inquisition any spark of scandal should rise towards' Katherine.[9]

The first person to be examined was Roger Cotes, formerly Duchess Agnes's tailor who had gone into Katherine's service, who was interrogated on 4 November. Cotes's involvement is something of a mystery because it is not clear how he came to the notice of the investigators. He confessed to making hose – perhaps the hose Katherine gave Dereham. He also explained his financial situation, saying that his money had come from the Duchess Agnes as well as careful investment. Cotes admitted that Queen Katherine gave him £10 before the progress.[10] Somewhat indelicately, he also admitted to having said that if Katherine 'were advanced he expected a good living'. However, he denied 'ever saying he was in such favour that he might have married her'.

As it turned out, Roger Cotes was of little consequence, but John Lascelles was a different matter entirely. Since he was the one who had brought the news of Katherine's early life to the council's attention, it was essential to establish whether he would 'stand to his saying'. To that end, the Earl of Southampton was despatched to London, where Lascelles was 'secretly kept', to question him.

Lascelles, examined on 5 November, 'answered that his sister so told him',[11] which was that Francis Dereham was 'so familiar' with Katherine 'afore her marriage to the king that he did lie with her a hundred nights in the year in his doublet and hose abed between the sheets'. One of the maidens who lay next to Katherine was shocked and annoyed by the couple's behaviour and wished they would lie elsewhere. Mary had also told him that 'once Henry Mannock did know her [Katherine's] privates from all others by a privy mark.' Moreover, 'Dereham did fly into Ireland at the time that the king's grace was in love with the lady Katherine [afore] her marriage.' Mary had described to him how 'Dereham did fight Henry Mannock and that the said Dereham did take her divers times [to] use the jakes', that is, he would take Katherine to the privy for sex. Finally, Dereham had boasted that he was 'so in favour' with Katherine 'that he might have married her if he had list'. He was warned to 'beware of such matters for it is no little jeopardy'.

Lascelles was anxious to point out that he had revealed what he had learned about Katherine 'for the discharge of his duty and for none other respect'. He very well 'knew what danger was in it nevertheless he had rather die in declaration of the truth as it came to him, seeing it touch the King's Majesty so nearly, than live with the concealment of the same'.[12]

In this way, Lascelles was able to avoid being charged with misprision, but were his motives so principled? In view of his concerns for the reformist cause following the fall of Cromwell and his earlier conversation with his co-religionists, it is possible to see another purpose to Lascelles's actions, which was the desire to cause considerable damage to the Duke of Norfolk by initiating the fall of the Howard queen.

Having confirmed that Lascelles did indeed 'stand to his saying', Southampton immediately left for Sussex to examine Lascelles's sister, Mary. As it stood, Lascelles's story was second-hand. When the earl heard the story direct, would he uncover some discrepancy in the two accounts; or would Mary confirm all that her brother had deposed? At this stage, secrecy was essential; arriving later on 5 November, Southampton made 'pretence to the woman's husband of hunting and to her of receiving hunters'.

Mary began her testimony[13] by establishing her credentials, describing her employment, first with Lord Howard and then with the Duchess of Norfolk. She went on to speak of Katherine and her relationship with Henry Mannock, her music teacher. Mary rehearsed the events that followed: how the affair was brought to her attention, how she had confronted Mannock, his defiance. She recounted how she had accompanied Katherine when the girl went to confront Mannock, and that she had seen the two of them walking in the orchard a few days later.

When asked what she knew 'by Dereham' and Katherine, Mary said that she 'well perceived that Dereham and she was far in love together for she had seen them kiss after a wonderful manner for they would kiss and hang by the bills[14] together an [as though] they were two sparrows'.

Mary recalled the time when she was 'living in the chamber where my said lady lies'. Her mistress had implemented a rigidly observed ritual: 'every night my said lady would [cause] the keys for the chamber where [the] said gentlewomen lay to be brought in to her chamber; the said Mistress Katherine would desire this deponent to steal the key and bring it to her and so she did.' Katherine would then kiss Mary, after which she 'would go to naked bed and draw the curtains and the said Dereham would lie down upon the bed in his doublet and his hose'. There were 'many times the said Mistress Katherine would come in and steal the keys herself and let him in when my lady was in bed'.

Mary spoke about Alice Wilkes, who had told her that Dereham would remain with Katherine 'till it was almost day'. Alice had wittered on, saying that 'many times there was such a puffing and blowing between them as she never heard.' She had requested Mary to come and lie with her one night, saying that 'she was a married woman and wist what matrimony meant and what belonged to that puffing and blowing'. Mary, however, was less than sympathetic, telling Alice to 'leave Katherine alone, for an [if] she hold on as she begins we shall here she will be nought within a while'.

When asked whether she had mentioned any of this to her employers, Mary replied that she had not; she had told only her brother. However, she did name members of the duchess's household who were privy to what had been going on: John Walsheman, John Baynet and Richard Faver, grooms of the chamber, who would confess what they had seen, as would Margery, the duchess's chamberer. Having taken Mary's statement, Southampton made his way back to Hampton Court. How was he to present these confessions to the king?

While Southampton was busy with the Lascelleses, Thomas Wriothesley had gone to London to question Henry Mannock and to 'take' Francis Dereham. The arrest of Dereham was made on 'pretence of piracy, because he had been before in Ireland, and hath been noted before with that offence'. Again, subterfuge was being employed so that 'no spark of suspicion should rise of these examinations'. It was equally important to prevent collusion among the witnesses.

The Henry Mannock who gave his deposition to Wriothesley and Cranmer was a very different man to the one who had been confronted by Mary Lascelles. Not long after he had left the duchess's service, he had married and moved to Streatham with his new wife. Older and wiser now, Mannock displayed none of the boast and swagger that had been evident in Mary's description of the events. He began his testimony by explaining how he had entered the Duchess of Norfolk's household, that he and Mr Barnes had been engaged to teach Katherine to play on the virginals. It was 'in the execution thereof' that Mannock fell in love with his pupil and would 'many times' fall into 'familiarity' with her; for, as he believed, 'she hath shown to be of like inclination towards him'.

On one occasion, Mannock continued, the duchess happened 'to find them talking together [at night] in a chamber', whereupon she 'gave the said Mistress Katherine two or three blows' and 'charged they never more be alone together after'. For this reason they 'used not another's company'. He then spoke of Dereham, who loved Katherine as he did and who haunted her 'chamber where she lays nightly, and where he would commonly stay 'til two or three of the clock in the morning'.

Mannock explained how he and Barnes had written an

anonymous letter to the duchess warning her of what was going on in the maidens' chamber at night. He spoke of how the duchess had railed with her maidens and Dereham, telling them how she had learned of their mischief, and described how Katherine had stolen the letter and given it to Dereham, who copied it. Dereham, he said, had confronted him and called him a knave. In the end, Mannock was completely open about his relationship with Katherine, explaining that he had extracted a promise from her to allow him to handle her intimately and about his clumsy fumbling in the duchess's chapel. He was equally honest when he confessed upon his damnation that he never knew Katherine carnally.[15]

Having finished with Mannock, Wriothesley went on to speak with Dereham, who now waited anxiously within the confines of his prison deep inside the Tower.[16] He admitted that he 'hath had carnal knowledge with the queen afore [her] marriage, lying in bed by her in his doublet and hose diverse times and six or seven times in naked bed with her', even though she shared her bed with Katherine Tylney or Alice Wilkes. He 'did not open this thing before this time', saying that 'he loved the queen as at his first coming out of Ireland'. Dereham then spoke of how he had 'bought habiliments and other things for the queen afore marriage to the value of viii*l* [£8]'. He went on to confess that he 'was with the queen since her marriage at sundry times' and that he 'was in the queen's privy chamber diverse times since her marriage to the king'. He admitted that Katherine had felt it necessary to warn him to 'take heed what words you speak'. Finally, he mentioned that the queen had sent him, 'since her marriage at one time 3*l* for his hose, at another time she delivered to him 10*l* in her privy chamber'.

Between them, Wriothesley, Southampton and Cranmer now had four pieces of evidence that confirmed John Lascelles's original story. They made their way back to Hampton Court where, towards midnight on 5 November, another council meeting was called. They were joined by other members of the council, including Charles, Duke of Suffolk, who had been at his house in the country and was not due to return until Christmas. The seriousness of the situation was made clear when a summons was sent to the Duke of Norfolk. Because of the presence of plague in his house, the duke had been told not to come to court for another fifteen days, but now he was to repair to Hampton Court as quickly as possible.[17] As the meeting got under way, Southampton and Wriothesley made their reports to the king.

Southampton reported that John Lascelles did indeed 'stand to his saying', as did Mary Lascelles, whom the earl described as 'constant in her former saying'.[18] As though that were not bad enough, Wriothesley, who had Francis Dereham's confession, faced the unenviable task of advising his king that his beloved Katherine had not been pure when he married her. Not only had Dereham confessed to knowing Katherine 'carnally many times', he could also call to witness 'three sundry women one after another that had lain in the same bed with them when he did the acts, that the matter seemed most apparent'.[19] What was worse, however, was that Dereham had confessed to being in Katherine's chamber after her marriage. The import of this detail hung unspoken in the air; at least for now.

As Henry listened to the accounts and conclusions of his investigators, the hope he had cherished that Katherine had been falsely accused quickly faded. He fell into an 'inward sorrow'. The great king's 'heart was so pierced with pensiveness that long it was before his Majesty could speak and utter the sorrow of his heart to us'. Finally, 'with plenty of tears (which was strange in his courage) opened the same'.[20]

At this point the history of Katherine Howard gives way to an enduring legend. Henry, having ordering the queen to be confined to her apartments, made plans to leave Hampton Court. Just before his departure, he went once more to his closet in the Chapel Royal to hear mass. At that point Katherine, in a desperate attempt to see her husband, managed to escape from her guards and flee her chamber. She ran down the Queen's Staircase and into a gallery now known as 'The Haunted Gallery', towards the chapel. Just as she reached the door to the king's closet, her guards caught up with her and dragged her back to her own apartments. Her piercing screams were ignored by her once adoring husband, who quite calmly returned to his devotions. If indeed Katherine had tried to reach Henry while he was at prayer, it must have been on Sunday 6 November, shortly before he left Hampton Court.[21]

Later that day, Norfolk and Audeley joined their king and, using the pretext of a hunting expedition, dined at a little place in the fields, no doubt in an attempt to lessen the risk of the matter becoming common knowledge. Here, Henry informed them of what had happened and how it had come to his notice.

As night fell, the king secretly left Hampton Court for London. He did not say goodbye to Katherine and she would never see him again. At midnight, another meeting of the council was called. Held at the Bishop of Winchester's house at Southwark, it went on until four or five o'clock on the Monday morning.[22]

So far, the activity at court had been so secret that not even the ambassadors knew for certain what was going on. Marillac noted that the 'lords have been ever since in Council morning and evening'. He added that 'Henry himself was attending these meetings, which he is not wont to do.' Everyone showed 'themselves very troubled'; Norfolk, he noted, was particularly worried, although he 'is esteemed very resolute, and not easily moved to show by his face what his heart conceives'.[23]

Clearly, it was a matter of great weight and this inspired much speculation. It was conjectured that bad news had arrived from Ireland. Then it was thought that the Scots were threatening war. It was even suggested that 'justice is to be done upon certain lords who have [mis]managed the finances'.[24]

Attention now turned to Queen Katherine. It was noted that she had not seen her husband for several days. Furthermore, Hampton Court was being 'closely guarded, with only officers admitted'. Almost from the moment of her return from the summer progress, the queen had 'taken no kind of pastime', but had 'kept in her chamber'. Previously, 'she did nothing but dance and rejoice, and now when the musicians come they are told that it is no more the time to dance.'

If the ambassador found it hard to puzzle out what exactly was going on, matters were even worse for Katherine. Effectively she was under house arrest; her husband had slipped away without a word to her and her amusements had been curtailed; but, as yet, she had received no formal notice that anything was wrong.

15

'Most vile wretch in the world'

~

T HE SHADOW OF uncertainty beneath which Katherine had
lived since her return from the summer progress was lifted
when she received a delegation of councillors in her apartments.
It was 7 November; five days after Cranmer had slipped the note
with its terrible message on to Henry's pew. Now the archbishop,
accompanied by Chancellor Audeley, Robert Radcliffe, Bishop
Gardiner and the Duke of Norfolk entered her chambers. Whatever
comfort Katherine might have taken from her uncle's presence was
quickly dispelled when she was informed of the accusations against
her. At first Katherine 'constantly denied it', and it was only with
'the matter being so declared unto her' that she 'perceived it to be
wholly disclosed'.[1] In other words, Katherine was advised that she
faced serious charges and that the delegation had come, not to
hear her defence, but to gather the evidence against her.

The councillors then extracted a confession from Katherine.[2]
It began, as many such statements do, with the 'guilty' party
humbling herself before the one who holds the power of life and
death over her: 'I your grace's most sorrowful subject and most
vile wretch in the world, not worthy to make any recommend-
ations unto your most excellent majesty do only make my most
humble submission and confession of my faults.' She invoked the
times in the past when she had successfully petitioned her husband
to show mercy to others, asking him to extend the same favour to
her while showing herself, nevertheless, to be unworthy of it:
'And where no cause of mercy is given upon my part yet of your
most accustomed mercy extended unto all other men undeserved

most humbly on my hands and knees do desire one sparkle thereof to be extended unto me although of all other creatures most unworthy either to be called your wife or subject.' Katherine then conveyed her regret for her misdeeds, once again asking her husband to be merciful: 'My sorrow I can by no writing express; nevertheless I trust your most benign nature will have some respect unto my youth my ignorance my frailness my humble confession of my fault and plain declaration of the same referring me wholly unto your graces pity and mercy.' Now she asked Henry to consider how she came to commit her errors:

> First, at the flattering and fair persuasions of Mannock, being but a young girl suffered him at sundry times to handle and touch the secret parts of my body which neither became me with honesty to permit nor him to require. Also Francis Dereham by many persuasions procured me to his vicious purpose and obtained first to lie upon my bed with his doublet and hose and after within the bed and finally he lay with me naked and used me in such sort as a man doith his wife many and sundry times but how often I know not.

Katherine pointed out that the company she had kept with Dereham had 'ended almost a year before the King's majesty was married to my lady Anne of Cleve and continued not past one quarter of a year or little above'. She went on, further demeaning herself: 'Now the whole truth being declared unto your majesty I most humbly beseech the same to consider the subtle persuasions of young men and the ignorance and frailness of young women.' True to the social conditioning of the time, Katherine took her share of the responsibility for what had been done to her, even though she was the one who had been exploited.

Katherine explained that she had kept the secret of her earlier encounters because she was 'so desirous to be taken unto your grace's favour and so blinded with the desire of worldly glory that I could not nor had grace to consider how great a fault it was to conceal my former faults from your majesty, considering that I intended ever during my life to be faithful and true unto your majesty after'.

Katherine had found it difficult to live with her 'offences' and her sadness and sense of shame was, at times, almost overwhelming. Nevertheless, 'the sorrow of my offences was ever before mine eyes considering the infinite goodness of your majesty towards me from time to time ever increasing and not diminishing'.

It remained only to commit her cause to her husband, with the hope that he would be merciful, for the consequences of her offences, she well knew, were deadly serious. She referred 'the judgement of all mine offences with my life and death wholly unto your most benign and merciful grace to be considered by no justice of your majesty's laws but only by your infinite goodness, pity, compassion and mercy without the which I knowledge myself worthy of most extreme punishment'. The confession was then signed in the hand of Kateryn Howard.

The delegation had reason to be pleased with their day's work. Having got what they came for, they left Katherine alone in her chambers. She was in a dreadful state, badly frightened and almost hysterical.

Cranmer reported to Henry on the visit he and his colleagues had made to the queen. However, as Henry listened, he found Cranmer's account wanting. Katherine had spoken about Mannock's furtive fumbling. She had confessed that she and Francis Dereham had been involved in a full sexual relationship. But what did it really mean? Was it fornication? Was there something more to it, perhaps sex between a woman and a man bound by contract? In other words, was Katherine Dereham's legal wife?

Henry instructed the archbishop to return to Katherine and dig deeper into the affair. It was a measure of Henry's continued love for Katherine that he asked Cranmer to assure her that he was inclined to be merciful. Equipped with these fresh instructions, the archbishop returned to Katherine's apartments that evening where he interrogated her further.

The image of Katherine afterwards portrayed by Cranmer was

not that of a composed queen angry at the calumnies being heaped upon her. Instead, it is a distressing picture of a terrified young woman.[3] The archbishop had found Katherine 'in such lamentation and heaviness, as I never saw no creature, so that it would have pitied any man's heart in the world to look upon her'. In fact, Katherine had continued in a 'vehement rage' from the time Cranmer and the council had left her; now, she was 'far entered toward a frenzy'. As he noted, 'if Your Grace's comfort had not come in time, she could have continued no long time in that condition, without a frenzy, which nevertheless I do yet much suspect to follow hereafter'.

The approach Cranmer had intended to use with Katherine was 'first to exaggerate the grievousness of her demerits, then to declare unto her the justice of Your Majesty's laws, and what she ought to suffer by the same; and last of all, to signify unto her your most gracious mercy'. However, when he saw the condition she was in, he thought it best to 'turn my purpose, and to begin at the last part first, to comfort her by Your Grace's benignity and mercy'. Cranmer feared that, otherwise, he might have 'driven her unto some dangerous ecstasy, and else into a very frenzy, so that the words of comfort coming last, might, peradventure, have come too late'.

Having been assured of Henry's mercy, Katherine 'held up her hand, and gave most humble thanks unto Your Majesty, who had showed unto her more grace and mercy, than she herself thought meet to sue for, or could have hoped of'. The queen became calmer now, although she still 'sobbed and wept'. Yet, 'after a little pausing, she suddenly fell into a new rage, much worse than she was before'.

Whenever Katherine fell into such 'extreme braides', Cranmer, who showed that he had a warm and compassionate side to his character, would 'travel with her to know the cause, and then, as much as I can, I do labour to take away, or at the least to mitigate the cause'. On this latest occasion, he told Katherine that 'there was some new fantasy come into her head, which I desired her to open unto me'. When she had recovered herself sufficiently and was able to speak, the weeping Katherine lamented:

> Alas my Lord, that I am alive, the fear of death grieved me not so much before, as doth now the remembrance of the King's goodness, for when I remember how gracious and loving a Prince I had, I can not but sorrow; but this sudden mercy, and more than I could have looked for, showed unto me, so unworthy, at this time, maketh mine offences to appear before mine eyes much more heinous than they did before; and the more that I consider the greatness of his mercy, the more I do sorrow in my heart, that I should so misorder my self against His Majesty.

No matter what words of comfort Cranmer spoke, he was unable to soothe the young queen and she 'continued in a great pang a long while'. Still, she rallied again and 'came to her self', so that the archbishop was able to have 'very good communication with her', now that he had 'brought her into a great quietness'. Eventually, he managed to extract a signed statement from Katherine.[4] In it, she declared that:

> Being again examined by my Lord of Canterbury of contracts and communications of matrimony between Dereham and me, I shall here answer faithfully and truly as I shall make answer at the last Day of Judgement, and by the promise that I made in Baptism, and the Sacrament that I received upon All-hallows Day last past.

Although this is a standard preamble, it nevertheless demonstrates that Katherine regarded her promise to tell the truth as a solemnly sworn holy oath.

Katherine acknowledged that Dereham 'hath many times moved unto me the question of matrimony, whereunto, as far as I remember, I never granted him more than I have confessed'. Moreover, she denied that she had ever said to him, 'I promise you, I do love you with all my heart.' She did not remember ever speaking such words to Dereham. As to the words 'that I should promise him by my faith and troth, that I would never other Husband but him,' she was certain she never spoke them.

The queen next described the tokens and gifts she and Dereham had exchanged. The reason for the question was obvious: Cranmer wanted to know if she and Dereham had exchanged love tokens. Katherine answered that she had given Dereham a band and sleeves for a shirt; he had given her a heart's ease of silk and an old shirt of fine Holland or cambric. These were nothing more than New Year's presents, and not very expensive ones at that. The shirt had been second-hand, having previously belonged to Lord Thomas Howard. Beyond that, as far as she could remember, she gave Dereham nothing except £10 at the beginning of the progress.

Cranmer asked her if she had given Dereham a ring of gold upon condition that he should never give it away. Her reply was that, 'to my knowledge I never gave him no such ring, but I am assured upon no such condition'.

Cranmer then returned to the subject of the band and sleeves for the shirt that Katherine had given Dereham as a New Year's gift. He wanted to know if they had been her own work. This is an important point because making shirts for husbands was seen as a wifely duty. Katherine denied that she had made them: 'They were not of my own work, but as I remember Clifton's wife of Lambeth wrought them.'

The archbishop touched on a bracelet of silkwork, but Katherine avowed that she had never given Dereham one, 'and if he have any of mine, he took it from me'. The matter of a ruby came up, which Katherine was supposed to have given Dereham to set in a ring. Again, she knew nothing about it, saying that she had not given a ruby to Dereham for any purpose.

Cranmer next mentioned the French fennel; Katherine accepted that she had asked Dereham to arrange for one to be made for her. She explained about the little woman with the crooked back who made such things and how she had promised to pay Dereham for the flower when she had the money.

Cranmer spoke about a small ring with a stone, with the implication that Dereham had given it to Katherine and that she had lost it. Again, she knew nothing about it, saying, 'I never lost none of his, nor he never gave me one.'

Other items for which Dereham had lent Katherine money to buy were velvet and satin for habiliments, a velvet cap with a feather, and a quilted cap of sarcenet. He had also lent her money for unspecified reasons. Katherine repaid Dereham for all these things when she came to court. In other words, Katherine had used her first stipend to repay Dereham for the items he had bought for her, handing over to him some £5 or £6 that, in all truth, she needed for herself. She then explained that Dereham did not give her the sarcenet cap but only the material to make it. She gave this to Mr Rose, an embroiderer at the duchess's house, who made up the cap and decorated it with friar's knots, which Dereham took as a play on his name, Francis.

Cranmer next broached the subject of an indenture and obligation for £100 that Dereham had left in Katherine's custody when he went away. Dereham had told her that, should he never come back, she was to keep this money. This was a substantial sum, and the only realistic justification Dereham had for leaving it with Katherine was that he considered her to be his wife or his betrothed.

This brought Cranmer to the material point of the interview: had Katherine and Dereham entered into a contract of marriage? Katherine responded:

> Examined whether I called him husband and he me wife, I do answer, that there was communication in the house that we two should marry together, and some of his enemies had envy thereat, wherefore he desired me to give him leave to call me wife, and that I would call him husband. And I said I was content. And so after that, commonly he called me wife and many times I called him husband. And he used many times to kiss me, and so he did to many other commonly in the house. And I suppose, that this be true, that at one time when he kissed me very often, some said that were present, 'They trowed that he would never have kissed me enough.' Whereto he answered, 'who should let [prevent] him to kiss his own wife?' Then said one of them, 'I trowe the matter

will come to pass as the common saying is.' 'What is that,' quoth he. 'Marry,' said the other, 'that Mr Dereham shall have Mrs [Mistress] Katherine Howard.' 'By St John,' said Dereham, 'you may guess twice and guess worse.' But that I should wink upon him and say secretly 'what and this should come to my Lady's ear,' I suppose verily there was no such thing.

To call each other husband and wife was one thing. It suggested a commitment to their relationship, but as a contract, it was dissolvable. The crucial factor was whether or not they had sealed their contract sexually. In fact, Cranmer already knew that they had but, wanting to be absolutely certain in so important a matter, he asked Katherine outright whether or not she and Dereham had 'carnal knowledge' of each other. She replied:

> I confess as I did before, that diverse times he had lain with me, sometimes in his doublet and hose and two or three times naked, but not so naked that he had nothing upon him, for he had always at the least his doublet, and as I do think, his hose also, but I mean naked when his hose was put down.

The word 'naked' did not necessarily mean completely unclothed or nude; it often meant to be in one's undergarments. However, the phrase 'to lie with' was a euphemism for sexual intercourse. Whatever doubts Cranmer might have had were finally laid to rest.

Katherine continued, speaking about the times Dereham would come to the maidens' chamber with wine, strawberries, apples 'and other things to make good cheer' after the duchess had gone to bed. 'But that he made any special banquet, that by appointment between him and me, he should tarry after the keys were delivered to my Lady, that is utterly untrue.'

Cranmer was aware that Mary Lascelles had also mentioned the keys to the maidens' chamber, alleging that Katherine had stolen them or had required Mary to steal them on her behalf; he asked Katherine to elaborate. She asserted that 'I never did steal the keys myself, nor desired any person to steal them, to the intent and purpose to let in Dereham.' There were, nevertheless, 'other causes' for which the doors were opened, sometimes overnight, and sometimes early in the morning, 'as well at the request of me, as of other'. What these 'other causes' were Katherine did not say. Dereham had sometimes taken advantage of these occasions to 'come in early in the morning, and ordered him very lewdly', but this was 'never at my request, nor consent'.

Katherine told the archbishop: 'that [Alice] Wilkes and [Dorothy] Baskerville should say what shifts should we make, if my Lady should come in suddenly. And I should answer that he should go into the little gallery.' Katherine denied that she had said any such thing. Rather, Dereham had been the one to devise the strategy, 'and so he hath done indeed'.

Cranmer returned to Katherine's relationship with Dereham. He asked her what had passed between them upon her leaving Norfolk House to go to court in the service of Anne of Cleves. She answered that Dereham had avowed that he would not tarry long in the house if she were to leave. Katherine had merely dismissed him, saying 'that he might do as he list'. Moreover, she was adamant that she had not cried at their parting, 'but that I should say, it grieved me as much as it did him, or that he should never live to say thou hast swerved, or that the tears should trickle down by my cheeks, none of that be true. For all that knew me, and kept my company, knew how glad and desirous I was to come to the court.'

Finally, Cranmer asked about their communication after Dereham returned from Ireland. Katherine replied that Dereham had confronted her about reports that she was to marry Mr Culpeper. Katherine had countered with a withering retort and denied that she had any intention of marrying Culpeper.

Katherine had finally managed to convey her side of the story, but she was still very distressed. Night had fallen, and 'about six of the clock, she fell into an other like pang', although this time 'not so outrageous as the first was'. This time, her anguish was caused by 'remembrance of the time; for about that time, as she said, Master Hennage was wont to bring her knowledge of Your Grace.'

Cranmer left Katherine then and began to write up his report for Henry. However, he was too busy with other things to present it to the king in person. He referred the rest of his account to Sir John Dudley 'saving that I have sent, herewith enclosed, all that I can get out of her, concerning any communication of matrimony with Dereham'.

Although the matter of Katherine's relationship with Dereham was not as much as Cranmer had thought, he did 'suppose, surely, it is sufficient to prove a contract, with carnal copulation following'. Katherine, on the other hand, adamantly refuted this, saying that 'she think it be no contract'. Cranmer would have agreed with her but for certain conditions: 'as in deed the words alone be not, if carnal copulation had not followed thereof.' However, their relationship had clearly been sexual. It was the fact that Katherine and Dereham had known each other carnally that had transformed their contract from one that could be dissolved to one that was legally binding and indissoluble.

Cranmer then mentioned Master Baynton, the queen's brother-in-law and vice-chamberlain. Katherine had sent him to the king on her behalf after her first interview. The archbishop explained that it was 'partly for the declaration of her estate [condition]' and partly because, after Cranmer and the other councillors had left her earlier, 'she began to excuse and to temper those things, which she had spoke unto me, and set her hand thereto'. This Cranmer would explain more fully when he next saw Henry, 'for she said, that all that Dereham did unto her, was importunate [persistent] forcement, and, in a manner, violence, rather than of her free consent and will'.

At her first interview with the delegation of councillors, Katherine had been confounded and intimidated by the men confronting her and shocked at the accusations that had been made against her. Having no counsel to advise her, she had signed her name to a confession that did not represent the whole truth.

Afterwards, when she was left alone and the pressure had relented, Katherine recalled a vital point that had eluded her under the strain of her examination. She wanted it to be known that she had never consented to her relationship with Francis Dereham. In reality, Dereham had used violence against her, forcing himself upon her, raping her.

This was the reason why Katherine refused to acknowledge the existence of her contract, binding or otherwise, with Francis Dereham. It had nothing to do with Howard pride or her desire to remain queen. Rather, she regarded any contract that might be understood to exist between herself and Dereham as invalid. Despite the consummation of their relationship, it had all been against her will and without her 'interior consent'. From the queen's point of view, she and Dereham were not a couple legally bound by contract, nor had they ever been.

Katherine's status in this matter was ambiguous. Since she was in all probability effectively married to Dereham, whether she liked it or not, he was protected by the law that stated that a man could not be accused of raping his wife; sex was a conjugal right. On the other hand, that Katherine had not become pregnant by Dereham indicated that she had not enjoyed sex with him, suggesting that he had indeed raped her.[5]

Notwithstanding the technicalities of her case, who would believe Katherine? In view of the way women were regarded – by both sexes, not just men – and the nature of 'interior consent', her allegation of rape against Dereham would never have been taken seriously.

Despite the continued efforts to preserve the secrecy surrounding Katherine's case, enough information had leaked out to allow Marillac to write a report to King François.[6] He summarised the events of the past few days and the speculation at court over what it all meant. Although matters were still far from clear, he concluded that, 'it is to be presumed that this King wishes to change his wife'. The reasons for this were that Katherine 'is newly accused of being entertained by a gentleman [Dereham] while she was at the home of the old duchess of Norfolk' and because 'physicians say she cannot bear children'. Marillac is the only source to suggest that

Queen Katherine was unable to have children. How he came to this conclusion is impossible to guess; he probably assumed it as a result of Katherine's failure, so far, to become pregnant, notwithstanding his own assertions to the contrary. He went on, noting that 'the way taken is the same as with Queen Anne who was beheaded'; the ominous connotations for Katherine are obvious. Another ill omen was that Katherine's brother, Charles, who had been serving as a gentleman of the privy chamber, was 'banished from court without reason given'.

Already rumours had begun to circulate about who the king would take as his next wife. 'Everyone' thought he would return to Anne of Cleves, 'who conducted herself wisely in her affliction, and is more beautiful than she was, and more regretted and commiserated than Queen Katharine [of Aragon] was in like case'. Henry, however, showed no inclination towards any other lady.

The imperial ambassador, Eustache Chapuys, was also making 'diligent inquiry'. So far, he had learned that 'the King pretends' that Francis Dereham 'had actually been betrothed to the Queen before her marriage to him, and, therefore, that his own is invalid and null'.[7]

Meanwhile, King Henry contemplated the evidence against Katherine and reached a decision. His orders were that his wife should be removed from Hampton Court and sent to the dissolved Abbey of Syon. Until then, she was to keep her privy keys. Henry was treating Katherine with a degree of compassion, but his benevolence disguised a dark purpose.[8]

16

'Blind youth hath no grace to foresee'

~

WITH KATHERINE'S TRANSFER to Syon imminent, it was time to release the news of her rustication and the reasons for it. Henry ordered Chancellor Audeley to assemble the councillors, lords and judges and 'declare unto them the abominable demeanour of the Queen'. However, there was to be one significant omission. Audeley was to make no mention of Dereham or the precontract, 'which might serve for her defence'. Rather, he should 'open and make manifest the King's Highness's just cause of indignation and displeasure', so that 'the world may know and see that, which is hitherto done, to have a just ground and foundation'.

The king then issued a direction to all those councillors who already knew not only 'the whole matter, but also how it was first detected, by whom, and by what means it came to the King's Majesty's knowledge, with the whole of the King's Majesty's sorrowful behaviour and careful proceeding in it'. He ordered them to assemble the ladies, gentlewomen and gentlemen of the queen's household and explain the situation to them on the following Sunday. As before, they were to be careful not to mention the precontract; indeed, the plan to keep it a secret worked perfectly. Chapuys spoke of the 'most intimate connection' between Katherine and Dereham, during which 'there had been no question nor talk of a marriage between them'.[1]

These new developments inspired a gentleman of the privy chamber to conclude 'that Katherine shall no longer be queen'.[2] Whoever this gentleman was, he was incorrect. That is to say, his prophecy was not to be realised just yet.

The silence the council were to observe concerning Dereham and the precontract reflects the extent of the dilemma they faced regarding how they should proceed. By the statute dated July 1540, a precontract was held to be an impediment to any subsequent marriage unless the precontracted relationship was unconsummated.[3] Katherine had admitted that she and Dereham had called each other husband and wife; Dereham admitted to having sex with Katherine before her marriage. Therefore, a binding contract between Katherine and Dereham did exist. In this case, Katherine could be charged with bigamy and her marriage to King Henry dissolved.

Even so, it was not as simple as that. Katherine's steadfast refusal to accept that she had been precontracted to Dereham, whatever the evidence suggested, cast doubts over the whole affair. For this reason, 'all the prelates who are not commonly heard in affairs of state, are summoned hither'[4] in a bid to overcome the difficulty.

Meanwhile, the council focused their attention on Dereham. Had he not mentioned that he had entered the queen's privy chamber at 'diverse times since her marriage to the king and at one time the queen said to the said Dereham take heed what words you speak'? Had Katherine not had taken him 'into her service, and trained him upon occasion as sending of errands and writing letters, when her secretary was out of the way, to come into her privy chamber'? What is more, had Katherine not engaged Katherine Tylney 'to be one of her chamberers, one of the women which had before lain in the bed with her and Dereham'? The council concluded, 'what this pretended is easy to be conjectured'.[5] Yet, conjecture was not enough. Another visit to Dereham was in order. He would be questioned again to see if there was anything more he could tell them.

Under fierce interrogation, Dereham confirmed that he had entered Katherine's chambers after her marriage to the king. Of course he had, his post necessarily gave him right of access. However, he emphatically rejected any suggestion that he and the queen had revived their former association. Whether or not Dereham was tortured is unknown, and the usual phrases implying torture, 'extreme question' or 'seriously examined' or similar, are missing here. Certainly, there were several methods available to his interrogators. The rack, known euphemistically as being married to the Duke of Exeter's daughter, was one, that cruel frame upon which the suspect would be stretched until his joints were torn out. Then there were thumb-screws, pillywinks and iron boots, any of which could help loosen a reluctant tongue. Whatever the case, pressed to breaking-point and desperate to prove his innocence, Dereham blurted out that he had been replaced in the queen's affections by Thomas Culpeper.[6]

This was an interesting and entirely unexpected turn. Although the council was aware that Katherine's name had once been linked with Culpeper's – she had mentioned him herself during her interview with Cranmer – they had assumed that any relationship between them had long ago come to an end. Now Dereham had revealed that this was far from being the case.

Thomas Culpeper was arrested on 11 or 12 November 1541 and his questioning began immediately. Because of his position as a gentleman of the privy chamber, and as one of the king's favourites, Culpeper was not subject to the merciless treatment inflicted on Dereham. Nevertheless, he surely must have been shocked by his sudden detention. As Culpeper gave his deposition, his words were hastily scribbled down.[7]

He began by recounting the events of the previous Maundy Thursday at Greenwich, recalling that Katherine had sent for him and given him a decorated hat as a gift. He noted that Katherine had instructed him to hide it under his cloak, repeating the words he had spoken to her and her admonition. He recalled the dishes of meat and fish she had sent him when he was sick.

Culpeper next spoke of the progress time, when he had taken a cramp ring from Lady Rochford's finger 'which she said was the queen's'. When she told her mistress about it, Katherine 'took another cramp ring from her own finger and bade the lady Rochford give it' to Culpeper, 'saying it was an ill sight to see him wear but one cramp ring and therefore she did send him another'.

Lady Rochford had told Culpeper that 'she was bidden many nights by the queen to send for him both before and after'. Then, at Lincoln, 'the Lady Rochford appointed him to come into a place under her Chamber being, so he thinketh, the queen's stool house'. Here he had 'found the queen and the Lady Rochford and no other body about at eleven of the clock in the night, and then he talked with her and none present but the Lady Rochford till three of the clock in the morning or thereabout'. Culpeper recalled that they 'had there fond communication of themselves and of their loves before time and of Bess Harvey', a Culpeper conquest.[8] Culpeper and Katherine 'had a long talk then', although the queen 'always in that time started away and returned again as one in fear lest somebody should come in'. On one occasion, when Culpeper left Katherine's company, 'he kissed her hand saying he would presume no further'.

He remembered that, despite the queen's caution, every now and then a servant would come too close. He mentioned Lufkyn, one of Katherine's chamberers, who 'came close [to] where he was with the queen and the queen put him out'.

At Lincoln and again at Pontefract, Culpeper 'had word by the Lady of Rochford that diverse times he should have spoken with the queen of this being any place that would fain serve of the queen's own, saving for the queen would in every house seek for the back doors and back stairs herself'.

Culpeper had spoken with the queen twice at Pontefract, although their first rendezvous had almost been thwarted. Lady Rochford had 'showed him that he should have spoken with the queen'; however, 'the back door, which way he should have come, the queen feared lest the king had set a watch there'. Lady Rochford put one of her servants 'to watch the door one night and the next to see if any of the watch or any other went in or out'. When they were sure nobody was about, 'the next night the queen sent for the said Culpeper and then talked with him till the king went to bed'.

The second meeting at Pontefract was less fraught with difficulties than the first. As they talked, Katherine said, 'I marvel that you could so much dissemble as to say you loved me so openly and yet would and did so soon lie with another, called Anne Herbert'.[9] Culpeper's response was that 'the queen was married afore he loved the other and that he found so little favour at her [Katherine's] hands at that time that he was rather moved to set by others'. Katherine replied, 'if I listed I could bring you into as good a trade as Bray[10] hath my lord Parr in'. Culpeper answered that he thought Katherine 'no such woman as Bray was'. To this, Katherine said, 'well, if I had tarried still in the maidens' chamber, I would have tried you.'

During their stay at York, Katherine had 'laughingly' told Culpeper that she had a 'store of other lovers at other doors as well as he', to which he replied, 'it is like enough'. A version of this curious statement later reached Ambassador Marillac. As he summarised the trial of Culpeper and Dereham for his master, King François, he remarked that Katherine had spoken about Culpeper to Lady Rochford using words to the effect that 'if Culpeper would not listen to her there was behind the door another *qui ne demandoit pas meilleur party* (who would not be the best match)'.[11]

Also at York, Culpeper 'spoke with the queen at the back stairs at which time she had communication with him how much she loved him and showed him how when she was a maiden how many times her grief was such that she could not but weep in the presence of her fellows'.

While at Sheriff Hutton,[12] Culpeper 'sent a ring to the Lady Rochford and the queen sent him two bracelets with this message that they were sent [to] him to keep his arms warm'.

Culpeper recalled that he 'another night at York was with the queen in the Lady Rochford's chamber; then the queen told him at Lincoln that now she must indeed love him, wherefore the said Culpeper answered that she had bound him both then and now and that he both must and did love her again above all creatures.'

At some point Katherine had cautioned Culpeper 'that she doubted not that he believed that the king was supreme head of the church and therefore the queen bade him beware that when-so-ever he went to confession he should not shrive him of any such thing as should pass betwixt her and him for if he did, surely the king, being supreme head of the church, should have knowledge of it'. Katherine worried that words spoken in the confessional would be passed on to Henry. Culpeper assured her, 'no madam, I warrant you'.

Finally, Culpeper told his inquisitors that 'the Lady Rochford provoked him much to love the queen', and it had been she who had told him 'how much the queen loved him by which means he was tricked and brought into the snare which blind youth hath no grace to foresee'. He added that he had 'at divers times sent many familiar messages to the Lady Rochford and that she was the conveyer of all messages and tokens between himself and Katherine'. One message, which the queen sent to him at Pontefract read: 'as you find the door so to come.' He ended with the remarkable claim that 'he intended and meant to do ill with the queen and that in like wise, the queen so minded to do with him'.

Culpeper's deposition is an honest account of his association with Queen Katherine as he saw it. In the end, though, whatever his feelings for her, Culpeper portrayed himself as the victim of women's craft which he was powerless to withstand and that he was 'tricked' into loving her. In spite of this, he anticipated that his relationship with the queen would at some point progress beyond the emotional to become a physical one.

Culpeper represented Queen Katherine as a young woman very much in love with him; she was flirtatious perhaps, but sincere. However, her love had been frustrated by the attentions of another man. This new man being King Henry, Katherine was in no position to refuse his advances, even if she had wanted to. Later, Katherine had revived her love for Culpeper and was ready, as he was, to consummate it.[13]

Culpeper could not have given a worse account of the woman he claimed to love. In saying that they intended to 'do ill' with each other, he had sealed Katherine's fate as well as his own. It made no difference whether or not they had engaged in sexual activity or had merely planned to. The 1534 Treason Act classed as traitors any who 'do maliciously wish, will or desire by words or writing, or by craft imagine, invent, practice or attempt any bodily harm to be done or committed to the King's most royal person'.[14] This could be interpreted in so many ways that it would be impossible for anyone to escape once the terms of the Act had been applied to their case. Equipped with the information given to them by Culpeper, the members of the council turned their attention back to Katherine.

As dreadful as her examination over Dereham had been, the possibility that Katherine's renewed association with Thomas Culpeper might be disclosed was the thing that frightened her the most. Her relationship with Dereham had been prior to her marriage, not after it. Many people, surely, had been in the same situation and had been none the worse for it. However, her audiences with Culpeper had been after her marriage, carried out in secret and in private places. Well aware of how they could be interpreted, she was terrified that the council would find out about them.

'Three or four times daily since she was in this trouble', Katherine would ask Jane, Lady Rochford, what she had heard of Culpeper.[15] She felt that, 'if that matter came not out she feared not for no thing'. She had assured Lady Rochford that 'she would never confess it and willed the Lady Rochford to deny it utterly'[16] and 'in no wise disclose this matter'. Katherine warned Lady Rochford that 'they would speak fair to you and use all ways with you but and [sic] if you confess you undo both your self and others'. Lady Rochford promised her mistress that she 'will never confess it to be torn with wild horses'. She advised Katherine to 'hold her own for Culpeper was yesterday merry a hawking'. To this, Katherine answered that she marvelled that Lady Rochford had not yet been examined, saying, 'it would out, what hold your own I warrant you, be you afraid'. Neither woman knew that Culpeper had already been taken.

The council drew up a list of questions to be put to Katherine. These questions are not recorded, but their area of focus can be discerned from the answers the queen gave. They were interested only in the most incriminating aspects of her relationship with Culpeper: primarily, what form it took and who had initiated it.[17]

The first item concerned how Katherine had come to renew her relations with Culpeper. She explained that Lady Rochford 'hath sundry times made instans [urgent solicitation or entreaty] to her to speak with Culpeper, declaring him to bear her good will and favour'. Eventually, Katherine had given in: 'she did at the last grant he should speak with her', having been persuaded by Lady Rochford's 'affirmation that he desired nothing else but to speak with her and that she durst swear upon a book [that is, the Bible], that he meant nothing but honesty'. As a result, Katherine granted Culpeper an audience, and they spoke 'in a little gallery at the stair head at Lincoln when it was late at night about ten or eleven of the clock an hour or more, another time in her bed chamber at Pomfret [Pontefract] and another time in my lady Rochford's chamber at York'. Although Katherine agrees with Culpeper's statement at this point, it is clear that she had forgotten about the earlier meetings at Greenwich.

Just how persuasive had Lady Rochford been? Katherine answered that, whenever Lady Rochford 'moved her' for Culpeper, Katherine would warn her, 'alas, madam, this will be spied one day and then we be all undone'. At which Lady Rochford answered, 'fear not, madam, let me alone I warrant you' ('Trust me, I assure you').

As far as Katherine was concerned, Culpeper, having assisted her during the king's illness, had done what she had asked of him and she had no further need of him. Moreover, she could not have been unaware of the opprobrium that would be attached to her as a married woman if she entertained male friends privately. One authority, Anne de France, warned ladies to eschew 'all private and gracious acquaintances', because many such things, even if they have 'honest beginnings', will end up being 'dishonest and injurious' to them.[18] If only Katherine had heeded this sage advice.

Katherine was then asked whether Lady Rochford was involved only as a go-between, or did she provide some other service? She said that when Culpeper was talking to her, Lady Rochford 'would many times, being ever by, sit somewhat far off or turn her back'. Katherine would say to her, 'for God's sake, madam, even near us'. In other words, Katherine had expected Lady Rochford to act as chaperone. Katherine then spoke of her fears since the council had first come to her and the advice she had offered Lady Rochford not to disclose anything about Culpeper.

The inquisitors next asked Katherine about the cap with aglets and chain that she had given to Culpeper. This was a major point because of the importance of gifts in courtship ritual, and which could be interpreted as evidence of adultery, as the indictment against Anne Boleyn amply shows. Katherine confirmed that she had given him the cap and also that Lady Rochford had sent him a cramp ring that she had taken from the queen and that Katherine had sent him another 'of her to match it'. This differs slightly from Culpeper's deposition in that he claimed to have stolen the cramp ring from Lady Rochford, but perhaps Katherine did not know that. Katherine agreed with regard to the second ring, which she had sent to Culpeper because she thought he should have more than one.

Katherine added that the Lady Rochford had bought presents for Culpeper, having 'prayed her she might buy somewhat to send him and of her own choice bought a pair of bracelets to send him when he sent a certain pheasant'. These were the bracelets Culpeper thought Katherine had sent him to keep his arms warm. They had not come from Katherine after all, but from Lady Rochford.

To judge by the brusqueness of Katherine's answer, the question that was next put to her had been direct and to the point: 'as for the act [sex] she denied [it] upon her oath, or touching any bare of her but her hand'. This was an important point, as touching had been included in Anne Boleyn's indictment and used as evidence that she had committed adultery. Once again, however, Katherine corroborated Culpeper's testimony, saying that he had merely kissed her hand. The council could not have been unaware that the relationship between Katherine and Culpeper was not and had never been sexual. Katherine had denied having sex with Culpeper.

The subject now returned to Lady Rochford. Katherine told them that her lady would 'at every lodging search the back doors and tell her of them if there were any, unasked'. Furthermore, since the progress, Lady Rochford had told Katherine 'that when she came to Greenwich she knew an old kitchen wherein she might well speak with' Culpeper. Here, Katherine's confession differs from Culpeper's. He believed that Katherine had searched the back doors, not Lady Rochford. Also, he was unaware of the old kitchen, or did not disclose that he knew about it.

Katherine then said that 'my lady Rochford told her also that she thought Paston bear her favour but he never spoke with her'. This suggests a penchant for matchmaking on the part of Lady Rochford. Indeed, Katherine's next statement reveals much about who she thought had encouraged her to renew her relationship with Culpeper. She explained that 'lately, but the time she remembered not, my lady Rochford spoke with her of Culpeper'. Katherine had said to her, 'alas, madam, will this never end. I pray you, bid him desire no more to trouble me or send to me.' Then, after Lady Rochford 'had done my message his answer was that he besought me to send him no such word for he would take no such answer'. Culpeper, however, 'still sent to me as he might have a message'. At this point Katherine called him 'little sweet fool'.

More than anything else, this apparently casual remark betrays Katherine's true feelings for Culpeper. Her use of the word 'little' implies endearment, especially as she used it with 'sweet'. The word 'fool' also implies endearment, but can be an expression of pity too. Katherine is saying that Culpeper's attention to her is charming, perhaps even flattering, but ultimately of no interest to her. Katherine is effectively dismissing him.

Once again, Katherine had confirmed Culpeper's testimony, at least in part. She said, as did Culpeper, that the Lady Rochford had carried messages and tokens between them. She differed in that she attributed the motivating force behind the relationship to Culpeper, while he had said that Lady Rochford had taken the initiative. Katherine drove her point home when she explained that, 'when she took her rights last', she gave Lady Rochford 'warning to trouble her no more with such light matters'. Even so, Lady Rochford had insisted, 'yet must you give men leave to look for they will look upon you'.

Of course men would look upon Katherine; it was part of the game of courtly love for men to praise and woo her. Since Katherine was queen, she would expect to receive more devotion than any other lady at court. However, Culpeper had gone too far, taken too many liberties for Katherine to feel comfortable with his attentions. As such, she made several attempts to end their acquaintance, or at least to ensure the young man knew his place.

Katherine exhibited a desire to act within the norms of decency and proper behaviour, not only for a queen, but also for a woman. Although she did have some fondness for Culpeper, she was careful to keep him in his station. Her instruction to him to come only when Lady Rochford was with her[19] is evidence of this. Katherine used Lady Rochford as a chaperone, the presence of the senior member of the household serving to show that propriety was being observed and to ensure that the reputation of all concerned was protected.

The examination ended at that point. Katherine's testimony was written out and given to her to sign. Even so, King Henry was not satisfied.[20] He thought that Katherine 'hath not, as appears by her confession, so fully declared the circumstances of such communications as were between her and Culpeper at their sundry meetings'. As a result, the king commanded Archbishop Cranmer and the rest of the council to return once again to Katherine and 'get out of her, if she be in such frame and temper of her wits, as you think you may well enough press her'. However, they were to do this 'without too much troubling or inquieting her, so as might, in any case, be dangerous unto her'. As there were still concerns about Katherine's health, a second examination concerning Culpeper might not have taken place; if it did, the transcript has been lost.

Once Katherine's assignations with Culpeper became known the worst possible interpretation was applied to them, as she had feared. The once virtuous and pure Queen Katherine was now reduced to Katherine the seductress, the wanton. Just like any other woman, she had been unable to control her desires and had followed the way of all her sex by leading men astray.

Once Culpeper had confessed his intention to do ill with Katherine and she with him, things moved at lightning speed. By Sunday, 13 November, the queen was deemed an adulteress, her guilt firmly established. That day, Alice Wilkes and Mary Lascelles were 'bound in two several recognisances upon pain of their lives to appear at any time upon lawful warning before the Council'. They would be required 'as well to affirm such things as they have already confessed, as to answer also to any other thing that may be laid to their charge'.[21] At the same time, Sir Thomas Wriothesley went 'to the Queen' at Hampton Court.[22] He assembled her gentle-women and other servants in the great chamber and related to them 'certain offences' that Katherine had committed 'in misusing her body with certain persons before the King's time'. Wriothesley explained to the queen's entire household that Katherine had forfeited her honour and would be proceeded against by law; hence-forth, she would be named 'no longer queen, but only Katherine Howard'.[23]

Following this public shaming of the queen, Wriothesley discharged her household. However, before they went their separate ways, certain matters had to be addressed. Lady Margaret Douglas, who had no involvement in Katherine's downfall, nevertheless had been entangled in a scandal of her own. At some point during the summer progress, she had fallen in love with Katherine's brother, Charles. This was the second time she had become involved with a Howard,[24] and the king was most displeased. Lady Margaret was ordered to be removed from the court and sent to ponder her folly in the quiet comfort of the Norfolk residence of Kenninghall. Before she left, however, she was to receive a telling-off from Archbishop Cranmer, who had orders to 'declare unto her how discreetly she hath demeaned herself towards the King's Majesty, first with Lord Thomas, and secondly with Charles Howard; in which part ye shall, by discretion, charge her with overmuch lightness, and finally give her advice to beware the third time.'

Katherine's sister was to be 'released as innocent'. This was because 'she had been dismissed from her sister's chamber in favour of Lady Rochford'. As to the queen's maidens, they were ordered to 'repair each of them to their friends; there to remain'. Anne Bassett, whose step-father, Viscount Lisle, was still in the Tower, having been arrested for having treasonable communications with Cardinal Pole, was a special case: 'in consideration of the calamity of her friends' the king would provide for her at his own expense. Assistance would also be given to any servant who had no home or friends, or 'no means convenient to live'. Some of the queen's servants, however, were required to remain behind: 'the woman who knew of the matter with Dereham' and eight others were imprisoned for further questioning. The woman in question was Katherine Tylney, whose examination would begin later that day.[25]

Having heard Wriothesley's announcement of her mistress's downfall, Katherine Tylney was under no illusions about what she would be asked and how she was expected to answer. Her examination began with the question 'whether she know and deposes that the queen went out of her chamber any night or nights whenever it was late at Lincoln and where she went and who went with her'. She remembered that 'at Lincoln, the queen went two nights out of her chamber when it was late to my lady Rochford's chamber, which was up a little pair of stairs by the queen's chamber'.

Tylney described how, on the first night, she and Marget Morton tried to follow Katherine, but the queen made them both come down again. Mistress Tylney obeyed and went to bed but the inquisitive Marget went back up the stairs. Then, when it was late, Tylney thought 'about two of the clock', Marget came to bed. Mrs Tylney asked her, 'Jesus; is not the queen a bed yet?' Marget answered, 'yes, even now.'

On the second night, Katherine made all her servants go to bed, but this time she took Mistress Tylney with her. The servant 'tarried also in manner as long as she did the other night', during which time she sat to one side with Lady Rochford's woman. As such, she was unable to see 'who came into the queen and my lady Rochford, nor hear what was said between them'.

She then spoke of certain 'strange messages' the queen had asked her to carry to Lady Rochford. So strange were they that 'she could not see how to utter them'. Finally, at Hampton Court lately the queen sent Tylney to Lady Rochford 'and ask her when she should have the thing she promised her'. Lady Rochford replied that she 'sat up for it and she would next day bring her word herself'. Tylney then added that 'a like message and answer was at my lord of Suffolk's'.[26]

It was all very intriguing, but this is only in view of what later came out regarding Katherine's night-time activities while on progress and how they were interpreted. In the oppressive atmosphere of interrogation and investigation, half-remembered details take on meanings quite apart from their original intent. In reality, there was no reason why the queen and her senior lady should not have communication that they wished to keep private from the lower members of staff. As it was, the 'thing promised' Katherine by Lady Rochford must always remain a mystery. However, that the Duke of Suffolk had received a similar message from the queen indicates that there was nothing dishonest about it. In the end, Katherine Tylney's testimony amounted to nothing more than that the queen had gone into Lady Rochford's chamber late at night where she met someone Tylney could not see.[27]

While Wriothesley was busy with Katherine Tylney, Sir Anthony Browne was questioning her colleague, Marget Morton.[28] Casting her mind back to the summer, Marget recalled that she 'never mistrusted the queen till she was at Hatfield, when she saw the queen look out of her privy chamber window on Mr Culpeper after such sort that she thought in her conscience that there was love between them'. She had not drawn this conclusion at the time, but only later. 'For when she saw that and the queen gave commandment in the same house that neither Mistress Lufkyn nor no nother should come in to her bedchamber without they were called, then she remembered what she had seen.'

Marget then spoke of an incident when Katherine had sent her to the Lady of Rochford carrying 'a letter without any superscription, sealed, bidding her show my lady that she was sorry that she could write no better'. This was, in fact, a 'privy letter' sent by the queen to 'Lady of Rochford at Lyddington being then there sick'.[29] The Lady Rochford then bade Marget 'desire the queen to respite her till the next morning for an answer'. The next day, Katherine sent Marget back to Lady Rochford, who sent 'a nother letter to the queen without any superscription'; it was sealed and Lady Rochford prayed 'her grace to keep it secret and not to lay it abroad'.

As Marget's testimony continues, it becomes obvious that she harboured feelings of resentment towards Queen Katherine. The reason for this was clear: it was 'after Katherine Tylney was come that the queen could not abide Mistress Lufkyn' or herself. She thought 'my lady of Rochford the principal occasion' of the queen's 'folly'. She even implied that Lady Rochford had more influence over Katherine than perhaps she should have done because, 'at Pomfret the queen was angry with Mistress Lufkyn and with her, and that the queen said she would put them both away and she says yet she knows not why, but she thinks if they had been put away that the queen would a taken other of my Lady of Rochford's putting.'

Finally, Marget recalled that 'at Pomfret every night, the queen being in her bedchamber having no nother with her but my Lady of Rochford, did not only lock the bedchamber door but also bolted it on the inside.' On one occasion, Anthony Denny, a gentleman of the privy chamber who had been sent to Katherine from the king, 'found it bolted himself'.

As with Katherine Tylney, Marget Morton's testimony contained little of any substance. Her recollection of Katherine looking out of the window at Culpeper was a highly subjective interpretation of the event influenced by the news that had just been broken to her about the queen's alleged immoral behaviour. Beyond that, all Marget Morton could really say with any certainty was that 'secret', that is to say private letters had passed between Katherine and her chief female servant regarding business that was none of Marget's concern.

However, there was one lady whose close proximity to the queen would make her testimony highly valuable. Her name had already been mentioned several times: Jane, Lady Rochford. Notwithstanding all that it was thought she knew, in the event, her deposition proved to be relatively short.[30] She began by pointing out that 'the queen and Culpeper talked so secretly that she heard not their conversations', although she did hear them 'speak of Bess Harvey'.

Culpeper had also mentioned Bess Harvey, but he had not gone into details. These were supplied by Lady Rochford, who suggested that Katherine had felt sorry for the lady and had made some attempt to compensate her for Culpeper's neglect: 'to the which Bess Harvey the queen gave a damask gown'. Lady Rochford also appears to have felt some sympathy for Bess: 'this deponent said to Culpeper that he did ill to suffer his tenement to be so ill repaired and that she for to save his honesty had done some cost of it.' This and the bracelets Lady Rochford sent to him suggest that she harboured some affection for Culpeper.

Regarding the meeting between Katherine and Culpeper at Pontefract, Lady Rochford denied knowing what was said. She explained that she had kept watch at the door while 'Culpeper stood upon the stairs ready always to slip down if noise came and the queen stood upon the uppermost step afore him where they might speak and do together, this deponent being never the privier.'

She spoke of their time at Lincoln. Here, Katherine and she had 'stood waiting at the back door for Culpeper at eleven of the clock in the night and one of the watch, having a light in his hand, came that way'. The two ladies had withdrawn as the 'watch man pulled to the door and locked it, and so departed'. Shortly afterwards, 'Culpeper came in and they marvelled how he came in and Culpeper said that he and his man did pick the lock.'

Still at Lincoln the queen and Culpeper 'were secretly together', during which time the Lady Rochford slept 'until the queen did call her to answer Lufkyn'. This accorded with the confessions of both Culpeper and Marget Morton. The inquisitive Mrs Lufkyn seems to have been determined to find out what her mistress was getting up to.

Lady Rochford kept her best for last. She told her interrogators outright that 'she thinketh that Culpeper hath known the queen carnally considering all things that this deponent hath heard and seen between them'. It was a curious assertion to make considering her insistence that she knew nothing of what was said or took place between Katherine and Culpeper; she had even claimed to have been asleep during at least one of their trysts. However, by these words, Lady Rochford further condemned Katherine, Culpeper and herself.

17

The Trial and Execution of
Dereham and Culpeper

~

O N MONDAY, 14 NOVEMBER Katherine, banished from
Hampton Court and the life she had come to know, made
her way by water to the former Abbey of Syon. She was kept 'in
the estate of a Queen',[1] but her conditions were much reduced.
Her lodgings comprised three chambers 'hanged with mean stuff,
without any cloth of estate'. Only two of these chambers were for
Katherine's own use; the third was intended for Sir Edward Baynton
and the other attendants to dine in. Sir Edward was appointed to
'attend upon the Queen, to have the rule and government of the
whole house; and with him the Almoner[2] to be also associate'.

Henry, who had meticulously organised every aspect of
Katherine's life at Syon, allowed her 'a mean number of servants'.
She could also have 'at her election, four gentlewomen, and two
chamberers'. Nevertheless, Henry insisted that Isabel, Lady Baynton
should be one of them. Other servants could be appointed at Sir
Edward's discretion to carry out duties as needed in preparation,
but they were to depart upon the queen's arrival.

Just as Henry dictated the smallest details of his wife's household,
he also regulated her wardrobe. Katherine was allowed 'six French
hoods with their accessories and edges of goldsmith's work, so
there be no stone nor pearl in the same'. She was also to be given
six 'pairs of sleeves, six gowns, and six kirtles of satin damask, and
velvet'. These were to be adorned with 'such things as belong to
the same, except always stone and pearl'.[3] Katherine's jewels had

already been taken away from her. They, together with other items belonging to the queen, were currently in the care of Thomas Seymour, who took them to Hampton Court for inventory.[4]

At Syon, a careful watch was placed on Katherine. She had never fully recovered from the fear and frenzy that had gripped her since her first interrogation by the council a week earlier. Because 'she would neither eat nor drink since this matter was known, but intended to kill herself', the precaution was taken to remove 'knives and all such things as wherewith she might hurt herself'.[5]

Now that proceedings had come so far with Katherine, Henry felt it necessary to inform his ambassadors abroad of the situation.[6] Letters detailing 'the whole order and story of the most lamentable misdemeanour of the Queen' were sent to William Paget in France,[7] Sir Henry Knyvett, ambassador with Emperor Charles, as well as the ambassador of Flanders and the deputy of Calais. Within a week, Paget wrote back to King Henry to tell him how he had disclosed the news to François and hinted that there was more to come:[8]

> we have not yet heard all, but there is vehement presumptions by that we know already, that she hath wonderfully abused the King our master's goodness, for she hath found the means not only to train the same Dereham, that you spoke of, in her service, and to find sundry occasions for him to haunt often in to her privy chamber, but also she hath retained, to be chamberer of her privy chamber, one of the women that lay in bed with Dereham and her, when they used their ribaldry.

Upon hearing this news, François had laid his hand on his breast, exclaiming that Katherine 'hath done wonderous naughtly'. He commiserated with Henry that he should 'have such occasion of inquietness'. Paget explained that they were glad that François should know the truth, not because they doubted that 'he would conceive otherwise than uprightly' of Henry's proceedings, but, 'because if it should fortune him to hear in this matter any untrue tales forged maliciously, he might be of a certain knowledge to reprove the same'. François assured Paget that he 'would not fail to do unfainedley, if he heard any such'.

Marguerite d'Angoulême, who had shown so much interest in Queen Katherine, expressed her sorrow that Henry should be 'thus disquieted'. Nevertheless, she was 'glad that she knew the truth of the matter at length, to the intent that she might declare the same when time and place required'. She told Paget that there had been, and there were still, those at the French court 'that be the gladdest men in the world to deprave the King's Majesty's doings'.

This had been Henry's intent. He wanted it known that Katherine deserved her punishment, whatever it might be, and that the world should see that he treated her justly.

With Katherine now established at Syon, Jane, Lady Rochford and Thomas Culpeper, along with several others, were 'had to the Tower'.[9] Their goods were inventoried at the same time.[10] No mention was made of Katherine's letter to Culpeper; it had certainly been found by this point, but it was not seen as important, and had not been taken for a love letter. Instead, it was merely marked 'sent to Culpeper' and stored with the rest of his things.

Ambassador Marillac wrote to King François on 14 November, the very day that Katherine went to Syon.[11] He noted that he had spoken with the Duke of Norfolk, who told him what he knew so far about his niece's crimes. Norfolk spoke with 'tears in his eyes of the King's grief, who loved her much'. He particularly expressed his dismay over the 'misfortune' to his house 'in her [Katherine] and Queen Anne, his two nieces'.

Marillac reported that Katherine 'is proved to have had, before this King married her, several servants familiar with her, and although the first accusation spoke of two, upon further enquiry and the Lady's written confession, confirmed by the confessions of the guilty persons and of the women who conducted these practices, it is found that she has prostituted herself to seven or eight persons'.

Again on the word of Norfolk, Marillac went on to say that since Katherine became queen, 'there are great presumptions that she has continued her incontinence'. One of her accomplices 'being her earliest favourite, a gentleman of a poor house named Dereham', who had 'continued of her chamber in such favour with his mistress that he spent more angelots that her three brothers together'. He added that Katherine had thought that, following her confession, they would make no further enquiries. As it turned out, the opposite was true.

Before Marillac could send his despatch, the duke asked to speak to him once more. This time Norfolk admitted that he had been deceived about Katherine's having so many lovers, for only one, Dereham, had been proved. Norfolk's next statement, therefore, came as a shock. He had since learned that the situation was much worse than had been thought. For, during the royal progress to the north, Katherine had made the acquaintance of another man, 'a young gentleman of the King's chamber named Culpeper, who had been with her five of six times in secret and suspect places'. One such place was Lincoln, 'where they were closetted together five or six hours, and considering the words, signs, and messages between them it was held for certain that they had *passé oultre*'. Already the rumour mill was exaggerating Katherine's activities.

A few days after this, Andrew Maunsay, former servant to the Duchess of Norfolk, confessed to having thrice witnessed Katherine 'lie in her bed and Dereham, a gentleman then in the house, lie suspiciously on the bed in his doublet and hose'. This occurred twelve months before Katherine came to court.[12]

As so often happens during interrogations, Maunsay named others who would be able to corroborate his story. As a result, several people who had known Katherine at Horsham and Lambeth were questioned, their depositions jotted down.[13] Margaret Benet, Malyn Tylney, Edward Waldegrave, Henry Mannock and Joan Bulmer all testified to familiarity between Katherine Howard and Francis Dereham at Norfolk House. Katherine Tylney, interviewed again, had nothing further to add. Lady Margaret Howard related that, since the marriage, she had heard one Stafford say, 'if I were as Deram I would never tell to die for it' and that 'ther was a thyng that stakk apon his stomack' (i.e., left a painful impression on his mind). This was George Stafford, who had alerted Joan Bulmer to Katherine's rise and urged her to ask for a place in the new queen's household.

Robert Damport told his interrogators about Dereham's altercation with Mr Johns shortly after Dereham had joined Katherine's household. All this really revealed was that Dereham was resentful at having lost the woman he considered to be his own and he was taking out his anger on her other servants. His behaviour had been injudicious and childish certainly, but there was no real crime in it.

It was, perhaps, due to this fact that the imperial ambassador, Chapuys, having spoken to the Earl of Southampton, was able to report that Henry did 'bear the blow' of Katherine's case 'more patiently and compassionately than most people thought'. The king would certainly be more tender with Katherine than would her own relatives; the Duke of Norfolk, it was said, had declared that 'he wishes the Queen to be burnt alive'.[14]

At this point, Marillac offered his master another description of Katherine that differed markedly from the one he had presented at the beginning of her reign. Katherine, he said, 'had everything necessary not only to content the king her lord, but also to win the hearts of his subjects; for, apart from her excellent beauty, in which she surpassed all the ladies in England . . . she has a very gentle face, gracious of speech, her bearing moderate, restrained and her conversation humane [courteous]'.[15]

Katherine's merits, both personal and as queen, as well as the great love he once had for her, added to the emotional turmoil Henry now felt. One moment he wanted to show her compassion, the next he was threatening to kill her with his own hands; as Marillac, writing news 'which a servant ought to write to his master',[16] noted, Henry had now 'changed his love for the Queen to hatred'. He had 'taken such grief at being deceived that of late it was thought he had gone mad, for he called for a sword to slay her he had loved so much'. While sitting in council, the king would suddenly call for his horses 'without saying where he would go'. Occasionally his anger spilled over into cruel words, for he would avow 'that wicked woman had never such delight in her in incontinency as she should have torture in her death'. He would then burst into tears, 'regretting his ill luck in meeting with such ill-conditioned wives'. Predictably, he laid the blame 'for this last mischief' upon his council.

Chapuys confirmed Marillac's report. Henry, he wrote, had 'wonderfully felt the case of the Queen, his wife, and that he has certainly shown greater sorrow and regret at her loss than at the faults, loss, or divorce of his preceding wives'.[17] He goes on:

> In fact, I should say that this king's case resembles very much that of the woman who cried more bitterly at the loss of her tenth husband than she had cried on the death of the other nine put together, though all of them had been equally worthy people and good husbands to her: the reason being that she had never buried one of them without being sure of the next, but that after the tenth husband she had no other one in view, hence her sorrow and her lamentations. Such is the case with the King, who, however, up to this day does not seem to have any plan or female friend to fall back upon.

Chapuys's attempt at psychoanalysis captures Henry's predicament perfectly. Quite simply, the much married king had hoped and expected to live out the rest of his days with Queen Katherine by his side. Now that dream was gone, and it took with it the last remnants of Henry's youth. The gallant lover that had been reawakened in the king gave way to a vengeful monster, a tyrant.

On 1 December 1541 the Privy Council did not sit because they were required to serve as commissioners at the arraignment of Thomas Culpeper and Francis Dereham.[18] In fact, the process of the 'Trial and Conviction of Thomas Culpeper and Francis Dereham for High Treason in committing Adultery with Queen Katharine Howard' had begun some time before. Starting on 16 November, special commissions of oyer and terminer had been established in Yorkshire, Middlesex, Lincolnshire, the City of Lincoln, Surrey and Kent, all places where the alleged adultery was said to have taken place. The commissions had been appointed to read the indictments against Queen Katherine, Jane, Lady Rochford, Thomas Culpeper and Francis Dereham and to reach a verdict. One by one, their findings were returned to Chancery. They were unanimous. 'Indictments found against Queen Katherine, Lady Rochford, Culpeper, and Dereham, alleging the several acts of adultery, &c, to have been committed' at Hampton Court and Westminster (Middlesex), Gainsborough and elsewhere in the country of Lincoln (Lincolnshire), the county and the city of Lincoln (City of Lincoln), Lambeth, Oatlands, and elsewhere, in the country of Surrey (Surrey) and Greenwich, and elsewhere, in the county of Kent (Kent).[19]

The indictment returned by the county of Yorkshire, whose commission was held at Doncaster on 24 November, shows the full range of charges facing Culpeper and Dereham. It begins by stating that Katherine, Queen of England, 'before her marriage with the King, committed promiscuous fornication'. It also stated that she had engaged in 'specific acts of criminality with Francis Dereham' on 20 May 1541 and with Henry Mannock on 24 May 1541, even though there was not one shred of evidence to suggest that either of these two men were at court on these dates.

The indictment went on: 'Queen Katherine conducted herself so craftily as to make the King believe she was a virgin.' Then, 'the King, believing her to be chaste, and free from any matrimonial contract, took her in marriage'.

Next: 'the Queen and Francis Dereham having been examined before divers of the King's Council could not deny their offence.' Instead, they had alleged 'for their excuse, that they were contracted in marriage before the solemnization of the marriage between the King and the Queen'. They had concealed this contract, 'to the intent of preferring the Queen to her Royal marriage'. As such, they had 'deceived the King, to the great damage of any issue to be had between them, and the manifest injury of the whole kingdom of England'. This, then, is the basis of the treason charge. The perniciousness of the alleged crime lies in the threat it poses to the safety of the succession by its potential to violate the sanctity of royal blood.

The special commission next found that after the marriage

between the king and Queen Katherine, she and Dereham 'not intending to desist from their offences, on 25 August 33 Hen. 8 (1541), at Pomfret, traitorously imagined and procured' that Dereham should be 'retained in the service of the Queen', so that they could 'continue their wicked courses'. As such, Katherine did retain Dereham in her service two days later, and 'had him in open favour above all other persons', she 'frequently had conversation with him alone in her secret chamber and in other suspect places', as well as having 'frequently committed her private affairs to him, as well by word of mouth as by writing'. This ignores the fact that, as her secretary, Dereham had access to Katherine's privy chamber, where she would necessarily speak with him and assign tasks, some of which would entail written documents.

The special commission found that Katherine, 'in order to fulfil her wicked intent, traitorously gave various gifts to Dereham'. From this, the jury decided that 'the Queen and Dereham being united and confederate, 27th of August, at Pomfret, compassed and planned that they should continue their vicious course of life'. This, then, was the evidence against Francis Dereham.

The indictment now turned to Thomas Culpeper. It was found that, 'in order to continue her wicked course of life', Katherine had an 'unlawful meeting' with Culpeper at Pomfret on 29 August 1541 'for the purpose of inciting him to have criminal intercourse with her, being so much in love with him', that, on the day following, 'she intimated to him that she loved him above the King and all other men'. This is a highly inventive interpretation of events that intimated nothing of the sort. Culpeper had deposed that Katherine had told him of the love she had once had for him, but that had been before she had met Henry, and Katherine had never verified the assertion.

The Yorkshire commission went on to note that Katherine had given Culpeper 'various gifts and tokens the more to excite him'. As a result, Culpeper 'not only consented, but excited the Queen by various tokens, &c, asserting that he loved her, the Queen, more than the King or any other person'. This was one of the things that had most concerned Katherine, that her gift of the velvet cap, with aglets and chain, would be misconstrued as a love token. She had urged him to hide it under his cloak for this very reason.

Then, Katherine and Culpeper 'in order to carry on their illicit intercourse with more ease and secrecy' had 'retained with great affection Joan [sic] Lady Rochford . . . and took her into their counsel'. For her part, Lady Rochford 'gave her consent, and as a common procuress' between the queen and Culpeper, 'procured meetings' between them. These meetings took place in Lady Rochford's chamber at Pomfret, the queen's privy chamber and stool house, 'and that when the Queen and Culpeper were alone in such chambers she, the Lady Rochford, watched at the doors to prevent their being surprised'. The finding against Lady Rochford was that she 'aided and abetted the Queen and Culpeper in their illicit intercourse' on 1 September 1541.

Finally, the special commission of oyer and terminer for Yorkshire gave its verdict. This was that, 'by which actings and doings of the Queen, Lady Rochford, Culpeper, and Dereham, they conspired, imagined, and compassed, not only the danger of the Royal person and the scandal of the Royal Marriage, but also the final destruction of the King.'

On the morning of the trial, 1 December, Lord Chancellor Sir Thomas Audeley brought the indictments from the various counties into the court. At the same time, Culpeper and Dereham were escorted from the Tower to the Guildhall by Sir John Gage, constable of the Tower. They would face a panel of judges led by the Lord Mayor of London, Michael Dormer, who presided as chief. Audeley sat at his right hand and the Duke of Norfolk to his left. Also present were Charles Brandon, Duke of Suffolk, William Fitzwilliam, Earl of Southampton, and the Earls of Sussex and Hertford and others of the king's council.[20]

At the urging of his imperial master, Ambassador Chapuys sent one of his secretaries to the Guildhall, as had the French ambassador, Marillac, the Venetian secretary and the gentlemen of the Duke of Cleves.[21]

Culpeper and Dereham listened as the indictments were read out. Mayor Dormer then read aloud the queen's signed deposition concerning her relations with Dereham before marriage, and her conversations with Culpeper.[22]

When asked to speak, Dereham confessed to having known Katherine 'familiarly before she was either betrothed or promised to the King'. He insisted, however, that 'he did not know that there was any wrong in that, inasmuch as they were then engaged to each other'.[23]

Dereham refused to allow his judges to believe that he and Katherine had attempted to conceal their contract in order to advance her royal marriage. Although the council had specified that the contract could not be used as a defence, Dereham knew it was his, and possibly Katherine's, only chance. He had to invoke it in a desperate attempt to save his own life, if not the queen's.

Similarly, Culpeper 'persisted in denying the guilt of which he was accused'. He maintained 'that he never solicited or had anything to do with' Katherine; on the contrary, it had been she who had 'impor-tuned him through Mme de Rochefort', who had requested him to go and meet the queen 'in a retired place in Lincolnshire, to which she appointed him'. On that occasion, the queen told Culpeper, 'as she had on the first instance sent him word through Mme Rochefort, that she pined for him, and was actually dying of love for his person'.[24]

Culpeper had decided to maintain his stance, formulated at his earlier examination, that the queen and Lady Rochford were behind the secret meetings and that he, a defenceless man, was merely the innocent victim of women's craft.

When asked how they pleaded, Culpeper and Dereham answered not guilty.[25] The two men having had their say, a jury for the county of York was assembled and sworn in. However, before it could retire to give its verdict, 'and after sufficient evidence on the part of the Crown had been given against Culpeper and Dereham', the two men changed their pleas to guilty.

The judgement was then read out, the sentence, 'as is usual in such cases of High Treason: execution to be had at Tyburn'. In all, the trial had lasted six hours.[26]

Throughout the trial, Katherine's uncle of Norfolk had 'laughed as if he had cause to rejoice'. The duke had been accompanied at court by his son, Henry, Earl of Surrey, but of Katherine's brothers there was no sign. Instead, they, together with those of Culpeper, had taken to parading on horseback through the town. 'It is the custom,' explained Marillac, 'and must be done to show that they did not share the crimes of their relatives.'[27] Shortly after the trial, Norfolk withdrew to his estate of Kenninghall. Rumour had it that he had not gone of his own free will, 'but was sent on some pretence or other, to have him away from the Privy Council now that business touching his own family must necessarily be discussed therein'.[28]

Chapuys thought that Culpeper and Dereham would be beheaded that same day,[29] but that was not to be the case. Rather, they were ordered to be 'taken back to the Tower and thence drawn through London to the gallows at Tyburn, and there hanged, cut down alive, disembowelled, and (they still living) their bowels burnt, beheaded, and quartered'.[30]

As Culpeper and Dereham were returned to their dismal cells in the Tower, one very important conclusion was left unexpressed. Although it was the two men who had been tried that day, it was clear that Queen Katherine's guilt had already been established. It had been determined by Culpeper at his examination and confirmed by Lady Rochford. Katherine's denials and protests to the contrary were, quite simply, ignored. It was the certainty of her guilt that had allowed the condemnation of Culpeper and Dereham.

The only crime with which Katherine could reasonably be charged was misprision of treason for failing to disclose the exist-ence of a prior contract; her betrothal to Dereham rendered her marriage to Henry illegal and endangered the succession because, had she borne Henry's children, they would have been illegitimate. This stood even though Katherine consistently denied that any such contract existed.

Another potential charge against Katherine was that of commit-ting bigamy. However Henry, informed by the findings of the council and the revelation of Katherine's relationship with Dereham, rejected the existence of the precontract as a defence. This he did even though Katherine and Dereham had not actually committed adultery. Katherine, then, was found guilty of presumptive treason, and was condemned not for what she had done but for what others said she had intended to do.

Francis Dereham could only legally be charged with misprision of treason, for he too had failed to disclose the prior contract between Katherine and himself. Morally, though, he had committed a much worse crime than that. He had taken Katherine's virginity, her inno-cence, and ruined her for the king. What was worse, the revelation that Katherine had never really been his had robbed Henry of the exquisite but fragile illusion that he had recaptured his lost youth.

As to Thomas Culpeper, there were no charges that could real-istically be levelled against him. The only thing he could be accused of was indulging a creative imagination which had led him to suppose that Katherine continued to love him as much as he did her. Still, Culpeper had denied that his relationship with the queen had been sexual, although he did claim that they meant to 'do ill' with each other.

Katherine had also insisted that they had not had sex. She had given every indication that she never intended to let Culpeper have his way and that she was unwilling to allow the relationship to develop any further. On the other hand, while Marget Morton suspected that the relationship between them was not platonic, Lady Rochford was in no doubt at all that it had been sexual.

Such ambiguity might have favoured Katherine and Culpeper had it not been for two vital factors: Henry's relationship with God and the 1534 Treason Act. Henry understood his kingship to have been divinely appointed. He spoke to God and believed that God spoke to him. He knew with absolute certainty that the disclosure of Katherine's past life, no matter how it had come about, had been the work of God. The subsequent investigations, confessions, even denials, merely confirmed God's agenda. There had to be a reason for this divine intervention, and it was found to be 'the danger of the Royal person and the scandal of the Royal Marriage, but also the final destruction of the King'. Then there was the danger to the succession that had been posed by the queen's actions. Faced with such overwhelming proof, Henry had no option but to act. God had shown him in the strongest terms that Katherine was guilty, as were Culpeper and Dereham.

The application of 1534 Treason Act to the case proved to be every bit as conclusive as the word of God. Once caught in the Act's malicious web, anyone could be deemed a traitor. It, therefore, made no difference whether or not Katherine and Culpeper had engaged in sexual activity. No longer was it necessary to actually commit an act of treason or to speak treasonous words. Malicious intent was enough. When it came to the safety of the king and the realm, anything could be considered malicious. In saying that they had intended to 'do ill' with each other, even though they had not yet done so, Culpeper had sealed Katherine's fate as well as his own by indicating that Katherine was willing to commit adultery with him. As such, Culpeper was sentenced to death even though 'he had not passed beyond words'. What mattered was that he had 'confessed his intention to do so' and 'having been found alone together in a private place for over five hours, his conversation, so offensive and improper, being held by a subject to a Queen, deserved death'.[31]

As to Dereham, he was condemned 'for having not only kept the lady from the time he violated her', but also 'for having since been of her chamber'. In addition, Dereham had 'brought thither the woman who had been his accomplice before, which is presumptive evidence that they continued in their first purpose'.[32] Here, Marillac was referring to Katherine Tylney, whom the queen had taken into her household the previous autumn.

The consequences of adultery in a queen were deadly serious. It 'weigheth no less that the wrong reign of a bastard prince, which thing for a commonwealth ought specially to be regarded'.[33] As a sin against king and country, Katherine's crimes were punishable by death. Katherine, therefore, 'was found an harlot before he [Henry] married her, and an adulteress after he married her'.[34] The conviction of Culpeper and Dereham was a natural consequence of Queen Katherine's guilt.

18

The Bottom of the Pot

~

FOR THE TIME being, Katherine remained at Syon. It was rumoured that, 'to show clemency', the king would 'make no innovation whatever with regard to her, or do more than he has hitherto done'. Rather, he would wait 'until Parliament meets and decides what her fate is to be'.[1] Considering that Parliament was not due to sit until 16 January, Katherine's state of suspense would be long-lived.[2]

Katherine was not the only one to be held in uncertainty. Lady Rochford remained in the Tower and the stress of her situation was proving too much for her. The trial of Culpeper and Dereham had shown that she was regarded as Katherine's accomplice. This placed her in a very dangerous position. Chapuys felt that she would have been sentenced on the same day as Culpeper and Dereham 'had she not, on the third day after her imprisonment, been seized with a fit of madness by which her brain is affected'.[3] Although 'now and then she recovers her reason', Lady Rochford's condition was very delicate. She was sent to the home of Lord Russell, there to be cared for by his wife, Anne.[4] King Henry ensured that his own physicians paid daily visits to her 'for he desires her recovery'. The king's concern was not for Lady Rochford's welfare, but 'chiefly that he may afterwards have her executed as an example and warning to others'.[5] At present, the law did not allow the execution of 'mad' persons.

Lady Rochford was not the only lady to be troubled. From the moment she had heard of Katherine's detention and Francis Dereham's arrest, Agnes, Dowager Duchess of Norfolk, had lived in fear. Her first reaction was to send her servant, William Pewson, to Hampton Court on the pretext of getting faggots. In reality, he was to see what he could find out.[6]

The duchess then approached Robert Damport with news that 'Dereham is taken, and also the Queen'. She asked him if he knew what was the matter. Damport was dismissive, but Agnes feared 'lest there be some ill'. She asked him again if he knew anything. Her fear, at this stage, was that Queen Katherine would be repudiated and that she 'shall come home to me again'.[7]

Duchess Agnes took some of her servants, one of them an elderly man called William Ashby, into the room that was used by Dereham when he stayed at Norfolk House. She broke open the two coffers he kept there and removed some items. The Privy Councillors had ordered seals to be placed on all coffers and chests of those with the queen at Hampton Court. Dereham's coffers were missed because he had kept them at Lambeth. A few days later, the Duke of Norfolk arrived with orders to search Dereham's coffers.[8] When he discovered that they had already been broken into and that certain items were missing, he was obliged to report the matter to the king. Thus the investigation into the Duchess Agnes, her household and the events that took place during Katherine's childhood began.

It would take almost a month before the true investigation got under way; the council was busily compiling evidence to convict Culpeper and Dereham. The first witness to be examined with a view to building a case against Agnes was her kinswoman, Katherine Tylney, whose examination took place on 30 November.[9]

Asked whether the duchess knew of familiarity between Katherine and Dereham, Katherine Tylney assured them that she 'only knew that there was love between them'. Asked about what Dereham did after Katherine had gone to court, Mistress Tylney said that, according to the duchess, 'Dereham was now always asking leave to go.' However, she asserted that Agnes did not know that Dereham had gone to Ireland, 'for when Katherine Howard, then one of the maidens in the Court, came to see her she asked if she knew where he was, and Katherine answered she knew not'. The duchess knew nothing about Dereham's going to Ireland, although Mary Lascelles did, or she claimed to; Agnes's servants were keeping their own counsel.

Even on the day of the trial of Culpeper and Dereham some business was conducted. As part of their investigation into the Duchess Agnes, Chancellor Audeley, Norfolk, Suffolk, Southampton, Hertford, Gardiner, Sir John Gage and Richard Riche drew up a set of interrogatories to be ministered to the duchess, Queen Katherine, Francis Dereham and Lady Bridgewater. These were sent to the king for approval. In the meantime, Gage, Riche and Henry Bradshaw were appointed to examine Dereham, Damport and Joan Bulmer.[10] That Dereham was to be put on trial for his life that day made no difference to the council. If he had information that could assist in the case they were building against Agnes, they were determined to have it. Letters were sent out with orders for Joan Bulmer and Alice Wilkes to appear as witnesses.[11] Joan was finally able to leave her unhappy situation at York behind, at least for a time, but not in the way she had wished. Anthony Restwold, Alice's husband, went to Westminster to be near his wife during her examination. Overstaying his leave of absence, the council wrote on his behalf to the deputy of Calais asking for him to be excused.[12]

Across two days of questioning, Robert Damport[13] explained that, on hearing of Katherine's detention and Dereham's arrest, Agnes had sent him to the Duke of Norfolk, who was staying at the archbishop's house nearby. Damport was to invite the duke to spend the night at Norfolk House because it was too late for him to go home. The duke had refused, saying he had to go to court on the king's business. When Damport returned, the duchess asked him for news of Dereham. Damport merely palmed her off with 'some words belike be spoken by him to a gentleman usher or to some other'. The duchess would have none of it. She said, 'I fear it be for some matter done when they were here.' She then told him about the letter Mannock and Barnes had written to her, telling her to 'take heed', but she had taken it as a 'warning for me to take heed between Hastings' and another. She pointed out that 'if it were done when they were here, neither the Queen nor Dereham should die for it'. This was because the affair had taken place prior to Katherine's marriage, and so it was not adultery. The duchess then expressed her sorrow for the king, 'for he taketh the matter very heavily'.

Much of the evidence that had so far been gathered against the Duchess Agnes was nothing more than hearsay. It was time to speak to the lady herself. Therefore, the day after Damport's second examination, Agnes, who was now unwell, received a visit.[14] The Earl of Southampton, Thomas Wriothesley and Richard Pollard, the king's remembrancer of the Exchequer and one of the General Surveyors, went to Norfolk House 'as if only to visit and comfort her'. They discovered that, in their opinion, she was 'not so sick as she made out'. Rather, she appeared to them to be well enough to go to Chancellor Audeley, who had 'certain questions to demand of her', which, she was told, 'should much serve to the clearing of this matter'. They advised her to go, saying that things were not as bad as they thought and she could 'both shortly and truly answer'. At this point, the elderly duchess became unwell again 'even at the heart', as she told them. The councillors concluded that it was the 'sickness of mistrust', stemming from her fear 'that if she went, she should not return'.

In this the councillors were correct. The duchess's indisposition was caused by fear of what might happen to her. The memory of the awful fate of the old Countess of Salisbury, who had been executed several months before, could not have helped. The countess's brutal death showed Agnes that her age and present infirmity would not protect her.

In the event, Agnes was persuaded to go to the chancellor. The three councillors repaired to Wriothesley's house, where they watched until they had seen her barge go by. Mr Pollard then returned to the duchess's home, while arrangements were made to despatch Mr Petre, a senior administrator, to her house in Horsham later that evening; both men were sent 'to put the house in order'; that is, to make preparations for the inventory of the duchess's goods.

In the meantime, Southampton and Wriothesley continued their investigation and 'somewhat travailed' with William Pewson, who was 'yet stiff'. He confessed that he had gone to Hampton Court after Dereham's arrest, but it was only to buy boards for the duchess and faggots for himself at Kingston. His interrogators found his answers unpersuasive; they thought that Pewson 'can, and shall, tell another tale'.[15]

At his second examination, Pewson initially claimed that he had first heard about the matter of the queen and Dereham at Hampton Court.[16] He then changed his mind, saying instead that he had heard it at home from servants of Sir John Dudley and Dover of the Pastry. He had told the duchess about it, pointing out that either they had stolen her key or had another. Pewson then said that, if 'it were true that was said of the Queen, Dereham, the lady of Rochford, Culpeper, Davenport and Katherine Tylney, they were worthy to be hanged one against another, and if your Grace be true and my lord William I pass not of none of them [I care not for any of them]'. At that 'the Duchess held up her hands and said she was as innocent as the child new-born'.

The council were gathering evidence against Duchess Agnes. Before they questioned her once more, 'to the intent that we might be better armed for the purpose', they thought it expedient to speak again with her man, William Ashby.[17] He was held in the custody of Richard Riche, who brought to the council 'three or four leaves of paper' upon which Ashby had written his deposition.

Ashby deposed that he had been present when the Duchess Agnes opened Dereham's chests. Also present were her comptroller, a priest and the smith who picked the lock on one chest and broke open the other. He deposed that the duchess had removed all the writings she found and 'carried them to her chamber, saying she would peruse them at her leisure, without suffering anybody to see them with her'. She did the same with the writings in Dereham's 'male' (mail). In order to keep these items secret, the duchess asked Ashby to take a satin coat in lieu of the thirty shillings and eight pence Dereham owed him, but Ashby refused.

Ashby spoke of the duchess's fear that Alice Wilkes had told Lord William of the familiarity between Katherine and Dereham. She had wanted to send someone to Calais to inform her son of the matter, but had been advised to the contrary.

Next, Ashby confessed that he had helped his mistress search for the pardon, a thing of great import to the duchess.[18] This was the general pardon that had been issued in July 1540.[19] Typically vague, it covered all crimes except 'heretical opinions touching the sacrament, treason, murder, and some other crimes'. The duchess was anxious to know if the pardon would also apply to those who 'knew of the naughty life of Dereham and Mrs Katherine and did not reveal it'.[20] In other words, even at this early stage, Duchess Agnes of Norfolk had realised that she was open to charges of misprision. She had told Ashby that 'if there be none offence done since the marriage, she [Katherine] ought not to die for that which was done before'.

As he continued his deposition, Ashby wrote that his mistress had also broken open a chest and two coffers belonging to Robert Damport following his committal to the Tower. As she had done with Dereham's, she had taken out letters and writings. Again, she had been assisted by Ashby and her comptroller, while Dunn, a yeoman of her cellar, had played the smith's part.

The council were not entirely satisfied with Ashby's deposition, and they questioned him a third time to see if he had anything more to add.[21] Ashby explained that his mistress had wanted 'to see what writings were in Dereham's chests that were meet to be sent to the King's council'. She had found writings and ballads and a ballad book. As she turned the leaves of the book, Ashby saw that there were ballads in it as well as notes for playing on the lute. This book he later saw again in the duchess's hands.

However, the duchess had discovered more than ballads and

music books; she had also found a 'bill', a letter. It was, as she explained to Ashby, a copy of the bill that 'was laid in her pew in Lambeth Church which Katherine Howard stole and took out of her gilt coffer in her chamber in the night when she was abed'. The duchess told Ashby that it was because of this bill that 'Dereham and her fell out about the beginning of the King's progress and [she] commanded him out of her gates.' Agnes knew that it was dangerous to be in possession of the bill; she told Ashby that it 'belongeth to me and to nobody else and would do me no good'. Ashby agreed and urged her to burn it, but she did not heed his warning, placing it with Dereham's ballads instead. Then, at eight o'clock one night, the duchess gave him 'a good handful of bills rolled together and named by her ballads' to take to the Duke of Norfolk in the morning.

Ashby recalled how, 'a long time since', the duchess had said to him that she 'mistrusted Katherine Howard and Dereham', to which he answered, 'I do see no such cause.' Ashby, however, did know of the relationship between Katherine and Dereham; he had been told about it by Henry Mannock.

Ashby closed his deposition by confirming that he had 'written and opened unto your Lordships and confessed as I do know'. He then begged 'your Lordships to be good and have pity of me thus greatly troubled in my old age . . . by a wilful woman'.

As the council were going over Ashby's deposition, news arrived that Robert Damport had asked to speak with one of the councillors. Sir John Gage and Sir Richard Riche were immediately despatched to the Tower. Damport wanted to tell them something Dereham had confided in his dismay when the king first began to favour Katherine: 'I could be sure to Mistress Katherine, and I would, but I dare not. The King beginneth to love her; but, and he were dead, I am sure I might marry her.' Damport also told them that Dereham had been present when the duchess pointed him out to a gentlewoman in the queen's chamber and said, 'this is he that came in to Ireland for the Queen's sake'.[22]

These new pieces of information were of great interest to the council. The comment about Dereham's going to Ireland provided further confirmation that the duchess was aware of the nature of the relationship between Katherine and Dereham. However, Dereham's avowal that he would marry Katherine if the king were dead was particularly significant. It showed that he had imagined the king's death, and that was treason.

Because of the timing of Damport's confession, which he 'would not do it for any torture he could before be put to', they decided that both he and Dereham would be 'seriously examined again, this day, of certain points, which we have noted for the purpose'.

The phrase 'seriously examined' implies torture or, at the very least, the threat of it. Their tactic clearly worked, and Dereham, on the strength of his co-operation, made 'humble suit for the remission of some part of the extremity of his judgement'. Certainly, it was in Henry's power to grant such a request, and Sir Anthony Browne and Ralph Sadler were sent 'to know His Majesty's pleasure therein'. However, given the circumstances, they must have known beforehand what the king's pleasure would be.

Amid all else they had done that day, the council still found time to interrogate Duchess Agnes.[23] Most likely they drew their questions from the list of interrogatories they had compiled a few days previously,[24] asking the duchess to confirm the evidence that had been gathered during the examinations of Ashby and Pewson. They also wanted to know about how she had brought up Katherine and what changes of apparel she had given her. They questioned her about Katherine's familiarity with Dereham, how the duchess knew of it and when. Had the duchess ever had occasion to discipline Katherine over the affair or for any 'light and wanton behaviour' between the two? What exchanges had she had with Damport concerning Katherine and Dereham? What did she know of the precontract and to whom had she spoken about it? When they had finished the interrogation, the council sent a report to the king.

Henry had gone on a hunting progress in an attempt to find solace in the peace of beautiful landscapes and the excitement of the chase. It did little to cheer him. Despite being surrounded by 'musicians and ministers of pastime',[25] Henry could not forget his grief, especially when he received daily reminders of it in the letters sent to him by his councillors. As he read their latest report about the duchess's interrogation, he found that her inquisitors had not been as thorough as they should have been.[26] He instructed them to find out why the duchess had opened Dereham's coffers. If it was so that she could send the writings and papers to the king or the council, why had she not done so? Henry thought her actions and the secrecy that surrounded them 'importeth a marvellous presumption, that the writings should contain matters of treason, considering the act, with the vehement presumption, and joining thereto all circumstances of the likelihood that the Duchess knew of the former naughty life betwixt the Queen and Dereham'. This had provided the council with grounds to make Dereham's case treason and to presume that he had entered the queen's service with the intent that he should renew his 'former naughty life'. Henry ordered the council to examine the duchess and her senior ladies to find out what had happened to the writings she had taken from Dereham's coffers.

Henry now turned to the duchess's fears that Alice Wilkes had told Lord William about the familiarity between Katherine and Dereham, and that she would have sent word to Calais to warn her son had she not been persuaded to the contrary. This Henry thought to be 'another presumption, and circumstance to prove that she knew of the naughty life betwixt the Queen and Dereham'. Southampton was ordered to 'pick out any pithy or material matter of Alice Wilkes' concerning Lord William. He was then to keep Lord William, who had been returned to England on 3 December,[27] occupied so he could keep an eye on him.

Henry found Agnes's search for the general pardon rather interesting, particularly her enquiry 'whether the pardon would not serve other that knew of their naughty life before marriage'. This, together with her breaking into Damport's coffers 'and the conveying of his letters and writings' once he had been taken to the Tower, 'must needs weigh grievously against her'.

This brought the king to Damport's confession that the duchess had pointed to Dereham as the man who had gone to Ireland 'for the Queen's sake'. Henry ordered Dereham and Damport to be 'seriously examined' again to find out to which gentlewoman the duchess spoke. In view of this, Dereham's execution was to be stayed for a time in anticipation of further evidence coming out.

Henry then asked for a copy of the interrogatories that had been remitted to the council by Wriothesley, and which the king had amended in some part while at Esher. As to Dereham's request for some remission of the extremity of his judgement, Henry 'thinketh he had deserved no such mercy at his hand, and therefore hath determined, that he shall suffer the whole execution'. This came as no surprise. Legally, Dereham's only crime had been misprision, hardly justification for such a cruel death. Rather, it was his moral offence that, in Henry's eyes at least, demanded such terrible punishment. Henry could not forgive Dereham for his violation of Katherine and for shattering Henry's blissful illusion that he had recaptured all the vigour and prowess of his youth.

After they had examined the duchess one more time and perused all the evidence they had gathered so far, the council now considered that 'all presumptions and circumstances' pertaining to the duchess and Lord William 'will extend to misprision of treason'. Likewise, the ladies Margaret Howard and Katherine, Countess of Bridgewater, together with Alice Wilkes, Katherine Tylney, Robert Damport, Edward Waldegrave, Malyn Tylney, Mary Lascelles, Joan Bulmer, William Ashby, Anne Howard and Margaret Benet 'be in the same case, if it shall please His Majesty to proceed against them'.[28]

Meanwhile, plans were made to question further Lady Bridgewater, Joan Bulmer and Alice Wilkes, as well as two servants, Mynster Chamber and one Philip, principal witnesses against Lord William and Lady Bridgewater. With these people, the council promised to 'travail and labour to find out the bottom of the pot'. In the end, however, all they learned was that the duchess had known of the familiarity between Katherine and Dereham, although it is clear that she had not known the extent of it; that is, she had not known of the precontract.

The Duchess Agnes, most of the senior members of her family and certain members of her household, past and present, were expected imminently to be committed to the Tower. Until now, they had been kept under house arrest at Wriothesley's house.[29] At the same time, their 'goods put in safe custody to His Majesty's behalf'. There was to be only one exception. Having considered how the whole affair had come to light, Mary Lascelles, 'who not only refused the Queen's service, but, also, at the first opening thereof to her brother, seemed very sorry and lament that the King's Majesty had married' Katherine, was to be spared. This was so that the king's 'clemency and mercy, showed now to the said Mary, might be a mean to give courage and boldness to others to reveal things in like cases'.[30]

After all the interrogations, and the passing back and forth of reports and letters between themselves and the king, the council now felt that the need to proceed with the indictment of Duchess Agnes, her family and retainers for misprision of treason had become pressing. They worried that the duchess, being 'old and testy', might, upon her committal, 'take it so to heart, as might put her in peril of her life'. The concern was not for Agnes's wellbeing, but so that the 'Parliament shall have better ground to confiscke their goods, if any of them should chance, before their attainder, to die'.

During all this time, Culpeper and Dereham had continued to languish in the Tower awaiting their execution. In Dereham's case, the delay was so that he could be further examined; whatever information he gave was to be used against his former mistress. For Culpeper, who had nothing to do but compose himself for the ordeal ahead, and perhaps hope that some remission of his punishment might be granted, the wait must have been unbearable.

As it was, the council now felt that they had got as much out of Dereham as they ever would. It was time for the two men to 'prepare themselves to God for the salvation of their souls' in readiness for their execution.[31] The following day, the council confirmed that they 'shall get no more of Dereham than is already confessed; and therefore, unless we shall hear otherwise from the King's Majesty, we have resolved that they shall suffer tomorrow'.[32]

At the last moment, there was a remission of sorts for Culpeper. Henry had decided to commute his sentence from drawing, hanging and quartering to simple beheading. Even so, the council considered that his offence was 'very heinous, and that it is necessary that his execution be notable'. They issued orders that he should be drawn to Tyburn, 'and there only to lose his head', unless they heard the king's 'pleasure to the contrary'.[33]

The day eventually appointed for the execution of Culpeper and Dereham was 10 December 1541. During their last few hours on earth, they would participate in a carefully orchestrated ritual of death. They dressed accordingly in formal mourning or in wedding costume; their clothes were a perquisite of the executioner. Then, fastened face down to wooden hurdles, they were drawn through the winding and uneven streets between the Tower and Tyburn, the crowds jeering and shouting on either side.

The route took them past the gates of St Sepulchre-without-Newgate where, according to custom, they would each be given a nosegay. The bells of the church rang out as the bellman recited a verse calling upon the victims to repent and the spectators to pray for their souls. Further on, they passed St Giles-in-the-Fields, established by Matilda, the queen of Henry I, as a leper hospital and dedicated to the patron saint of outcasts. Following a tradition established by Matilda, Culpeper and Dereham were offered a mug of ale, their last refreshment before they met their deaths. Arrived at last at Tyburn, they were released from the hurdles and led to a triangular gallows that had been erected for the occasion.[34]

Culpeper, as the highest ranking prisoner, was the first to be executed. He stood next to the gallows and exhorted the people to pray for him. Then, 'he standing on the ground by the gallows, kneeled down and had his head stricken off'.[35]

Now it was Dereham's turn. If a prisoner's family could afford it, they could pay the executioner to hang the victim until he was dead before cutting down the body and inflicting the rest of the punishment on it. There was also the option of despatching him with a knife before his bowels were drawn out.[36] Unfortunately, Dereham would be granted no such favour. He climbed the ladder of the gallows where the hangman placed the rope round his neck. He was strangled for several moments before being cut down while still alive and carried to the quartering block. Here, his privy parts were cut off before his abdomen was opened and the entrails drawn out and burned before his eyes. Only then did the axe deliver the *coup de grâce*.

What remained of Dereham was chopped into quarters, the pieces to be sent wherever the king deemed fit. Culpeper's body was buried in the St Sepulchre-without-Newgate. His head and Dereham's were carried to London Bridge, where they were parboiled before being set on spikes. So died Thomas Culpeper and Francis Dereham, not for anything they had done, but for what it was presumed they had intended to do.

19

Condemnation

~

ON THE VERY day that this gruesome scene was played out,
Henry ordered the 'serious examination' of Agnes, Dowager
Duchess of Norfolk.[1] While he was aware of the testimony against
her, he thought it 'were much better to have her convinced
[convicted] by her own confession'. There was also the hope that,
if she were 'groundly examined, many things may appear and come
to light, which be not yet discovered'. Wriothesley, relishing his part
in the proceedings, expressed his satisfaction at the prospect of 'every
one's fault totted on their heads'. This especially applied to Agnes
who, although she had been aware of the familiarity between
Katherine and Dereham, did nevertheless 'commend her to the
King's Majesty and after was a mean to her to extend favour, or
rather renew favour to Dereham'. Then, following Dereham's arrest
and imprisonment in the Tower, she had secretly broken open two
chests belonging to Dereham and removed writings and letters 'as
might manifest the treason, and her own knowledge' of it.[2]

Lord William Howard, his wife, Lady Margaret, and Anne
Howard, Katherine's sister-in-law, had already been taken to the
Tower. Wriothesley noted that Lord William 'stood as stiff as his
mother', adding, 'I did not much like his fashion.' He continued,
'this day go my guests, and the Duchess herself unless we shall
hear otherwise'. He then made his way to Lambeth to assist in the
inventory of the duchess's belongings.[3]

Wriothesley did not have long to wait before his final guest
moved on. Agnes was committed to the Tower the following day,
11 December.[4] On the same day, a stray piece of evidence found

its way into the hands of the council. Anne Fox of Reading, while at supper with the chaplain and other servants of William Penison, commented that she 'did know for a year past that the Queen was of ill disposition'.[5]

Notwithstanding the evidence against the Duchess of Norfolk, the council were well aware that it was little more than gossip; she herself had confessed to nothing. Now that she was firmly in their clutches, her interrogators vowed that they would 'not fail to travail, as earnestly as we can' with her 'both to make her confess the things testified against her and also to "cough out" the rest, not yet discovered, if any such dregs remain among them'.[6]

There were now so many Howards and their 'gentlewomen chamberers, and light young men'[7] imprisoned in the Tower that there were not enough rooms to accommodate them all. Special arrangements had to be made, and an appeal was submitted to the king. Henry therefore allowed the prisoners to be held in the royal apartments, although the locks had to be changed because he could not find his keys. At the same time, the inventories at the houses of the duchess and others continued, while provisions were made for the children of Lord William and Lady Bridgewater.[8]

When news reached the Duke of Norfolk at Kenninghall that the senior members of his family were committed to the Tower of London, he wrote to the king.[9] He railed against 'mine ungracious mother in law, mine unhappy brother and his wife, with my lewd sister of Bridgewater'. Nevertheless, he doubted not that the king would have acted as he had but for 'their false and traitorous proceedings' against him. This and the 'most abominable deeds done by 2 of my nieces' had brought the duke 'to the greatest perplexity'. Now, fearing that His Majesty might 'conserve a displeasure' in his heart against the duke and all others of his kin, as well as 'abhor to hear speak of the same', he declared himself prostrate at the king's feet. He urged Henry to remember that much of the matter had come to light when he had declared to the king 'the words spoken to me by my mother in law, when Your Highness sent me to Lambeth to search Dereham's coffers'. This had led to the examination of the

Duchess Agnes and her 'ungracious children', that is, Lord William and Lady Bridgewater. Now, considering the duke's 'true proceedings' towards the king and the 'small love my two false traitorous nieces and my mother in law have borne unto me', he allowed himself to hope that the king would not extend his displeasure to him. He asked to be 'advertised plainly how Your Highness doth weigh your favour towards me'; for, unless he knew that he continued in the king's good favour, 'I never desire to live in this world any longer, but shorty to finish this transitory life.'

The duke's letter, written in the most obsequious and sycophantic terms, betrays the shock he felt. He had no idea how Katherine had been treated while at Norfolk House, no sense of what had taken place under his stepmother's roof. He felt betrayed by his relatives, all of whom should have known better. He was afraid that the king would take out his wrath on him, and he knew all too well that the consequences of royal anger were terrible. As he had once warned Sir Thomas More, 'by the Mass, Master More, it is perilous striving with princes. And therefore, I would wish you somewhat to incline to the King's pleasure; for by God's Body, Master More, *Indignatio principis mors est.*' If the unfortunate duke remembered More's answer, it could not have given him any comfort in his time of trouble: 'Is that all, my Lord? Then in good faith is there no more difference between your Grace and me, but that I shall die today and you tomorrow.'[10]

The duke was not to die for the actions of his family, and while he was lamenting his lot from the relative safety of Kenninghall, the prisoners in the Tower continued to receive visits from Southampton and Wriothesley.[11] The two councillors had come to interrogate them further, and they began with the Duchess Agnes. They found her on her bed, 'as it appeareth, very sickly', and no doubt feeling every day of her sixty-four years. Nevertheless, they pressed her 'as much as we might' to disclose more about 'the lewd behaviours of the Queen and Dereham, and of all other things done or spoken since that matter came to revelation'. Thankfully, they were able to promise her, on the king's behalf, 'of her own life'.

With this assurance, the duchess told them that she had 'never suspected any act' between Katherine and Dereham. She never thought
them 'to be of that abominable sort, she now knoweth them to
have been'. Even so, she could not deny that she 'perceived a light
love and favour between them, more than between indifferent
persons'. She had heard that Dereham would often give Katherine
money, but she thought it had 'proceeded upon the affection that
growth of kindred', Katherine and Dereham being related. Referring
to her silence about the affair before the royal marriage and her
breaking open the coffers belonging to Dereham and Damport,
she 'confessed herself to have offended God and His Majesty'. She
humbly beseeched the king to forgive her.

Knowing that her offence would necessarily lead to the confiscation of her goods and properties, she trusted wholly in the king's
mercy, that he would give her 'something to live on', praying him
'not to give away my house at Lambeth, for I can not long live
here' in the Tower.

Having left the duchess, Southampton and Wriothesley went to
Alice Wilkes, Joan Bulmer, Katherine Tylney and Anne Howard,
'one after the other, who be women much changed'. Their stay in
the Tower had made them 'very repentant and determined to confess
their faults'. In the end, however, all the councillors learned was that
Dereham would resort many times to Katherine's chamber; that he
would lie on her bed, sometimes in his doublet and hose and sometimes in 'naked bed'; that there was much 'puffing and blowing';[12]
that they would banquet and be merry;[13] that Dereham would take
Katherine in his arms and kiss her; and that Dereham and Mannock
had fought over the letter sent to the duchess.[14] There was nothing
they did not know already.

Southampton and Wriothesley then spoke to the Lady Howard,
the wife of Lord William, who seemed not to have known how
she had offended. Her inquisitors enlightened her, so that, when she
'once perceived the same, we never saw a more sorrowful woman'.
Yet, all they took from Lady Margaret was confirmation that there
had been 'much familiarity' between Katherine and Dereham before

Katherine married the king. She also mentioned Stafford, who had been aware of the relationship.[15] Again, there was nothing to add to the testimony they had already gathered.

Their final visit that day was to Lord William Howard. They wanted 'to see his state, because we hear the man is wonderfully troubled, and out of quiet'. To Sir William and his fellow prisoners, the councillors were able to give assurance of the king's mercy.

Southampton and Wriothesley left the Tower and returned to Hampton Court. They prepared their report and made the final arrangements 'to proceed to their arraignment'. It was decided that Lord William and Robert Damport should be tried in the afternoon, with Lady Howard and the others facing trial in the morning. This was, as they said, because they thought 'the being of Lord William and his wife together, at the bar, might much trouble the woman, and be to us no mean of expedition'. This arrangement was approved by the king.[16]

The charges in the indictment were that:[17]

> Katherine Queen of England, one of the daughters of Edmund Howard, before her marriage with the King, had illicit intercourse with divers persons in the mansion of Agnes Duchess of Norfolk, at Lambeth, where she was educated, and in particular that she was criminally connected with Francis Dereham and Henry Mannock, and that the said Queen Katherine and Francis Dereham acknowledged the same, as mentioned in the preceding indictments.

Moreover, that Katherine and Dereham, aware that Katherine was unchaste, 'and themselves, as they alleged, contracted in marriage', and Dereham, knowing that the king intended to marry Katherine, 'did, when the king sought Queen Katherine in marriage, and during the whole time before the marriage, conceal the wicked life of the said Katherine'. Then, Katherine, whom the king believed to be 'pure, chaste, and exonerated from any matrimonial contract', did contract marriage with the king at Oatlands on 28 July 1541.

The indictment now turns to events after the marriage. That Katherine and Dereham were 'so intent upon continuing their criminal intercourse', that she, 'of her own mind as at the instigation of Dereham and several friends', contrived that Dereham and Katherine Tylney, 'who was procuress between them', should enter the queen's service at Oatlands. In addition, Katherine had kept Dereham and Katherine Tylney 'in high love and favour, gave them various gifts, and employed Dereham in her secret affairs'.[18] By these means, Queen Katherine and Dereham 'not only deceived the King but also brought the King's royal person into great danger, and to the scandal of the marriage between the King and the Queen'.

It was found that Katherine Tylney, Alice Restwold (Wilkes), Joan Bulmer, Anne Howard, Robert Damport, Malyn Tylney and Margaret Benet had concealed from the king and his councillors 'the wicked life of the Queen and Dereham', that they knew 'the Queen before the said marriage with the King to be unchaste', and that 'the King intended to marry' Katherine, as well as that 'the Queen after marriage between her and the King retained Dereham in her service, and continued her illicit intercourses as well before the Royal marriage as after such Royal marriage'.

Next, Agnes, Duchess of Norfolk, William Howard, Margaret Howard, Katherine, Countess of Bridgewater, Edward Waldegrave and William Ashby,

> knowing the loose conduct of the said Queen whilst she was in the mansion of the Duchess, as well by many evil tokens, as by the intimidation of divers persons,[19] and also having vehement suspicion of an unlawful intercourse between her and Dereham; and also knowing that the Queen after her marriage retained Dereham in her service, and employed him in her affairs as well between the Queen and the Duchess as between other parties had concealed all this from the King so that Katherine might be promoted to the Royal Estate.

For this purpose, they did, on 20 July 1541, at Lambeth 'as well in the presence of the King as in the presence of other persons, falsely commend and praise the said Katherine for her pure and honest condition, by which the King was deceived concerning her'.

Finally, that, after Katherine and Dereham had been arrested, and after Dereham and Damport had been committed to the Tower, the Duchess of Norfolk and her man, William Ashby, had broken open chests belonging to the two men and taken out 'various chattels, writings, and letters, being in the chests, and concealing the same from the King for four days and upwards'.

The arraignment of Katherine Tylney, Alice Restwold (Wilkes), Joan Bulmer, Anne Howard, Malyn Tylney, Margaret Benet, Margaret Howard, Edward Waldegrave and William Ashby took place on the morning of Thursday, 22 December 1541.[20] They 'most humbly and lamentably knowledged their offences, and submitted themselves wholly to His Grace's mercy', each pleading guilty as charged. Therefore, they were to be returned to the Tower and 'in the same Tower or elsewhere, as the king shall direct', were to be held in perpetual imprisonment, their goods and chattels forfeited to the king and their lands and tenements seized into the king's hands.

The councillors who had attended the arraignments now found the prisoners so sorrowful and changed by their imprisonment, 'that we think divers of them cannot long live', unless the king was merciful and allowed them 'some liberty in the Tower, with some resort and comfort of their friends'. They asked the king's pleasure in the hope that Southampton and Wriothesley 'should tomorrow, in the morning, go to the Tower, to give them some further hope, that we would be suitors for them'.

In the afternoon, Lord William Howard and Robert Damport were brought to the bar and both pleaded not guilty. The jury of the county of Surrey were sworn in, 'but before they could retire to give their verdict, and after sufficient evidence had been given by the Crown against' them, Lord William changed his plea to guilty. This was done in 'such lowly and repentant sort, and with such advice to all men there present to beware by his example'. Lord William was sentenced to perpetual imprisonment, with the forfeiture of goods and chattels.

As with the prisoners who had been arraigned and imprisoned in the morning, the councillors were anxious to act as suitors on

Lord William's behalf. He had been so contrite that it would take them too long, it 'being now so late, to write all his words, used in his submission, but, to be short, it was both for the King's Majesty's honour in the confession of the offence, and for the example, as good as was to be desired'.

That left only Robert Damport, who 'stood thoroughly to his trial'. The jury, having been discharged from giving a verdict against Lord William, 'found a verdict of guilty against Damport'. He was condemned not only 'by the order of the law, but with such declaration of his offences', that it was thought that 'all the standers by did wonderfully both detest the man, and the manner'. His sentence was that of all the others: perpetual imprisonment, with the forfeiture of goods and chattels. There were no pleas of clemency for him.[21]

As it had been at the trial of Culpeper and Dereham, Katherine's guilt was accepted. Those convicted of misprision of treason were judged according to that fact. Their condemnation was a foregone conclusion, as was Katherine's, even though she had not yet been formally charged with anything.

Henry read the report of the trial that his councillors had sent to him. He noted particularly their plea for him to show his 'mercy and clemency' to the prisoners. He was unmoved. While he did intend at some point to do so, he thought it 'not meet' that the council should 'so hastily put them in such comfort, or so soon restore them to any liberty within the Tower'. For this, the king had 'sundry great respects and considerations'. He suggested, therefore, that Southampton and Wriothesley did not go to the Tower in the morning as they had planned.

It being close to Christmas, Henry made plans to repair to Greenwich; as it turned out, he would not arrive before Christmas Eve.[22] How different the festive season would be from the previous year, when Katherine had graced the court and brought her own light to the winter darkness. As the New Year dawned, the candles remained dark, the music silenced, 'the whole Court seemed confused, the King little joyous, and his ministers pensive and melancholy'.[23]

20

All Be-wept in Black, and Poor Estate

~

'The King's so many wives, whom he chopped and
changed at his pleasure'[1]

THERE WAS LITTLE to do now except wait for the opening
of Parliament. Marillac had heard that Norfolk was expected
to be back at court so he could attend, although 'whether in his
former credit is not certain'. He noted that 'Lord William is the
least charged, and will, it is hoped, soon be released.'[2]

On the appointed date, 16 January 1542, the new Parliament
duly began its sessions. In a lengthy speech, Chancellor Audeley
outlined the business that would be transacted over the coming
weeks. The real cause of the Parliament, the condemnation of
Queen Katherine and others, would certainly have been alluded
to, but was not recorded.[3]

Unlike Anne Boleyn before her, Katherine was not to be given
a trial. Instead, she was to be condemned by an Act of Attainder;
that is, the pronouncement of judgement and punishment passed
as law in Parliament. This development was almost inevitable, given
that her fate had been decided long ago.

The announcement of Katherine's attainder was passed over in
silence for two reasons. The first was that the Parliament was
attended by Henry, whose honour had to be protected at all costs.
It was well known that if a wife offended, her husband was urged
to examine his own life to 'find how the occasion came from
himself, and that he hath not used her, as he ought to have done'.[4]

A still more important reason was that the Lords were well aware that Katherine had never actually committed an offence, so there was nothing with which to charge her. This incongruity would be addressed within the bill itself.

Five days into the session, on 21 January, the Bill of Attainder against Queen Katherine and Jane, Lady Rochford for high treason was introduced. Another against the Duchess Agnes of Norfolk, Lord William and others for misprision was introduced at the same time.[5] Over the next week, the bill would be debated, until, on 28 January, Chancellor Audeley advised the House that they must proceed with caution.

The problem was that Katherine's guilt had been assumed but not proven. She had not definitively been found guilty and, more importantly, she had not been given a chance to speak in her own defence. This was an unacceptable state of affairs. Audeley reminded the Lords that Katherine was 'no mean or private person, but a public and illustrious one'. As such, 'her cause ought to be judged with that sincerity, that there should be neither room for suspicion of some latent quarrel, or that she should not have liberty to clear herself, if perchance, by reason or counsel she were able to do it, from the crime laid to her charge'.

The words 'reason or counsel' sum up Katherine's situation perfectly: she was still in as fragile a state as she had been at the beginning of her troubles, and she had been, throughout her ordeal, without adequate counsel. It was at this point, therefore, that the decision was made to send a committee to Katherine at Syon. They were to reassure her and soothe her 'womanish fears'. They would urge her to have 'presence of mind enough to say any thing to make her cause better', for 'it was just that a princess should be judged by equal laws' to the lords. Audeley made the point that, 'clearing herself in this manner would be highly acceptable to her most loving husband'.

Ambassador Chapuys thought that Henry, perhaps feeling some pang of conscience in allowing the condemnation of the queen he had once loved so much, had wanted to 'proceed with all moderation and justice'.[6] The real reason was so that the process against Katherine as well as her conviction should be incontrovertible. As a consequence, Archbishop Cranmer, the Duke of Suffolk, the Earl of Southampton and Bishop Gardiner were appointed to go to Katherine at Syon. Meanwhile, the passage of the bill was suspended.

At Syon, Katherine was said to be 'making good cheer'. Chapuys wrote that she was 'fatter and more beautiful than ever', taking care with her attire 'and more imperious and difficult to serve than when she was with the King', despite the fact that she 'expects death and only asks for a secret [private] execution'.[7] Chapuys's information came from an unnamed source; some of it can be believed. With no more time to dance, a healthy exercise, Katherine might have put on some weight. She may have taken to eating for comfort. Her imperiousness naturally stemmed from the difficulty of her situation; but to report good cheer in a woman facing death while still in the springtime of her life is surely incorrect.

Notwithstanding Katherine's disposition, her husband's spirits were considerably lifted. On 29 January Henry 'gave a supper and banquet to the ladies'.[8] Twenty-six of them shared his table with several lords, and a further thirty-five sat at an adjoining table. Henry 'showed much favour and attention' to certain ladies: Elizabeth Brooke, the repudiated wife of Sir Thomas Wyatt and sister to Lord Cobham; Madame Albart, the daughter of Sir Anthony Browne's niece; and Anne Bassett, the stepdaughter of Lord Lisle, currently imprisoned in the Tower. Rumours about this last abounded, fuelled by news that Lisle had been given liberty in the Tower, while his arms were ordered to be restored in St George's Chapel.

In the event, the visit to Katherine was delayed. Two days after agreement had been reached to send a delegation to her, Chancellor Audeley announced to the Lords that the Privy Council had not approved of the message that was to be sent to her. Instead, they had devised another way, 'less faulty', which should be 'altogether demanded' of the king. This was that Henry should consider that the 'whole state of the kingdom' depended upon his resolution to divert his mind from all trouble and solicitude. Second, that the attainder of Thomas Culpeper and Francis Dereham should be confirmed, as should the attainder for misprision against Lord William Howard, while Parliament should have 'leave to proceed to give judgement and to finish the Queen's cause, that the event of that business may be no longer in doubt'. Third, that when Parliament had concluded its work, the king should 'condescend to give his Royal Assent' to it without coming personally to Parliament, but *in absentia* by Letters Patent under the Great Seal of England. This was so as not to 'renew his grief and endanger His Majesty's health'. Finally, it was arranged that the council would be pardoned if 'by speaking freely on the Queen, they should offend against the Statutes then in being'. This version of events firmly resonated with Henry's intent on the case, and he gave his consent.[9]

As the Lords rose at the end of the session, 'a deputation of some principal members from the House of Commons' was admitted into the royal presence. What was said behind closed doors can be constructed from subsequent events: the Commons delegation had not been long gone before Henry recalled them as well as the Lords. The king reminded them that they did not work for themselves but for the good of the realm and the public. Every peer was urged to 'reflect how much he owes to the absent multitude' and that it behoved them to be unanimous in their deliberations and decisions and not to reject bills because they could not be understood by their opposers. The Lords and Commons were effectively ordered to co-operate with each other to implement the royal will and ensure the passage of important Acts.[10]

With the king's will and correct procedure established, Charles, Duke of Suffolk and his fellow deputies were finally able to visit Queen Katherine. This took place on the same day that she was removed from Syon, 10 February. That afternoon, the badly frightened Katherine was 'after some difficulty and resistance' bundled into the barge that was to carry her to the Tower.[11] In other words, the councillors who had come to hear Katherine's defence had planned, at the same time, to carry her to the Tower where they knew she would die.

Katherine travelled in a small covered boat with 'four ladies of her suite, besides four sailors to man the boat'. Ahead of her, in a large oared barge and accompanied by a sizeable retinue of servants, was William Fitzwilliam, Earl of Southampton, and several members of the Privy Council, who had done so much in the service of the king with regard to Katherine's case. Following the queen, 'in a big and well-manned barge, with plenty of armed men inside', was the Duke of Suffolk.[12]

The route carried Katherine past those places that had formed the backdrop for some of the most significant events of her life. Leaving Syon, the Thames meanders eastwards into London, eventually passing, on the right, Norfolk House, where Katherine had come to live while still a girl. Here, in this magnificent mansion, her association with Francis Dereham had ended her torment at the hands of Henry Mannock. Then, as fate would have it, her saviour, in his turn, became her assailant, and the pattern of her life turned towards a still more vicious course.

Directly opposite, on the left bank of the fast-flowing river, stood the Palace of Whitehall. Here, Katherine had found her redemption and achieved her ambition. Maiden to a queen, she could not have hoped that, one day, she would become queen herself. Yet she did reign; the beloved wife of a generous, passionate and indulgent king.

Slowly, the barge continued its journey, a cruel distortion of Katherine's triumphant entrance into London less than a year earlier. She passed the imposing Baynard's Castle, which was to have been part of her jointure, her security in widowhood. Then, all too soon, looming out of the encroaching darkness of the late afternoon was London Bridge, still ornamented with the severed heads of Thomas Culpeper and Francis Dereham, the terrible price they paid for presumed intimacy with the queen.[13]

Katherine now reached the Tower of London, her final

destination. Southampton and Suffolk landed first, followed by Katherine, 'dressed in black velvet', who was accorded 'the same honours and ceremonies as if she were still reigning'.[14]

Katherine entered the Tower through the sally door at Byward Tower. From here, she walked along Water Lane, which runs parallel to the Thames and is flanked by a high curtain wall, past the Garden Tower (now known as the Bloody Tower), and into the comfortable luxury of the royal lodgings that would be her home for whatever time she had left.[15]

The following day, 11 February, Chancellor Audeley produced two statutes that had been passed by the Lords and the Commons. The first concerned the method of proceeding against 'lunatics' who, before their insanity, had confessed themselves guilty of high treason. This was designed to facilitate the execution of Jane, Lady Rochford. The second was the Act of Attainder for Queen Katherine.

The Act opened by outlining the crimes imputed to the queen.[16] Katherine Howard, whom the king had taken to wife, thinking her to be 'chaste and of pure and honest living', was now said to have been nothing of the sort, as proved 'both by her own confession and others also'. This referred to her relationships with Henry Mannock and Francis Dereham before she met Henry.

After she had married the king, she 'took most traitorously into her service the same person with whom she used her vicious life before'. This was Dereham, who Katherine used 'in many secret conferences and messages after, as by his confession and attainder doth more plainly appear'. Dereham had been judged guilty based on Katherine's culpability; now Katherine's guilt is confirmed by Dereham's. Then, Katherine's engagement of Katherine Tylney as her chamberer, a woman who knew of the queen's 'naughty life' before, and could help her continue it after her royal marriage, was entered as further evidence against the queen.

The Act now turned to Jane, Lady Rochford, with whom Katherine had 'traitorously confederated' so that she might 'bring her vicious and abominable purpose to pass with Thomas Culpeper Esquire'. The queen met him 'in a secret and vile place, and that at an undue hour of eleven a clock in the night, and so remained there with him till three of the clock in the morning'. Here, Katherine entertained Culpeper, with no other company than 'that Bawd the Lady Rochford, by whose means Culpeper came thither'. Then, 'at other conferences together afterward most falsely and traitorously committed and perpetrated many detestable and abominable treasons, to the most fearful peril and danger of the destruction of your most royal person and to the utter loss, derision and desolation of this your Realm of England'.

These crimes having been revealed by God, and in a timely manner, Francis Dereham and Thomas Culpeper were convicted and attainted 'according to the laws of the Realm', and had 'justly suffered therefore pains of death according to their merits'. Similarly, Queen Katherine and Jane Lady Rochford should be 'lawfully indicted'.

The Lords then asked that the indictment and attainder of Culpeper and Dereham be passed into law. They proposed also that Katherine and Lady Rochford 'shall by the authority of this present parliament be convicted and attainted of High Treason', for which they would 'suffer pains of death' and loss of goods and chattels. All possessions owned by Katherine, Lady Rochford, Culpeper and Dereham as of 30 August 1541 and since would be forfeited to the king.

The Act was to be granted the royal assent by letters patent signed in the king's hand and placed under the Great Seal of England. By this means, Henry authorised his wife's death warrant, the Act then to be executed 'with convenient speed'.

The next clauses concerned Agnes, Dowager Duchess of Norfolk, her relatives and retainers who now languished in the Tower. They were each attainted, sentenced to perpetual imprisonment and their property forfeited to the king. Once again, Henry was to approve these attainders by letters patent placed under the Great Seal.

Provision was next made to pardon all those who had been concerned with the detection of the queen's crimes and those of her accomplices. This applied to Mary and John Lascelles, who had initially revealed the facts of the queen's past life, as well as Archbishop Cranmer, who had written the note that had first alerted Henry to Katherine's past. The clause also applied to those who had 'by their words spoken, uttered and published, but also in their deeds done and devised and set forth by writing' been involved in bringing 'this High Treason to light'. This concerned William, Earl of Southampton, Thomas Wriothesley and others who had interrogated witnesses, written out the testimonies and drawn up the indictments. They were 'pardoned, acquitted and discharged' for having carried out these duties 'against the King's Highness, his heirs and successors for ever'. This was a safeguard designed to ensure that those engaged in the detection of crimes would not, in future, be themselves implicated should the attainders be reversed.

The most malevolent part of the Act were the clauses that made it mandatory for anyone who knew of any past 'lightness of body in her which for the time being shall be Queen' to disclose what they know, although they should not 'openly blow it abroad nor privately whisper it in other folk's ears'. If they did not do so within twenty days, they would 'have like punishment and forfeiture as the offenders should'. Furthermore, if this king or any of his successors 'should take a fancy' to any woman 'in way of marriage, thinking and esteeming her a pure and clean maid', that lady should, if she were unchaste, declare this fact to the king. If she did not, she would be judged guilty of high treason, with all the penalties such a charge attracted, including death.

Finally, Katherine's Act of Attainder made consensual adultery in a queen an act of treason. Until then, provision had been made only for 'violation' of the queen. In other words, Katherine was sentenced to die by the very Act that had created the law under which she was condemned. This Act and the Act for lunatics were duly signed by the king in his own hand, upon which they were added to the statutes. Katherine's death warrant, having received the royal assent, became law.

When this was done the Duke of Suffolk, speaking on behalf

of the delegation he had led the previous day, rose and addressed the Lords. He announced that Katherine had 'openly confessed and acknowledged to them the great crime she had been guilty of' against God, the king, and the whole English nation. She begged them 'to implore His Majesty not to impute her crime' to her family, but that 'however unworthy she might be and undeserving', the king would 'extend his unbounded mercy and his singular beneficence to all her brothers, that they might not suffer for her faults'. She then asked them to beseech Henry to bestow some of her clothes on those maidservants who had been with her since the time of her marriage, 'since she had now nothing else left to recompense them as they deserved'. At this point, Suffolk sat down and the Earl of Southampton rose to speak. He confirmed Suffolk's words and added some of his own, but these were not recorded.[17] Then, it being a Saturday, the Parliament was prorogued until the following Tuesday.

There was only a short while to go now. Although she had been treated with the dignity of a queen throughout her ordeal, Katherine was unable to maintain her composure. Ambassador Marillac heard that, since she arrived at the Tower, 'she weeps, cries, and torments herself miserably, without ceasing'. So distraught was she that the ambassador, who expected her to be executed 'this week', speculated – a horrific thought – that her death would be 'deferred for three or four days' to allow her to recover and to compose her mind for the ordeal ahead.[18]

The merchant Otwell Johnson knew better. He wrote to his brother, John Johnson, a merchant of the Staple, that business had been held up because of 'provision of things for the Queen's household'. However, he expected that the situation 'will take an end very shortly for as tomorrow in the morning she is appointed to lose her life within the Tower aforesaid, where I am commanded to wait upon my master'.[19]

Johnson would be proved correct. On Sunday, 12 February, 'towards the evening', Sir John Gage, in his capacity of constable of the Tower, came to warn Katherine 'to dispose her soul and prepare for death, for she was to be beheaded next day'. Unlike Anne Boleyn before her, Katherine was to be executed with an axe. Her response was to ask to see the block because 'she wanted to know how she was to place her head on it'.[20]

This is not such an unreasonable request as it might appear. The axe was an awkward instrument which, if inexpertly wielded, could inflict terrible injury before the victim was finally killed, as had happened to the Countess of Salisbury. As to the block, there were two types in use: one was very low and would require Katherine to place her neck across it while lying on the ground; it would hardly be comfortable, and it would be difficult for the headsman to achieve an effective swing. The other type of block was higher, allowing Katherine to kneel against it and lean forward to place herself. This type, if nothing else, would make the headsman's task a little easier. The act of practising with the block would serve precisely the purpose Katherine gave, but it also allowed her to focus her mind on the minute details, providing a sense of control in a situation where, in reality, she had none. Her strange request was granted and the block was brought to her chamber. Katherine 'tried and placed her head on it by way of experiment'.

Katherine then made her confession.[21] She spoke of 'the miscarriages of her former life, before the king married her: but stood absolutely to her denial, as to any thing after that'. She 'took God and his angels to be her witnesses, upon salvation of her soul, that she was guiltless of that act of defiling her sovereign's bed, for which she was condemned'.

Early in the morning of Monday, 13 February, a crowd began to gather at the Tower: members of the Privy Council, foreign ambassadors and merchants working nearby.[22] Katherine's death was to be witnessed by the same men who had directed the process against her, who had interviewed the witnesses and drawn up the reports for the king, her husband, to view. Only the Duke of Suffolk, who was indisposed, and Norfolk were absent; Norfolk perhaps unable to face watching another of his nieces die. His son and Katherine's cousin, Henry, Earl of Surrey, did attend, as did several other lords and gentlemen. It can only be wondered whether John Lascelles stood among them to witness the results of an innocent remark made by his sister only a few months before; if so, he would witness an easier death than his own: he would be burned at the stake as a heretic in four years' time.

Katherine continued to be attended in her chamber as she prepared to die.[23] She was given breakfast before being dressed in a black velvet gown, one of those King Henry had allocated to her, the sombre colour of mourning befitting the cold and grey February dawn. A French hood, gloves of soft leather and a furred mantle finished the ensemble.

Soon the time came when all things of the world must pass. Just before the bells of St Peter ad Vincula were to chime nine o'clock, Sir John Gage went to the queen's lodgings to escort her on the short, final journey of her life. Leaving her chambers, Katherine emerged through the Coldharbour Gate, and passed the imposing White Tower on her right before arriving on Tower Green. Here, the scaffold awaited her. Some three to four feet high, draped in black, it stood on the same spot upon which Katherine's cousins, Queen Anne and Sir George Boleyn, had died not six years earlier. Katherine climbed the wooden steps, turned to face those who had come to witness her execution and addressed them.

There are two versions of the speech Katherine made on the scaffold. In one, the queen states:

> Brothers, by the journey upon which I am bound I have not wronged the King, but it is true that long before the King took me I loved Culpeper, and I wish to God I had done as he wished me, for at the time the King wanted to take me he urged me to say that I was pledged to him. If I had done as he advised me I should not die this death, nor would he. I would rather have him for a husband than be a mistress of the world, but sin blinded me and greed of grandeur, and since mine is the fault mine is also the suffering, and my great sorrow is that Culpeper should have to die through me.[24]

Katherine then turned to the headsman and bade him, 'Pray hasten with thy office.' He knelt before her and asked her pardon. Katherine's reply was 'I die a Queen, but I would rather die the wife of Culpeper. God have mercy on my soul. Good people, I beg you pray for me.' At that point, she fell to her knees and said her prayers. The headsman 'performed his office, striking off her head when she was not expecting it'.[25]

This story is wholly incorrect; it is so remarkable that, had it been true, it would have found its way into the reports of the ambassadors Marillac and Chapuys, and the accounts of other commentators on English affairs. As it was, Marillac reported that Katherine was 'so weak that she could hardly speak, but confessed in a few words that she merited a hundred deaths for so offending the King who had so graciously treated her'.[26] Naturally Katherine was fragile at this point, worn down as she was by prolonged fear, sleeplessness, the injustice of her situation and an overwhelming sense of helplessness. Chapuys, too, noted that Katherine had little to say, only confessing her guilt and praying for the king's welfare and prosperity.[27] In other words, her scaffold speech followed the standard pattern.

When Katherine had spoken, she handed the headsman a purse containing some coins: his fee and alms for the poor. Her ladies then removed her hood, gloves and mantle and caught her auburn hair into a white linen coif. Next, they bound her eyes with bandages so that she would not see the ground rising to meet her in those final few seconds before the darkness came. They then withdrew to the back of the scaffold. They still had one more duty to perform for their mistress.

Katherine knelt and said her prayers; then she positioned herself on the block just as she had rehearsed during the last short night of her life. Mercifully, the headsman removed her head with a single stroke of the axe. Katherine's ladies stepped forward now and covered her body with a black cloak before laying it to one side. The procedure was then repeated for Jane, Lady Rochford. Lady Jane, noted Chapuys, 'had shown symptoms of madness until the very moment when they announced to her that she must die'.[28] Now she was fully recovered and ready to face death with courage. She gave a 'long discourse of several faults which she committed in her life'.[29] Then, kneeling in the straw that was stained with the queen's blood, she too was beheaded.

A few days later, the merchant Otwell Johnson described the execution of Queen Katherine and Jane, Lady Rochford to his brother:

> I see the Queen and the lady Rochford suffer within the Tower . . . whose souls (I doubt not) be with God, for they made the most godly and Christians' end that ever was heard tell of (I think) since the world's creation, uttering their lively faith in the blood of Christ only, with wonderful patience and constancy to the death, and, with goodly words and steadfast countenance, they desired all Christian people to take regard unto their worthy and just punishment with death, for their offences against God heinously from their youth upward, in breaking of all his commandments, and also against the King's royal majesty very dangerously; wherefor they, being justly condemned (as they said), by the laws of the realm and Parliament, to die, required the people (I say) to take example at them for amendment of their ungodly lives, and gladly obey the King in all things, for whose preservation they did heartily pray, and willed all people so to do, commending their souls to God and earnestly calling for mercy upon Him, whom I beseech to give us grace with such faith, hope, and charity, at our departing out of this miserable world, to come to the fruition of his Godhead in joy everlasting. Amen.[30]

The mortal remains of Queen Katherine and Jane, Lady Rochford were carried to the nearby Chapel Royal of St Peter ad Vincula and buried in the sacred earth beneath the altar. The tragic young queen lies close to Anne Boleyn, George Boleyn, Jane, Lady Rochford and the Countess of Salisbury. On the floor a small plaque bears her name; it is the only memorial of Queen Katherine Howard.

Epilogue

~

K ATHERINE HOWARD HAD not been a queen long enough to allow history to judge her in that role. The evidence she left behind – her eagerness to show patronage, her intercession on behalf of felons, her willingness to fulfil her religious obligations and her kindness – suggests that she would have been as good a queen as any of Henry's wives.

It is equally difficult to speak of a legacy of Katherine Howard. Politically, her only significance lay in her replacement of Anne of Cleves as Henry's queen. The Cleves alliance had been forged primarily to secure a treaty between England and the duchy of Cleves with France against the Emperor Charles. As such, the idle gossip that Henry was thinking of dismissing Katherine and taking back Anne greatly alarmed the imperial ambassador, Chapuys, who referred to it several times and vowed to do all in his power to prevent it. For the same reason, it very much pleased the French ambassador, Marillac.

As it turned out, Katherine's fears that Henry would repudiate her were unfounded. Anne, having heard of her successor's fall, made her way to Richmond to be closer to the king. The Cleves ambassador, Karl Harst, was instructed to promote her cause with Henry and the council. In the end, it was made clear to him that the divorce had been based on just causes and that 'the king would never take back the said lady'.[1]

Katherine's true importance lay in the effect she had on the many lives she touched. For Henry Mannock, she was a plaything who enabled him to sow his wild oats in the last few months before marriage and responsibility.

For Francis Dereham, Katherine was the means to advancement, an alliance with an influential ducal house that would bring him prosperity and position. Then, having lost her to the king, he was angry and resentful, as his behaviour while a member of her household attests. His later testimony spoke of their relationship as it had once been and hinted at his unwavering belief that Katherine was still his wife and he had right of access to her. In spite of this, he honoured her royal marriage and did nothing to press himself upon her. Nevertheless, it was Katherine's relationship with Dereham that had spoiled her for the king, who thought she had been his alone; for this and the presumption that he had intended to renew his relations with the queen, Dereham was sent to a cruel and horrific death.

For Katherine, Thomas Culpeper was a kinsman who became a friend and then a suitor. Although married to the king, Katherine trusted him enough to renew their friendship at a time when she was worried about the king; even so, she kept it within the strict bounds of propriety. It was only when Culpeper sought to see Katherine privately that their friendship took on a more dangerous hue. Previously, any interaction between them could be seen as familial and innocent; that was no longer a possibility once Culpeper insisted on visiting Katherine in her chamber after hours and away from the prying eyes of other courtiers and household staff. In the end, it was Culpeper's words that condemned them both, as well as Lady Rochford, whose affection for the young man led her to believe in his honesty.

As to King Henry, he was captivated by Katherine's beauty, dazzled by her sparkle and enraptured by her charm. For him, Katherine represented something he thought was lost to him for ever: his precious youth. From the moment she came into his life, he was a new man. He was revitalised, looking forward once again to a glorious and happy future where previously he had seen nothing but an insecure succession shrouded in the encroaching twilight of old age. Henry dressed his beloved in the finest clothes, showered her with glittering jewels and indulged her every whim. His love for Katherine was intense, matched only by the anger and hatred that overwhelmed him when he thought his beautiful jewel had betrayed him. It could lead in only one direction, and that was Katherine's cold and bloody death on the scaffold.

Henry felt Katherine's loss keenly. It shook his faith in womanhood, and he turned for solace to God, with whom he so often spoke. In his copy of Miles Coverdale's translation of the Scriptures, he found the words that reflected his feelings, and he highlighted one passage in particular: 'for the lips of a loose woman drip honey, and her speech is smoother than oil; but in the end she is bitter as wormwood, sharp as a two edged sword'.[2] Still, the bereaved king took to socialising with ladies, much as he had done following the fall of Anne Boleyn; it was his way of focusing his anger and soothing his injured masculinity.

In the end, perhaps the person most affected by Katherine's death was her stepdaughter, Elizabeth. Although the child had not had time to become very close to the young queen, she was acutely aware, as she could not have been in her mother's case, of what it meant to be executed for treason. Katherine's death at the hands of her husband was cited as one of the reasons why Elizabeth refused to marry; and the death of Elizabeth brought with it the end of the remarkable Tudor dynasty.[3]

Katherine Howard had barely begun to make her mark on the world stage when she was swept aside in a catastrophic series of events that are only now beginning to be fully understood. Like a butterfly, her existence was ephemeral. She lived for so short a time, yet she left an indelible trace, a memory of her that is both charming and tragic.

Acknowledgements

~

My interest in Katherine Howard began many years ago when I read the story of a young queen who practised her own execution on the night before she was to die. I found someone who could do such a thing intriguing, and I wanted to know all about her. What was she like? How had she lived her life, and what had brought her to such a terrible death?

Over the years my interest grew and, as I read more about Katherine Howard, I found that there were many contradictions in the accounts, and much that had yet to be told. I felt her story deserved to be more than just a diversion, personal reading to pass the time and, as circumstances allowed, I gradually turned it into a project and then reached out to people who could help me bring it to fruition.

Writing is a solitary experience, yet every author relies on a network of people without whom their books would remain scribbled jottings in pretty notebooks or aimless musings on a computer. I am deeply grateful for the help and support of all those who understood the allure of Katherine Howard and her tragic life: my agent, Andrew Lownie, Roland Philipps and Becky Walsh of John Murray, and Alison Weir for her encouragement. I gratefully acknowledge the Society of Authors' Authors' Foundation for granting me an award which greatly assisted my research. I also thank the staff of the various libraries visited during the research and writing of this biography, particularly at the universities of Newcastle and York for allowing me access to books in their special collections. Finally, I would like to express my gratitude to the staff at the National Archives, who granted me the privilege of consulting the primary documents, sewn into beautiful leather-bound volumes, concerning Katherine and those associated with her. Nothing can ever compare with seeing the actual writings of the people whose history this is; their voices are made louder and clearer by the simple act of handling and reading the papers they left.

Dr Josephine Wilkinson
Kew, December 2015

Illustration Credits

~

Notes

~

1. A Calamitous Childhood

1. Tusser, xxxviii, f.49.
2. Howard, p.12; Head (p.14) suggests 1479.
3. Hall, p.511.
4. Hopwood, vol. 1, p.35.
5. *Letters and Papers* (henceforth *LP*) I, 1661.
6. Not marshal of the horse as is sometimes said. 'Host' simply refers to an armed company of men, an army.
7. Hall, p.562.
8. *LP* I, 2246 (4 ii).
9. Ibid., 3325.
10. Anne, daughter of Thomas Howard and Agnes Tylney: *Visitations of Norfolk*, vol. 2, p.16.
11. *LP* I, 3348 (3).
12. Ibid., 3483 (iii).
13. *LP* II (ii), 'The King's Book of Payments', p.1463. This loan was worth more than three times the Duke of Suffolk's half-year wages.
14. Smith, p.19.
15. Noble, online.
16. Hall, pp.589–91.
17. Ibid., p.600.
18. *LP* II (ii), 'The King's Book of Payments', p.1473.
19. Nichols, *Chronicle of Calais*, p.21.
20. Ibid., p.26.
21. Ibid., pp.31–2.
22. Elyot, vol. 1, p.29.
23. *Surrey Archaeological Collections*, LI, p.87.

24. Ibid., p.89.
25. The letter Sir Edmund wrote to Wolsey is not dated, but it is calen-dared in *LP* at December 1527, which means that the wife referred to might have been Jocasta, who was still alive as of May of that year, when her mother's will was proved. Since it is not known precisely when Jocasta died, it is equally possible that the wife concerned was Dorothy Troyes.
26. Ellis, third series, vol. 1, pp.160–3; this letter is printed in a much abbreviated form in *LP* IV, 3731, 3732.
27. Sir Edmund was supporting his own children by Jocasta Culpeper, including Katherine, as well as some of Jocasta's children from her previous marriage.
28. Brenan and Statham, vol. 1, p.243. This sister was Elizabeth Barham at Barham Court by Teston, near Maidstone.
29. Dorothy Howard's will is printed in an abbreviated form in *Surrey Archaeological Collections*, III, p.174.
30. *LP* V, 220 (14). The post is believed by some to have been awarded to him following intervention on his behalf by his niece, Anne Boleyn, whose influence with King Henry was now firmly established. It is not possible to verify or disprove this.
31. Ibid.,1042.
32. Margaret Jennings is the unnamed wife referred to in *LP* XI, 1098.
33. *LP* VII, 1179.
34. Nichols, *Chronicle of Calais*, p.183.
35. *LP* VII, 1219.
36. *LP* XIV, 906 (17); £80 in the 1530s is about £25,768 in today's money.
37. *LP* XIII (i), 465.
38. *LP* XII (ii), 466.
39. *LP* XIII, 717.
40. *LP* VIII, 1083, 1103.
41. It is not certain who this man was; he does not appear to be the Sir Robert Bowes of the Council of the North, who maintained his post from 1537 onwards.
42. *LP* XIV (i), 172.
43. Edmund had died before 29 April 1539, *LP* XIV (i), 906 (17).

2. Being but a Young Girl

1. Brenan and Statham, vol. 1, p.268.
2. *Visitations of Surrey*, p.21.
3. *LP* IV, 5778 (ii).
4. 'Horsham: Manors and other estates', *A History of the County of Sussex*, vol. 6, part 2: Bramber Rape (North-Western Part) including Horsham (1986), pp.156, 157–8.
5. Brenan and Statham, vol. 1, p.269.
6. Malyn Tylney's maiden name was Chamber. It is possible that she was the sister of Minster Chamber, who was a servant in Lord William's household. Edmund, the son of Philip and Malyn Tylney, was born in 1536 and would serve at the court of Elizabeth I (Dutton). Philip Tylney was one of the constabulary of Calais; see *LP* XV, 608 (p.275).
7. *LP* XVI, 1337.
8. Mother Emet is mentioned by Margaret Benet: TNA SP 1/167/155–6.
9. As will be seen, Agnes would later express the fear that Katherine would be sent back to her house, a prospect she did not relish. Also, on at least one occasion, Katherine had no qualms about speaking sharply to her step-grandmother, rebuking her for mistrusting her and Dereham (*LP* XVI, 1416; unfortunately, the original source for this is largely destroyed).
10. Wood, vol. 2, p.29.

3. Flattering and Fair Persuasions

1. *Calendar of State Papers, Spanish* (henceforth *CSP Sp.*) V (ii): item 35. Dr Ortiz had been Katherine of Aragon's proctor.
2. *LP* X, 200; Wriothesley also said that the king 'took no hurt' (*Chronicle*, p.33).
3. *LP* X, 282; Wriothesley had heard that Anne herself reckoned that she had been 'fiftene weekes gonne with chield' at the time of her miscarriage (*Chronicle*, p.33).
4. *LP* X, 282.

5. *CSP Sp.* V (ii), 29.

6. *LP* X, 282.

7. *CSP Sp.* V (ii), 29.

8. Muir, pp.208–9.

9. Ives, pp.14–15; Paget, p.166; *Correspondance de Maximilien et Marguerite*, vol. 2, p.461, n.2.

10. Byrne, vol. 4, pp.163, 199. Such matters were prescribed in Mrs Pole's 'book of reckoning'.

11. Russell, pp.63, 64.

12. Copinger, vol. 1, p.221. There is no reason to suppose that Henry Mannock is the same man who entered Parliament in Huntingdonshire in 1554. Katherine's music teacher was married and living with his wife by 1538 (see below and at *LP* XVI, 1416); Henry Mannock, MP is estimated to have been born *c.*1526, and was, therefore, too young to have married in 1538 (Bindoff, vol. 2, pp.564–5). It is entirely possible, however, that the two men were related.

13. Henry's father, George Mannock, was the son of John Mannock, who had married a daughter of Sir Thomas Waldegrave. George, in his turn, married Katherine Waldegrave, daughter of Sir William Waldegrave (Copinger, vol. 1, p.221; *Visitations of Suffolk*, p.151).

14. TNA SP 1/167/138 and 161: examination and confessions of Henry Mannock.

15. *LP* VI, 923.

16. *LP* XII (ii), 952.

17. Henry had, of course 'meddled' with Anne's sister Mary, who had been his mistress.

18. TNA SP 1/167/138 and 161: examination and confessions of Henry Mannock.

19. 'Confession of the Queen Katherine Howard', HMC, *Bath*, p.9.

20. *LP* XVI, 1334.

21. Today, Mannock would be guilty of sexual harassment and abuse. In the Tudor period there was no concept of child sexual abuse, and the term itself was not coined until very recently. This, however, does nothing to diminish Katherine's ordeal at Mannock's hands. The idea that Katherine was sexually abused was first promoted by Denny (pp. 86, 88–9, 115–16).

22. Schroeder, pp. 51, 63, 67, 95–6; McLaren, *Reproductive Rituals*, p.20.

23. TNA SP 1/167/135: examination of Henry Mannock.

24. *LP* X, 953, Lady Worcester is mentioned as Anne's chief accuser, along with Nan Cobham and 'one maid more'; *LP* X, 964, Lady Worcester is named as Anne's principal accuser.

25. *CSP Sp.* V (ii), 61.

26. *LP* X, 876.

27. Ibid., 793.

28. *CSP Sp.* V (ii), 54, 55; *LP* X, 909.

29. Wriothesley, pp. 40–1.

30. The grounds for the annulment of Anne's marriage will never be known; Cranmer never gave them and the papers pertaining to the case have disappeared.

4. 'To play the fool'

1. Brenan and Statham, vol. 1, pp.271–2.

2. *LP* XVI, 1320.

3. TNA SP 1/167/129: confession of Mary Lascelles.

4. Ibid.

5. Thomas, p.117.

6. *LP* XII (ii), 1004.

7. Ibid.

8. *LP* XII (ii), 1187.

9. Madge, or Mary, Shelton was youngest daughter of Sir John Shelton (*c.*1477–1539) of Norfolk. Sir John's wife was Anne Boleyn (d. 1555), the sister of Sir Thomas Boleyn, making her the queen's aunt.

10. *LP* XIII (i), 123.

11. *CSP Sp.* V (ii), 220. Chapuys would shortly leave court on assignment. He would return on 13 July (*State Papers, Henry VIII*, VIII, 400; *LP* XV, 885).

12. *LP* XIV (i), 1014.

13. Byrne, vol. 5, pp.491, 615–16, 665; *LP* XIV (i), 1014; XIV (ii), 22, 284.

14. Byrne, vol. 5, p.666; *CSP Sp.* VI (i), 468.

15. *LP* XII (ii), 922, 923.

16. Ibid., 1060.

5. Francis Dereham

1. *LP* XIII (i), 995; Castillon was writing on 14 May 1538.
2. Ibid., 1135.
3. Marie de Guise married James V by proxy in May 1538, and arrived in Scotland the following month. Her daughter, the future Mary, Queen of Scots, was born in 1542.
4. *LP* XIII (i), 1132.
5. Ibid., 387.
6. Ibid., 1133.
7. Ibid., 1126. As Supreme Head of the Church in England, Henry had competence to issue dispensations in such cases. However, in this case, he would be required to dispense his own affinity in order to allow him to marry one of his own relatives.
8. *LP* XIV (ii), 400; 'Memorial from George Constantine', pp.60–1.
9. *LP* XIII (i), 994.
10. Ibid., 1135.
11. Ibid., 1355.
12. *LP* XIII (ii), 77.
13. Brenan and Statham, vol. 1, p.272.
14. Hasted, vol. 12, p.349.
15. Blomefield, vol. 7, pp.310–14, 321–38.
16. Ibid., p.325. Philip had three daughters, Maud, Grace and Marion, but it is not clear which of them was Dereham's grandmother.
17. See http://www.sonic.net/~fredd/cousins.html. Dereham was connected to other members of the duchess's household. He was related by marriage to Mary Lascelles, who served Duchess Agnes at Lambeth. Mary's brother, George, was married to Dorothy, the daughter of John Paynell of Boothby Pagnell in Lincolnshire. Dereham's mother, Isabel, was also a daughter of John Paynell of Boothby. Moreover, the second wife of Dereham's grandfather was Jane (or Joan), daughter of a John Bennett (*Visitations of Norfolk*, vol. 2, p.227). Unfortunately, it is not known if she was related to the Margaret Benet who served Duchess Agnes.
18. *Visitations of Norfolk*, vol. 2, p.228. Dereham's father is called John in some sources and Thomas in others.

19. Ibid.

20. Strickland, vol. 3, p.113.

21. For the duties of a gentleman usher, see Banks, pp.321–5. If the duchess also employed a steward or comptroller, he would share some of his duties with Dereham.

22. Slightly younger than Dereham, Waldegrave was born in 1514–15, the third son of George Waldegrave and Anne Drury. He is not to be confused with Edward Waldegrave, MP, courtier and administrator, who served Mary I.

23. William Bulmer, Esquire, was the son of Sir William Bulmer, Warden of the East Marches and Steward of the Household to Henry Fitzroy, Duke of Richmond, in the Council of the North. Although Bulmer had been ordered by the Privy Council to return to his wife, the couple would part for good after Katherine's fall. Part of this process can be followed in *Acts of the Privy Council*, vol. 1, pp.48, 81, 82, 89, 148, 151. Reid, p.292n., confuses the elder William Bulmer with his son.

24. *LP* XVI, 1321: testimony of Henry Mannock.

25. 'Examination of Q. Katherine Howard' in Burnet, vol. 4, p.505.

26. Ibid.

27. 'Confession of the Queen Katherine Howard', HMC *Bath*, p.9.

28. Katherine displays some of the symptoms of sexual abuse accommodation syndrome; see Summit.

29. TNA SP 1/167/156: confession of Edward Waldegrave.

30. TNA SP 1/167/156: confession of Malyn Tylney.

31. TNA SP 1/167/161: confession of Robert Damport.

32. TNA SP 1/167/162: confession of Joan Bulmer.

33. TNA SP 1/167/151: confession of Andrew Maunsay.

34. TNA SP 1/167/161: confession of Robert Damport.

35. TNA SP 1/167/155: confession of Margaret Benet.

36. TNA SP 1/167/162: confession of Joan Bulmer.

37. TNA SP 1/167/155–6: confession of Margaret Benet. The word 'private' is partly cyphered. Joan Bulmer also spoke of Dereham going with Katherine to the jakes (TNA SP 1/167/162).

38. Kirkman, p.176.

39. *The Works of Aristotle*, p.19; see also Greene, part 1, f.8.

40. TNA SP 1/167/155–6; Malyn Tylney overheard a similar conversation (TNA SP 1/167/156).

41. Langham, p.680.
42. Dr Layton to Cromwell, in Wright, p.97; The story of Onan is in Genesis 38.
43. TNA SP 1/167/155–6.
44. Chaucer, *The Parson's Tale*, lines 575–6.
45. McLaren, *Reproductive Rituals*, pp. 19–21, 26–8, 146. This belief prevailed at least until the pre-Enlightenment dawn of the seventeenth century, when scientific principles began to be developed.
46. TNA SP 1/168/87–9; *LP* XVI, 1469.
47. TNA SP 1/168/87–9; *LP* XVI, 1416, 1469.
48. Nicolas, *Proceedings and Ordinances of the Privy Council of England* (henceforth *PCC*) VII, p.353.
49. TNA SP 1/167/130: testimony of Mary Lascelles.
50. *CSP Sp.* VI (i), 209.
51. 'Examination of Q. Katherine Howard' in Burnet, vol. 4, p.505.
52. Kelly, p.275; Finch, p.189.
53. *LP* XVI, 1416 (2).
54. TNA SP 1/168/87–9; TNA SP 1/168/87–9; *LP* XVI, 1469.
55. 'Examination of Q. Katherine Howard' in Burnet, vol. 4, p.504.
56. Ibid., p.505.
57. Ibid., p.504.
58. *LP* XVI, 1423. Mr Ashby referred to Master Molyneux, a variant of Mannock.
59. TNA SP 1/167/136: deposition of Henry Mannock. In this context, secretary means confidant.
60. *LP* XVI, 1400.
61. TNA SP 1/167/137: deposition of Henry Mannock.
62. TNA SP/1/167/135–8: confession of Henry Mannock; TNA SP 1/167/155: confession of Anne Howard; TNA SP 1/167/162: confession of John Lascelles.
63. *LP* XVI, 1416.
64. TNA SP 1/168/21–2; *LP* XVI, 1385; *LP* XVI, 1416 (2), TNA SP 1/168/87–9; *LP* XVI, 1469.
65. *LP* XVI, 1416 (2).
66. TNA SP 1/168/21–2; *LP* XVI, 1385; *LP* XVI, 1416 (2), TNA SP 1/168/87–9; *LP* XVI, 1469.

6. A Lady in Waiting

1. Wriothesley, pp.99–100.
2. *State Papers, Henry VIII*, VIII, p.5; *LP* XII (ii), 1172.
3. *LP* IV, 6364.
4. *State Papers, Henry VIII*, I, p.605; *LP* XIV (i), 552.
5. *LP* XIV (i), 920.
6. Ibid., (ii), 33, 117.
7. Ibid., (i), 920, 1193; (ii), 33.
8. Ibid., (ii), 169, 222, 328.
9. Ibid., 286.
10. Ibid., 572 (4).
11. Byrne, vol. 4, p.895.
12. Ibid., vol. 6, p.34.
13. *LP* XVI, 1409 (1).
14. 'Examination of Q. Katherine Howard' in Burnet, vol. 4, p.505.
15. Ibid.
16. TNA SP 1/168/87–9; *LP* XVI, 1469.
17. 'Examination of Q. Katherine Howard' in Burnet, vol. 4, p.505.
18. Byrne, vol. 4, pp.192–3, 198. Katherine's salary of £10 a year translates to about £3,075 today.
19. TNA E101/422/15.
20. Katherine's debt to Dereham amounted to roughly £1,650 today.
21. Byrne, vol. 4, 895, pp.192–3.
22. TNA SP 1/168/45.
23. Brathwaite, pp.139, 141.
24. *LP* XII (ii), 271.
25. Mary Howard, Duchess of Richmond, was the daughter of Thomas Howard, Duke of Norfolk, and therefore Katherine's cousin. She was the widow of Henry Fitzroy, the king's illegitimate son by Bessie Blount.
26. *LP* XIV (ii), 572 (1).
27. *LP* XVI, 14; Nichols, *Chronicle of Calais*, p.175.
28. *LP* XV, 850 (7). Sir Anthony Browne, one of Henry's confidants, had the dubious honour of being privy to the king's most intimate thoughts. A different version of the meeting is offered in Wriothesley (pp.109–10).

29. Sir Thomas Manners, Lord Roos, created Earl of Rutland 18 June 1525. He would serve both Anne of Cleves and Katherine Howard as chamberlain.
30. Katherine, Duchess of Suffolk, was the wife of King Henry's close companion Charles Brandon, Duke of Suffolk.
31. Hall, p.833
32. Ibid., p.836.
33. Ibid., pp.833–4.

7. In the Service of Anne of Cleves

1. *LP* XIV (ii), 718.
2. *LP* XV 850 (7).
3. Ibid.
4. Merriman, vol. 2, pp.270–2.
5. Wriothesley, p.111.
6. Kaulek, p.142; *LP* XIV (ii), 449.
7. *LP* XIV (ii), 732.
8. *LP* XV, 233; *State Papers, Henry VIII*, VIII, pp. 245–52, 254–60, 265–8; *LP* XV, 202, 222–4, 253; Merriman, vol. 2, pp.250–55.
9. TNA SP 1/168/87–9; *LP* XVI, 1469.
10. *Visitations of Kent*, 1619–21, p.62.
11. By 1533 Culpeper was in a position to have servants, one of whom was his cousin, Jasper Culpeper, the son of Richard Culpeper of Wakehurst (Bindoff, vol. 1, pp.737–8). That Culpeper appointed Jasper can be attributed to the moral obligation resting upon people in higher positions to advance one's relatives wherever possible.
12. Wilson, pp.115–16.
13. Ibid., p.116.
14. See, for example, awards and grants to Culpeper in *LP* VI, 1595 (25); *LP* XII (ii), 975; *LP* XII (ii), 1150 (31); *LP* XIII (i), 1; *LP* XIV, 781 (68); *LP* XVI, 380 (125); *LP* XVI, 264 (16), 1056 (28).
15. Letter from Richard Hilles to Henry Bullinger, printed in *Original Letters*, pp.226–7.
16. André, le chapelain, p.150.
17. Cavendish, vol. 2, pp.68–70.

18. 'Examination of Q. Katherine Howard', in Burnet, vol. 4, p.505.

19. Hume, *Chronicle of Henry VIII*, pp.75–6.

20. MacCulloch, p.258

21. Strype, vol. 1 (ii), p.437; *State Papers, Henry VIII*, VIII, p.234; *LP* XV, 243.

22. *LP* XV, 248 (p.91).

23. Bernard, p.561.

24. *LP* XV, 334, 401, 425.

25. Merriman, vol. 2, p.266.

26. Easter Sunday fell on 28 March (*LP* XV, note to entry 480).

27. *LP* XIII (ii), 847.

28. Brigden, p.378.

29. Thomas Wyatt was related to John Legh through the Skinner family of Reigate; see Brigden, pp.75, 680, n.116. By extension, Wyatt was also distantly related to Katherine Howard.

30. Muir, p.180.

31. *LP* XV, 369.

32. Merriman, vol. 2, p.260.

33. *LP* XV, 613 (12).

34. Ibid., 686.

35. Wriothesley, p.118.

36. Ibid., p.117.

37. Merriman, vol. 2, p.271.

38. Ibid.

39. Merriman, vol. 2, pp.266–7; *LP* XV, 776 (p.366). The timing coincides with the departure of Anne's 'strange maidens' to Cleves (*LP* XVI, 380, f.133b).

40. Strype, vol. 1 (ii), p.460. The account of the fall of Cromwell, intriguing though it is, is too extensive and multifaceted to relate here. The best treatments can be found in Bernard, pp.556–79 and Schofield, pp.337–413.

41. Kaulek, p. 134; *LP* XV, 123.

42. Kaulek, p.174; *LP* XV, 401.

43. Kaulek, pp.176–7; *LP* XV, 487.

44. Kaulek, pp.179–80; *LP* XV, 567.

45. Kaulek, pp.180–1; *LP* XV, 625, 626.

46. 2 June. *LP* XV, 831 (33).

47. Bouterwek, pp.163–4.

48. Kaulek, p.199; *LP* XV, 848.

49. Letter from Richard Hilles to Henry Bullinger, printed *Original Letters*, vol. 1, pp.201–2.

50. *LP* XVI, 660; Strickland, vol. 3, p.159.

51. It is no longer accepted that Gardiner was interested in promoting the interests of the Howards. Similarly, there is no evidence to suggest that Norfolk and Gardiner collaborated, whether to assist in Henry's courtship of Katherine or to bring down Cromwell. See, for example, Redworth, pp.118–20; Bernard, pp.557–8.

52. *LP* XVI, 1409 (3).

53. *LP* XV, 821, 822.

54. MacCulloch, pp.271–2; see also Harpsfield, p.263 *et seq.*

55. *Statutes of the Realm*, III, 32 Henry VIII, cap. 38, p.792.

56. See Kelly, p.263.

57. *LP* XV, 843.

58. Kaulek, pp.200–1; *LP* XV, 850.

59. Strype, vol. 1 (ii), p.461. The 1540 edition of the book, *The Byrth of Mankynde*, which was originally intended to be dedicated to Anne of Cleves, contained an expanded discussion of fertility remedies. By the time the book was ready, however, Anne of Cleves had been replaced by Katherine Howard.

60. Ibid., p.462.

61. *LP* XV, 860, 861. The Cleves marriage would be finally dissolved on 29 July 1540 (*LP* XV, 909, 925, 930, 943).

62. *State Papers, Henry VIII*, VIII, pp.398–9; *LP* XV, 886. Richard Pate's letter is dated 13 July, showing how quickly, and how far, news and rumour could spread.

63. Although a widow, Mary was still a maid because her late husband had been too ill to consummate the marriage. As such, she had never really been married and was eligible to marry Henry (Wriothesley, p.54).

64. TNA SP 1/161/101–2.

65. Strickland (vol. 3, p.119) incorrectly gives this man's name as Seaford.

66. *LP* XVI, 1317.

67. *LP* XVI, 1409 (9); Agnes was asked whether she had reported any special commendation of Katherine to anyone, implying it was believed that she had.

68. Kaulek, p.202; *LP* XV, 901. Marillac wrote on 21 July 1540.
69. Kaulek, p.203; *LP* XV, 902.
70. *LP* XV, 900.
71. Ibid., 916; the belief that Katherine was pregnant when she married Henry would continue.
72. *CSP Ven.* V, 226; *LP* XV, 916; *LP* XV, 981.
73. *LP* XVI, 84.

8. A New Howard Queen

1. Words spoken by Jane Rattsey upon learning that King Henry was to marry Katherine Howard (*LP* XVI, 1407).
2. Kaulek, p.218; *LP* XVI, 12.
3. Wriothesley, p.123.
4. Ibid., p.120.
5. *LP* XVIII (i), 873.
6. *LP* XV, 686.
7. Kaulek, p.210; *LP* XV, 953. Marillac's letter is dated 6 August 1540. Henry's visit to Anne had inspired the more cynical and malicious members of the court to speculate that he had changed his mind about marrying Katherine and wanted to take back Anne. Later, another malicious rumour would have it that Anne was pregnant, presumably the result of this encounter (Kaulek, p.231; *LP* XVI, 142).
8. Hall, p.840; cf. Wriothesley (pp.121–2), who thought that Katherine and Henry had married on this date at Hampton Court.
9. Kaulek, pp.213–14; *LP* XV, 976.
10. Such as Katherine Grey, the granddaughter of the Duke and Duchess of Suffolk and sister of Lady Jane (de Lisle, p.320, n.3).
11. Nothing further is known about these two ladies, although Lufkyn may have been the daughter of George Lovekyn, the comptroller of the King's Works at Greenwich. Mistress Lufkyn appears to have left Katherine's service or Katherine dismissed her, as she had threatened to do. Her name does not appear among those questioned after Katherine's arrest.
12. Lady Lucy had also worked as a chamberer for the Dowager Duchess of Norfolk; see *LP* XVI, 1337.

13. Howard, p.12; Fox, pp.7, 9–10.

14. Bindoff, vol. 1, p.338

15. Kaulek, p.367; *LP* XVI, 1366.

16. *LP* Addendum I (ii), 1513.

17. *CSP Sp.* VI (i), 223.

18. Kaulek, p.214; *LP* XV, 976.

19. *LP* XV, 848 (p.419).

20. Nicolas, *PPC* VII, pp.8–68.

21. Ibid., pp.16–17.

22. Kaulek, p.218; *LP* XVI, 12.

23. Hume, *Chronicle of Henry VIII*, p.77.

24. Byrne, vol. 4, 887 (p.152).

25. Starkey, *Six Wives*, p.810, n.17; Brooke, pp.175, 176; cf. Strickland (vol. 3, p.122), who misinterpreted the image and motto on the coinage.

26. Wayment, p.115; Siddons, vol. 2, lists the wives of Henry VIII and their heraldic badges, but gives no entry for Katherine Howard.

27. Ampthill Castle Community Archaeology Project: http://www.ampthill.info/AmpthillParkArchaeologicalDigReport.pdf.

28. Kaulek, p.223; *LP* XVI, 59.

29. *LP* XVI, 69.

30. Ibid., 1389, from BL Stowe MS, 559.

31. Carley, p.134.

32. *LP* XVI, 1389.

33. Nicolas, *PPC* VII, p.39.

34. *LP* XVI, 107 (34).

35. http://list.english-heritage.org.uk/resultsingle.aspx?uid=1015595.

36. *LP* XVI, 128, 787 (49).

37. Ibid., 1416 (2).

9. Royal Children

1. Kaulek, p.239; *LP* XVI, 223 (p.100); Nicolas, *PPC* VII, p.68.

2. Many thanks to Alison Weir for confirming this point.

3. *State Papers, Henry VIII*, VIII, p.462; *LP* XVI, 204.

4. *State Papers, Henry VIII*, VIII, p.475; *LP* XVI, 240 (p.105).

5. *State Papers, Henry VIII*, VIII, p.494; *LP* XVI, 306.

6. Nucius of Corcyra, p.48.

7. See Starkey, *Six Wives*, pp.xxv, 650; cf. Dolman, pp.124–6 for an alternative view.

8. Colvin, vol. 3, 193–4; Wayment, p.57.

9. *LP* XVI, 121.

10. Kaulek, p.247; *LP* XVI, 311; *State Papers, Henry VIII*, I, p.690. Sir Thomas Henneage was chief gentleman of the privy chamber.

11. *LP* XVI, 5.

12. Kaulek, p.242; *LP* XVI, 269; Redworth, p.134.

13. Kaulek, p.242; *LP* XVI, 269.

14. See, for example, *LP* XV, 821.

15. Carley, pp.134–7.

16. Ballentyne, p.302.

17. TNA KB 8/13/2 (Court of King's Bench, Crown Side: *Baga de Secretis*), in which it is incorrectly stated that the encounter took place at Oatlands.

18. Marillac (Kaulek, p.370; *LP* XVI, 1426) states that, when Dereham came to court, he brought with him 'the woman who had been his accomplice before', that is, Katherine Tylney. This is not strictly true: Tylney joined Katherine's household on 29 November 1540, while Dereham did not enter the queen's service until the following August (see below). This is confirmed by the transcripts of the trial of Culpeper and Dereham in the *Baga de Secretis* (TNA KB 8/13/1; printed in 'Appendix II of the Third Report of the Deputy Keeper of the Public Records', pp.264–5 and summarised in *LP* XVI, 1470). Elsewhere, Marget Morton (TNA SP/167/162; *LP* XVI, 1338, p.618) suggests that Katherine Tylney entered Katherine's service later than the other ladies and maidens. William Pewson (TNA SP 1/168/93; *LP* XVI, 1415) suggests that Tylney was closely associated with Dereham, Culpeper, Damport and Lady Rochford, all of whom were Queen Katherine's alleged accomplices.

19. Hume, *Chronicle of Henry VIII*, p.76.

20. *CSP Sp.* VI (i), 143; *LP* XVI, 314.

21. Porter, pp.90–1; *CSP Sp.* IV (ii), 1133; *CSP Sp.* VI (i), 151.

22. For the enmity between Princess Mary and Anne Boleyn, see Porter, pp.51, 74, 101.
23. *LP* XVI, 316.
24. Ibid., 1389.
25. Nicolas, *PCC* VII, p.89; *LP* XVI, 325.
26. *LP* XVI, 1389.

10. The First Christmas

1. Kaulek, p.253; *LP* XVI, 373.
2. Kaulek, p.255; *LP* XVI, 374.
3. Nicolas, *Privy Purse Expenses*, p.83: 'Item to Cornishe for setting of a carralle upon Cristmas day in reward.' The term 'carol' described a ring-dance and the songs that accompanied it. The songs were not always religious, some were quite bawdy.
4. Hutton, pp.14–15.
5. *LP* XVI, 1389, from BL Stowe MS, 559. Katherine enjoyed giving crosses. She would give one to Lady Elizabeth, another to 'the lady Carew, late Mrs [Mistress] Norrys, against her marriage' and a third to Lady Rutland 'for a token'.
6. *CSP Sp.* VI (i), 149; *LP* XVI, 436. Curiously, Chapuys writes that Mary had not yet visited Katherine. This can only mean that Mary had not visited the court so far that Christmas, as the two women had met, with disastrous results, at least as early as the beginning of December 1540; see above and *CSP Sp.* VI (i), 143; *LP* XVI, 314.
7. Kaulek, pp.258–9; *LP* XVI, 449.
8. *CSP Sp.* VI (i), 149; *LP* XVI, 436.
9. Except where stated, this description of Anne of Cleves's visit to court is taken from the account written by Eustache Chapuys (*CSP Sp.* VI (i), 149; *LP* XVI, 436).
10. Kaulek, pp.258–9; *LP* XVI, 449.
11. Ibid.
12. *LP* XVI, 1489 (165).
13. Kaulek, pp.258–9; *LP* XVI, 449.
14. Ibid.

15. *CSP Sp.* VI (i), 148: this entry incorrectly gives the addressee as Mary of Hungary instead of the Emperor Charles; *LP* XVI, 421.

16. Nicolas, *PPC* VII, p.105; *LP* XVI, 422, 423; Starkey, *Six Wives*, pp.655–7.

17. See *LP* XVI, 423, where four ballads are shown to have been printed by Mr Bankes.

18. Nicolas, *PPC* VII, pp.511–13, 519–21; *LP* XVI, 427, 449, 464 (1, 2).

19. Kaulek, p.258.

20. *LP* XVI, 454 (25, 26).

21. *LP* XVI, 517.

22. Kaulek, p.274; *LP* XVI, 590.

23. Kaulek, p.49; *LP* XIII (i), 995.

24. Nicolas, *PPC* VII, p.139.

25. Dr Mallett was paid 20s: *LP* XVI, 1489 (f.183b).

26. Kaulek, p.273; *LP* XVI, 589.

27. *CSP Sp.* VI (i), 204; *LP* XVI, 1328. Although this letter is dated 10 November 1541, Chapuys refers to another, now lost, which he had written the previous Lent. He added that Henry was giving serious thought to divorcing Katherine. 'During all that time,' he wrote, 'there had been much consultation and talk of a divorce', although this was dropped 'owing to some presumption' that Katherine was pregnant 'or because the means and ways to bring about a divorce were not yet sufficiently prepared'(*CSP Sp.* VI (i), 204; *LP* XVI, 1328). In fact, Chapuys was merely recycling the old gossip from the previous year. Marillac noted that Chapuys ought to be recalled because he had not left his room, and had scarcely left his bed, for six months (Kaulek, p.314; *LP* XVI, 903). Chapuys had suffered terribly from gout since 1539.

28. Kaulek, pp.273, 274; *LP* XVI, 589, 590.

29. Kaulek, p.274; *LP* XVI, 589.

30. Wriothesley, p.124; Kaulek, p.281; *LP* XVI, 662, 1489 (f.184b).

31. *CSP Sp.* VI (i), 155; *LP* VIII, pp.545–6; *LP* XVI, 660, 662; for background see Brigden, pp.530–47; Starkey, *Six Wives*, pp.657–9.

32. Kaulek, p.261; *LP* XVI, 466.

33. *CSP Sp.* VI (i), 150; Nicolas, *PPC* VII, p.119.

34. Kaulek, p.261; *LP* XVI, 466. The cause of Sadler's arrest never became known. It has been suggested that he had been the victim of a conservative plot (Starkey, *Reign of Henry VIII*, p.113; Head, pp.187, 189). If so, it would go a long way to explaining his assiduous persecution of Katherine and her family later.
35. *CSP Sp.* VI (i), 151.
36. Roper, p.83.
37. *CSP Sp.* VI (i), 155.
38. Starkey, *Six Wives*, p.659.
39. Wriothesley, p.124; Kaulek, p.281; *LP* XVI, 662, 1489 (f.184b).

11. Dear Master Culpeper

1. Kaulek, p.289; *LP* XVI, 712.
2. http://www.royal.gov.uk/RoyalEventsandCeremonies/RoyalMaundy Service/Maundyservice.aspx.
3. *LP* XVI, 503 (14).
4. Ibid., 779 (14).
5. Nicolas, *PPC* VII, p.156.
6. Ibid., p.159.
7. Ibid., pp.158, 183.
8. 'Examination of Queen Katherine', HMC, *Bath*, p.10.
9. Thomas Paston would go on to marry Agnes, the daughter of Katherine's cousin, Sir John Legh of Stockwell (Riordan, 'Henry VIII, privy chamber of', *ODNB* online).
10. Hume, *Chronicle of Henry VIII*, p.82.
11. TNA SP 1/167/ 157–9: Culpeper's deposition.
12. Henry Webb was a stableman; see *LP* XVI, 380 (136).
13. TNA SP 1/167/14: Katherine's letter to Thomas Culpeper.
14. Often rendered as 'bid', the original text clearly states 'behove'.
15. The editors of the *LP* have calendared this letter at August 1541, suggesting that it was written during the time of the royal progress to the north (XVI, 1134 and note; see also Warnicke, pp.69–70). Certainly, letters were passed between Katherine and Lady Rochford at that time; however, as will be seen, this letter was not one of them.

16. TNA SP 1/167/159–60: confession of Jane, Lady Rochford.

17. *LP* XVI, 1366

18. See, for instance, *LP* XVI, 864, 1325, 1332, 1359, 1366, 1372, 1387 and elsewhere.

19. See Nicolas, *PPC* VII, pp.188, 189; *CSP Sp.* VI (i), 161; *LP* XVI, 831, 835; Starkey, *Six Wives*, p.660.

20. *LP* XVI, 804.

21. Ibid., 1389: the brooch was deemed a 'little thing worth' by those who inventoried Katherine's jewels.

22. *CSP Sp.* VI (i), 161.

23. Nicolas, *PPC* VII, p.190.

24. *LP* XVI, 841.

25. *CSP Sp.* VI (i), 163; *LP* XVI, 864.

26. Scarisbrick (p.417) finds that a straight line can be drawn from the time of Henry's recovery from his illness in the spring of 1541 to his return to the battlefield three years later.

27. *CSP Sp.* VI (i), 163.

28. *LP* XVI, 766.

29. *State Papers, Henry VIII*, I, pp.538–9.

30. Ibid., p.552; *LP* XII (ii), 271.

31. *CSP Sp.* VI (i), 166, 897; Kaulek, p.309; *LP* XVI, 868; Wriothesley, p.124 and Hall, pp.841–2.

32. Kaulek, p.309; *LP* XVI, 868.

33. *CSP Sp.* VI (i), 166.

34. Nicolas, *PPC* VII, 194.

35. *LP* XVI, 1056 (16).

12. The Summer Progress

1. *CSP Sp.* VI (i), 163; Kaulek, p.309; *LP* XVI, 868.

2. Kaulek, p.317; *LP* XVI, 941.

3. *CSP Sp.* VI (i), 163.

4. See the lists of Henry's 'Gests', *LP* XVI, 677, although none of these was strictly adhered to.

5. Kaulek, p.320; *LP* XVI, 1011.

6. *State Papers, Henry VIII*, I, p.659.

7. *LP* XVI, 1033, 1034.

8. This is the present-day Lyddington Bede House.

9. TNA SP/167/153–4: confession of Marget Morton.

10. *CSP Sp.* VI (i), 186; *LP* XVI, 1126.

11. *LP* XVI, 961.

12. Tragically, the boys would die within half an hour of each other on 14 July 1551, having contracted the dreaded sweating sickness.

13. 'Account of King Henry the Eighth's Entry into Lincoln'; *LP* XVI, 1088.

14. That is, Lincoln Cathedral.

15. This dress has been replicated by Pauline Loven and is on display at Gainsborough Old Hall: http://periodwardrobe.wordpress.com/2010/06/13/his-rose-without-a-thorn/.

16. Hall, p.842.

17. *LP* XVI, 1391 (18).

18. Kaulek, p.327; *LP* XVI, 1089.

19. The name Burgh is occasionally given as Borough.

20. http://www.gainsborougholdhall.com/. Coincidentally, a son of the third Lord Burgh, Edward, had married Katherine Parr in 1529. She had been widowed on his death four years later, when she married John Neville, third Baron Latimer.

21. Bowes is named by Hall, p.842.

22. *LP* XVI, 1130.

23. TNA SP/167/153–4; *LP* XVI, 1338.

24. *LP* XVI, 1131.

25. *LP* XVI, 1389, from BL Stowe MS, 559.

13. Sinister Stirrings

1. TNA SP 1/168/87–9; *LP* XVI, 1469.

2. *LP* XVI, 1400.

3. Ibid., 1423.

4. Ibid., 1409 (5.15), 1416 (pp.661–2); TNA SP 1/168/87–9; *LP* XVI, 1469.

5. 'Third Report of the Deputy Keeper', Appendix II, p.261; *LP* XVI, 1395.

6. *LP* XVI, 1334; Nicolas, *PPC* VIII, p.355.

7. *LP* XVI, 1105.

8. Ibid., 1115.

9. Ibid., 1143.

10. Ibid., 1125; *State Papers, Henry VIII*, I, p.680.

11. *LP* XVI, 1130 (p.534); Kaulek, p.334.

12. TNA SP 1/167/161: confession of Robert Damport.

13. TNA SP 1/167/157: confession of Francis Dereham.

14. Ibid. £10 translates to about £3,075 in today's values and was equivalent to Katherine's annual salary as a maiden of honour.

15. *State Papers, Henry VIII*, I, p.681; *LP* XVI, 1141.

16. http://www.bl.uk/onlinegallery/onlineex/unvbrit/h/001cotaugi00002u00011000.html.

17. *Victoria History, The City of York*, p.529; Kaulek, p.338; *LP* XVI, 1183.

18. Kaulek, p.338; *LP* XVI, 1183.

19. *LP* XVI, 1183; Kaulek, p.337.

20. *LP* XVI, 1183; Kaulek, p.338; a similar promise had been made with regard to Jane Seymour (Thornton, p.237 and notes).

21. TNA SP/167/159.

22. Nicolas, *PPC* VII, p.245.

23. *LP* XVI, 1211.

24. Ibid., 1232.

25. *Victoria History, Bedfordshire*, vol. 3, pp.262–6. Like the Howards, Gostwick's ancestors were also associated with Willington, tracing their presence in the parish back to 1209.

26. TNA SP 1/167/131: confession of Mary Lascelles.

27. TNA SP 1/167/155: confession of Alice Wilkes.

28. For the background to John Lascelles, see Wilson, pp.94–5, 100, 106, 117–18.

29. *LP* XVI, 101.

30. Parliamentary Archives, HL/PO/PU/1/1534/26H8n1.

31. Nicolas, *PPC* VII, pp.352–6, esp. p.353; TNA SP 1/167/162: John Lascelles's deposition; see also Mary Lascelles's deposition: TNA SP 1/167/130. Wilson (pp.133 and 257, n.14) suggests that Lascelles did not acquire the information about Katherine in one conversation, but that he constructed it from a series of exchanges with his sister. This is entirely possible.

32. Kaulek, p.365; *LP* XVI, 1366.
33. Nicolas, *PPC* VII, pp.353–4.

14. 'It is no more the time to dance'

1. Kaulek, pp.350–1; *LP* XVI, 1297. Marillac refers to Edward as the Prince of Wales. In fact, he was Duke of Cornwall.
2. For an excellent appraisal of the pregnancies and miscarriages of Katherine of Aragon and Anne Boleyn, see Dewhurst.
3. *LP* X, 282. Dewhurst incorrectly gives the item number of Chapuys's letter as 284.
4. Nicolas, *PPC* VII, p.352.
5. Harpsfield, p.277. Although Harpsfield was writing during the reign of Queen Mary, he was contemporary with the events he describes.
6. The basis of the narrative in this section is Nicolas, *PPC* VII, pp.352–6 (summarised in *LP* XVI, 1334). Although it is dated 12 November 1541, this letter was despatched on 14 November or shortly afterwards; see the note to this entry in *LP* XVI, 1334 and the entry at 1341.
7. See Wilson, pp.129–30; Starkey, *Reign of Henry VIII*, p.105 *et seq.*; quotation from Nicolas *PPC*, p.xiv.
8. *State Papers, Henry VIII*, VI, p.417.
9. Nicolas, *PPC* VII, p.354.
10. *LP* XVI, 1317. The examination of Roger Cotes is not mentioned in the letter written to Paget by the Privy Council. This is probably because he was found to have had no connection with the events under investigation. There were legitimate reasons why Katherine should give money to a servant. Wages were paid on a quarterly basis, but certain situations would require extra expenses. As such, the £10 Katherine gave Cotes was probably an advance on his wages.
11. TNA SP 1/167/162: deposition of John Lascelles. This document is damaged at the top, making the first two lines impossible to read.
12. Nicolas, *PPC* VII, p.354.
13. TNA SP 1/167/128–31: Mary Lascelles's confession to the Earl of Southampton.

14. This word could be read as belles, i.e. 'bellies', and is often rendered as such; however, given Mary's use of a sparrows metaphor, bills is more appropriate.
15. TNA SP 1/167/138: deposition of Henry Mannock. He was examined on 5 November 1541.
16. TNA SP 1/167/157: Francis Dereham's deposition. It is not known whether Archbishop Cranmer was present on this occasion.
17. *LP* XVI, 1332.
18. Nicolas, *PPC* VII, p.354.
19. Ibid., p.355.
20. Ibid.
21. Law, pp.223–4.
22. *CSP Sp.* VI (i), 204; *LP* XVI, 1332; Kaulek, p.352.
23. *LP* XVI, 1332; Kaulek, p.352. Marillac incorrectly considered Norfolk to have been the 'author of this marriage'.
24. *LP* XVI, 1332; Kaulek, pp.352–3.

15. 'Most vile wretch in the world'

1. Nicolas, *PPC* VII, p.355.
2. 'The Confession of the Queen Katherine Howard', HMC *Bath*, pp.8–9
3. *State Papers, Henry VIII*, I, pp.689–91.
4. 'Examination of Q. Katherine Howard' in Burnet, vol. 4, pp.504–5.
5. East, pp.445, 446.
6. *LP* XVI, 1332; Kaulek, p.352 *et seq.*
7. *CSP Sp.* VI (i), 204; *LP* XVI, 1328.
8. *State Papers, Henry VIII*, I, p.691 *et seq.*; *LP* XVI, 1331.

16. 'Blind youth hath no grace to foresee'

1. *State Papers, Henry VIII*, I, p.691 *et seq.*; *LP* XVI, 1331;*CSP Sp.* VI (i), 207; *LP* XVI, 1359.
2. *LP* XVI, 1332; Kaulek, p.354.
3. *Statutes of the Realm*, III, p.792. Ironically, one of the other clauses

in this statute had allowed the marriage between Katherine and Henry, despite his marriage to Katherine's cousin, Anne Boleyn, and his relationship with Anne's sister, Mary.

4. *LP* XVI, 1332; Kaulek, p.354.

5. Nicolas, *PPC* VII, 352; *LP* XVI, 1334.

6. *LP* XVI, 1366; Kaulek, p.364.

7. TNA SP 1/167/157–9: deposition of Thomas Culpeper. It is summarised in *LP* XVI, 1339 (pp.618–19).

8. Bess Harvey had served Anne Boleyn, but had then been dismissed under mysterious circumstances. She asked Sir Francis Bryan if he would help her find a place with Lady Mary. When Bryan raised her petition with the king, he was told to 'meddle with other matters' (*LP* X, 1134 (4)). However, Bess did return briefly to court before retiring on an annuity of 10*l* in March 1541 (*LP* XVI, 678 (13)).

9. Anne Herbert, the wife of William Herbert, was the sister of Katherine Parr. A member of Katherine's household, she looked after the queen's jewels.

10. This is almost certainly Dorothy Bray, who had been one of Katherine's colleagues as maiden of honour to Anne of Cleves.

11. Kaulek, p.371; *LP* XVI, 1426.

12. This is the only evidence that the court visited Sheriff Hutton during the progress.

13. Culpeper's image of Katherine places her in a very similar position to that which faced Katherine Parr when Henry first noticed her. Having been in love with Thomas Seymour, whom she wanted to marry, she had to set her own happiness aside when Henry showed an interest in her.

14. *Statutes of the Realm*, III 26 Henry VIII, cap. 13, p.508.

15. 'Confession of Queen Katherine', HMC *Bath*, p.10.

16. TNA SP 1/167/159–60: confession of Jane Lady Rochford.

17. 'Examination of Queen Katherine', HMC *Bath*, pp.9–10.

18. *Les Enseignements d'Anne de France*, p.36.

19. TNA SP 1/167/14: Katherine's letter to Culpeper.

20. *State Papers, Henry VIII*, I, p.694; *LP* XVI, 1333.

21. Nicolas, *PPC* VII, 267; *LP* XVI, 1336.

22. Wriothesley, pp.130–1.

23. Kaulek, p.366; *LP* XVI, 1366.

24. Margaret Douglas, daughter of Archibald, sixth Earl of Angus, and Margaret, Queen Dowager of Scots, had been involved in a scandalous relationship with Thomas Howard, Queen Katherine's uncle, for which she had incurred the king's wrath (*LP* X, 1087 (7); *LP* XI, 108, 147; *LP* XVI, 1333).
25. TNA SP 1/167/149; *LP* XVI, 1337: deposition of Katherine Tylney.
26. Suffolk's home was Grimsthorpe, which the court visited on its way to York.
27. Strickland (vol. 3, p.146) makes the valid point that, had Katherine Tylney seen anyone of any importance or interest, their names would have been recorded.
28. TNA SP 1/167/153–4; *LP* XVI, 1338: deposition of Marget Morton.
29. Ibid. and TNA SP 1/167/162: confession of Marget Morton (summary).
30. TNA SP 1/167/159–60: confession of Jane, Lady Rochford.

17. The Trial and Execution of Dereham and Culpeper

1. *State Papers, Henry VIII*, I, pp.691–3.
2. Nicholas Heath, Bishop of Rochester, who was the king's almoner at this point.
3. *State Papers, Henry VIII*, I, p.695.
4. *LP* XVI, 1389.
5. *State Papers, Henry VIII*, VIII, p.636; summarised in *LP* XVI, 1363.
6. Nicolas, *PPC*, VII, pp.267–8.
7. Ibid., VII, p.267; *LP* XVI, 1341. The letter to William Paget is printed in Nicolas, *PPC* VII, pp.352–6; *LP* XVI, 1334.
8. *State Papers, Henry VIII*, VIII, p.636.
9. Wriothesley, p.131.
10. *LP* XVI, 1340, 1343, 1349.
11. *LP* XVI, 1342; Kaulek, p.355.
12. TNA SP 1/167/181; *LP* XVI, 1348.
13. TNA SP/1/167/155–62; they are summarised in *LP* XVI, 1339.
14. *CSP Sp.* VI (i), 207; *LP* XVI, 1359, letter dated 19 November 1541.
15. Kaulek, p.363.
16. *LP* XVI, 1426; Kaulek, pp.370–1.
17. *CSP Sp.* VI (i), 211.

18. Nicolas, *PPC* VII, p.276; *LP* XVI, 1393.
19. 'Third Report of the Deputy Keeper', pp.262–3.
20. Wriothesley, p.131.
21. *CSP Sp.* VI (i), 209; *LP* XVI, 1401.
22. *LP* XVI, 1426; Marillac, pp.370–1.
23. *CSP Sp.* VI (i), 209; *LP* XVI, 1401.
24. Ibid.
25. 'Third Report of the Deputy Keeper', pp.263–4.
26. *CSP Sp.* VI (i), 209; *LP* XVI, 1401.
27. Kaulek, p.371; *LP* XVI, 1426.
28. *CSP Sp.* VI (i), 213.
29. Ibid., 209; *LP* XVI, 1401.
30. Wriothesley, pp.131–2.
31. Kaulek, p.371; *LP* XVI, 1426.
32. Ibid.
33. Thomas, p.56.
34. Harpsfield, p.278.

18. The Bottom of the Pot

1. *CSP Sp.* VI (i), 209; *LP* XVI, 1401.
2. *LP* XVI, 1369.
3. *CSP Sp.* VI (i), 209; *LP* XVI, 1401.
4. Fox, p.302.
5. *CSP Sp.* VI (i), 209; *LP* XVI, 1401.
6. *LP* XVI, 1415.
7. Ibid., 1398.
8. The duke was sent to Norfolk House to make a search of Dereham's coffers on 14 November (*State Papers, Henry VIII*, I, p.721). The date is established by the indictment of Duchess Agnes, Lord William and the others (KB 8/13/2; 'Third Report of the Deputy Keeper', p.265).
9. TNA SP 1/168/21–2; *LP* XVI, 1385.
10. *LP* XVI, 1394.
11. Nicolas, *PPC* VII, p.277; *LP* XVI, 1397.
12. Nicolas, *PPC* VII, pp.274–5; *LP* XVI, 1379.

13. TNA SP 1/168/39, 55–6; *LP* XVI, 1398, 1400; Damport was questioned on 2 and 3 December 1541.
14. *State Papers, Henry VIII*, I, pp.695–6.
15. Ibid., p.696; *LP* XVI, 1408.
16. TNA SP 1/168/45; *LP* XVI, 1415.
17. *State Papers, Henry VIII*, I, pp.696–7; *LP* XVI, 1414.
18. See also, for instance, *LP* XVI, 1409 (1.8, 5.25).
19. *Journal of the House of Lords*, I, pp.151, 154, 155, 157.
20. *LP* XVI, 1409 (1.8).
21. TNA SP 1/168/104–5; summarised in *LP* XVI, 1423.
22. *State Papers, Henry VIII*, I, p.698.
23. Ibid., pp.702–3.
24. The questions to be put to the duchess are listed in *LP* XVI, 1409. Included are interrogatories to be ministered to Katherine, Dereham and Lady Bridgewater. Since there is no record that a visit was made to Syon House and no record of any answers Katherine might have given, it is impossible to know whether or not she was questioned.
25. *LP* XVI, 1426.
26. Henry's comments are given in *State Papers, Henry VIII*, I, pp.699–701.
27. *CSP Sp.* VI (i), 213; *LP* XVI, 1441.
28. *State Papers, Henry VIII*, I, pp.702–3.
29. *CSP Sp.* VI (i), 213.
30. *State Papers, Henry VIII*, I, p.704.
31. Ibid.
32. Ibid., p.707.
33. Ibid.
34. There were no permanent gallows at Tyburn until 1571.
35. Wriothesley, p.132.
36. Ridley, pp.80–1.

19. Condemnation

1. *State Papers, Henry VIII*, I, pp.708–9.
2. Ibid., pp.709–10.

3. Ibid., p.710.

4. Nicolas, *PPC* VII, p.282.

5. TNA SP 1/168/136; *LP* XVI, 1442; William Penison was Girolamo Penizon of the Stable.

6. *State Papers, Henry VIII*, I, pp.710–11.

7. Ibid., VIII, p.646.

8. Ibid., I, p.711.

9. Ibid, p.721. The duke's pleas fell upon favourable ears, for he was the only senior member of the Howard family not to face prosecution.

10. Roper, pp.71–2.

11. *State Papers, Henry VIII*, I, pp.722–4.

12. TNA SP 1/167/157: confession of Katherine Tylney; TNA SP 1/167/157: confession of Alice Restwold (Wilkes).

13. TNA SP 1/167/157: confession of Katherine Tylney.

14. TNA SP 1/167/155: confession of Anne Howard.

15. TNA SP 1/167/155: confession of Margaret, Lady Howard.

16. *State Papers, Henry VIII*, I, pp.724, 725.

17. TNA KB 8/13/2; 'Third Report of the Deputy Keeper', pp.264–5; the arraignment was based on the indictment found at Southwark on 16 December.

18. Dereham's duties in Katherine's household had been greatly distorted.

19. That is, Henry Mannock and his wife.

20. TNA KB 8/13/2; 'Third Reportof the Deputy Keeper', p.266; *State Papers, Henry VIII*, I, pp.726–7; the arraignment is also briefly mentioned in the *Chronicle* of Wriothesley's brother, Charles, pp.132–3.

21. All but Agnes, Dowager Duchess of Norfolk, and Lord William Howard were pardoned of misprision of treason on 28 February 1542 (*LP* XVII, 139 (9)); Agnes received her pardon on 5 May 1542 (*LP* XVII, 362 (25)); three weeks later she was granted those lands and manors she had forfeited (*LP* XVII, 362 (58)). Lord William Howard, who had been judged the least guilty, was pardoned of all treasons on 27 August 1542 (*LP* XVII, 714 (23)).

22. *CSP Sp.* VI (i), 221.

23. *LP* XVII, 2.

20. All Be-wept in Black, and Poor Estate

1. Thomas, p.55.
2. *LP* XVII, 2 (p.3); Marillac's sentiments are shared by Giovanni Stanchini, secretary to nuncio, Capo di Ferro (*LP* XVII, 19). As it happened, Norfolk did appear to have gained his former credit, at least as far as Marillac could tell (*LP* XVII, 35).
3. *Parliamentary History*, vol. 3, pp.176–7; *House of Lords Journal*, I, pp.164–571.
4. *The Court of Good Counsell*, p.6.
5. The passage of the Bill of Attainder against Katherine can be followed in *House of Lords Journal*, I, p.171 *et seq.* and *Parliamentary History*, vol. 3, p.177 *et seq.*
6. *CSP Sp.* VI (i), 232; *LP* XVII, 124.
7. *LP* XVII, Appendix B, 4.
8. Ibid., 6.
9. *House of Lords Journal*, I, p.171; *Parliamentary History*, vol. 3, pp.178–9.
10. *House of Lords Journal*, I, p.172; *Parliamentary History*, vol. 3, p.180.
11. Chapuys reports that, on 7 February, John Gage, comptroller of the household, had travelled to Syon to break up Katherine's household and dismiss her servants. He heard also that Gage was 'to take the Queen into his own lodgings'. Gage was constable of the Tower (*CSP Sp.* VI (i), 232; *LP* XVII, 124).
12. *CSP Sp.* VI (i), 232; *LP* XVII, 124.
13. Nucius of Corcyra (p.49) noted that 'the sculls are even at this time to be seen, denuded of flesh.' He was travelling in England in 1545–6 (pp.xxvi–xxvii).
14. *CSP Sp.* VI (i), 232; *LP* XVII, 124.
15. It is generally assumed that Katherine entered the Tower through the water gate in St Thomas's Tower, known today as Traitors' Gate (see, for example, Denny, p.248); however, kings and queens in the fifteenth and sixteenth centuries customarily used the Court Gate. The author wishes to thank Jason Woodcock, Yeoman Warder at the Tower, for confirming the route Katherine would have taken.
16. *Statutes of the Realm*, vol. 3, pp.857–60; summarised in *LP* XVII, 28(C.21).
17. *House of Lords Journal*, I, p.176; *Parliamentary History*, vol. 3, pp.181–2;

the *Journal* breaks off at this point in order, as is supposed, to protect the king's honour.

18. *LP* XVII, 100; Kaulek, p.388.

19. *LP* Addendum 1 (ii), 1522. This letter is badly mutilated.

20. *CSP Sp.* VI (i), 232; *LP* XVII, 124; Katherine's request to practise with the block is found only in Chapuys's letter to the Emperor Charles. It is unknown who his informant was on this occasion, but there is no reason to doubt the veracity of the report.

21. Burnet, vol. 1, p.496. It has been suggested that Katherine made a confession after her examination by the delegation of Lords who had visited her at Syon prior to her removal to the Tower. This is not impossible, although there is some confusion as to whom she would have made this confession. Strickland (vol. 3, p.166) suggests that it was to John Longland, the royal confessor; Burnet (vol. 4, p.496) and the editors of *Parliamentary History* (vol. 3, p.182) suggest Dr John White. However, the list of men who visited Syon in order to examine Katherine includes neither Longland nor White (*House of Lords Journal*, vol. I, p.171). The most appropriate time for Katherine to confess would be as she was preparing to die, hence the inclusion of her words at this point. The name of the priest to whom she made her final confession cannot be known for certain.

22. Chapuys states that the councillors began to assemble at seven in the morning (*CSP Sp.* VI (i), 232; *LP* XVII, 124); Marillac wrote that the executions of Katherine and Lady Rochford began some two hours later, at about nine o'clock (Kaulek, p.389; *LP* XVII, 100).

23. The names of Katherine's attendants in the Tower are not recorded. It is possible that they were her half-sister, Lady Baynton, and other senior ladies who had attended the fallen queen at Syon, but this is speculation.

24. Hume, *Chronicle of Henry VIII*, p.86. If Katherine and Culpeper had ever been pledged, it was an informal arrangement and their relationship had not been consummated.

25. Although she was the common law wife of Francis Dereham, the only man whose wife Katherine had actually wanted to be was King Henry. It was a trick of headsmen to strike while the victim least expected it.

26. *LP* XVII, 100; Kaulek, pp.388–9.

27. *CSP Sp.* VI (i), 232; *LP* XVII, 124.
28. Ibid.
29. *LP* XVII, 100; Kaulek, p.389.
30. *LP* XVII, 106.

Epilogue

1. *State Papers, Henry VIII*, I, pp.714, 716, 718; Kaulek, p.373; *CSP Sp.* VI (i), 220; *LP* XVI, 1445, 1449, 1453, 1457; 1482 (p.694).
2. Proverbs 5:3–4; see also Carley, p.105.
3. See Borman, pp.76–7, 214.

Bibliography

~

Unpublished Primary Sources in the National Archives, Kew

KB 8/13/1
KB 8/13/2
SP 1/161
SP 1/167
SP 1/168
SP 1/169

Printed Primary and Secondary Sources

'Account of King Henry the Eighth's Entry into Lincoln in 1541', *Archaeologia*, vol. 23, 1831, pp. 334–5

Allen, Thomas, *History of the Parish of Lambeth* (London: 1826)

Ampthill Castle Community Archaeology Project, http://www.ampthill. info/AmpthillParkArchaeologicalDigReport.pdf

Amyot, Thomas, 'Transcript of an original Manuscript, containing a Memorial from George Constantyne to Thomas Lord Cromwell. Communicated by Thomas Amyot, Esq. F.R.S., Treasurer, in a Letter addressed to Henry Ellis, Esq. F.R.S., Secretary', *Archaeologia*, vol. 23, 1831, pp. 50–78

André, le chapelain, *Art of Courtly Love* (trans. J.J. Parry) (New York: Columbia University Press, 1941)

Aubrey, John, *The Natural History and Antiquities of the County of Surrey* (London: Printed for E. Curll, 1718–19)

Ballentyne, J.W., 'The "Byrth of Mankinde"', *Journal of Obstetrics and Gynaecology of the British Empire*, vol. 10, July–December 1906, pp. 297–325

Banks, Sir Joseph, 'Copy of an Original manuscript, Entitled, a Breviate Touching the Order and Government of a Nobleman's House, etc.', *Archaeologia*, vol. 13, 1800, pp. 315–89

Barnard, Francis Pierrepont, 'The Kinship of Henry VIII and his Wives', *Miscellanea Genealogica et Heraldica*, 5th series, vol. 3

Becon, Thomas, *The Catechism of Thomas Becon* (Cambridge: Cambridge University Press, 1844)

Bernard, G.W., *The King's Reformation: Henry VIII and the Remaking of the English Church* (New Haven, CT; London: Yale University Press, 2005)

Betteridge, Thomas and Suzannah Lipscomb (eds.), *Henry VIII and the Court, Art, Politics and Performance* (Farnham; Burlington, VT: Ashgate Publishing, 2013)

Bindoff, S.T., *The History of Parliament: The House of Commons 1509–1558,* 3 vols. (London: Secker & Warburg, 1982)

Blomefield, Francis, *An Essay towards a Topographical History of the County of Norfolk* (Fersfield: 1739–75)

Borman, Tracy, *Elizabeth's Women: The Hidden Story of the Virgin Queen* (London: Jonathan Cape, 2009)

Bouterwek, Karl Wilhelm, 'Anna von Cleve, Gemahlin Heinrichs VIII', *Zeitschrift des Bergischen Geschictvereins*, vol. 6, 1869

Brathwaite, Richard, *The English Gentleman containing Sundry Excellent Rules or Exquisite Observations, Tending to Direction of every Gentleman, of Selecter Ranke and Qualitie* (London: Printed by John Haviland, and are to be sold by Robert Bostock at his shop at the signe of the Kings head in Pauls Church-yard, 1630)

Brenan, Gerald and Edward Phillips Statham, *The House of Howard,* 2 vols. (London: Hutchinson & Co., 1907)

Brigden, Susan, *Thomas Wyatt, the Heart's Forest* (London: Faber, 2012)

Brooke, George C., *English Coins* (London: Methuen & Co., 1932)

Burnet, Gilbert, *The History of the Reformation of the Church of England*, vol. 4 (Oxford: Clarendon Press, 1865)

Byrne, Muriel St Clare (ed.), *The Lisle Letters*, 6 vols. (Chicago: University of Chicago Press, 1981)

Calendar of Letters, Despatches and State Papers Relating to Negotiations between England and Spain, Preserved in the Archives at Simancas and Elsewhere (ed.) G. A. Bergenroth *et al.*, 13 vols. in 20 (London: Longman, Green, Longman & Robertrs, 1862–1954)

Calendar of State Papers and Manuscripts Relating to English Affairs, Existing in the Collections of Venice and in Other Libraries of Northern Italy (ed.) R. Brown *et al.*, 38 vols. in 40 (London: Longham, Green, Longman & Roberts, 1864–1947)

Camden, William, *Remains Concerning Britain* (London: John Russell Smith, 1870)

Campbell, Rebecca, Tracy Sefl and Courtney E. Ahrens, 'The Physical Health Consequences of Rape: Assessing Survivors' Somatic Symptoms in a Racially Diverse Population', *Women's Studies Quarterly*, vol. 31, no. 1/2, *Women, Health, and Medicine: Transforming Perspectives and Practice*, spring–summer 2003

Carley, James P., *The Books of King Henry VIII and his Wives* (London: British Library, 2004)

Cartwright, J.J. (ed.), *Calendar of the Manuscripts of the Marquis of Bath preserved at Longleat, Wiltshire*, Historical Manuscripts Commission, no. 58

Cavendish, George, *Life of Cardinal Wolsey, Metrical Visions* (London: Harding, Triphook and Lepard, 1825)

Caxton, William, *The Boke yf Eneydos . . . translated oute of latyne in to frenshe, and oute of frenshe reduced in to Englysshe by me Wyllm Caxton* (Westminster: W.C., after 1490)

Chaucer, Geoffrey, *Canterbury Tales* (London; New York: Routledge, 1985)

Childs, Jessie, *Henry VIII's Last Victim* (London: Vintage, 2008)

Clarke, Hughes (ed.), *Miscellanea Genealogica et Heraldica* (London: Mitches Hughes Clarke, 1918–19)

Colvin, H.M. (ed.), *The History of the King's Works*, 6 vols. (London: Her Majesty's Stationery Office, 1975)

'The Confession of the Queen Katherine Howard' in Cartwright, J.J. (ed.), *Calendar of the Manuscripts of the Marquis of Bath preserved at Longleat, Wiltshire*, Historical Manuscripts Commission, no. 58, pp. 8–9

Copinger, W.A., *The Manors of Suffolk, Notes on their History and Devolution* (London: T. Fisher Unwin, 1905)

Correspondance de l'Empereur Maximilien I. et de Marguerite d'Autriche sa Fille, Gouvernante des Pays-Bas, de 1507 à 1519. Publié d'après les manuscrits par M. Le Glay (Paris, 1839)

The Court of Good Counsell (London, 1607)

Cyclopaedia: or, An Universal Dictionary of Arts and Sciences (London: Ephraim Chambers, 1728)

Dasent, J.R. (ed.), *Acts of the Privy Council of England*, 46 vols. (London: Her Majesty's Stationery Office, 1890)

de Lisle, Leanda, *The Sisters who would be Queen* (London: Harper Press, 2009)

Denny, Joanna, *Katherine Howard: A Tudor Conspiracy* (London: Portrait, 2005)

Dewhurst, Sir John, 'The Alleged Miscarriages of Catherine of Aragon and Anne Boleyn', *Medical History*, vol. 28, 1984

Dolman, Brett, 'Wishful Thinking: Reading the Portraits of Henry VIII's Queens in Betteridge and Liscomb' (eds.) *Henry VIII and the Court, Arts, Politics and Performance* (Farnham; Burlington, VT: Ashgate Publishing, 2013)

Dugdale, William, *The Baronage of England* (London: Printed by T. Newcomb, 1675–6)

Duncan, L.L., *Medieval & Tudor Kent P.C.C. Wills*, Book 54

Dutton, Richard, 'Tilney, Edmund (1535/6–1610)', *Oxford Dictionary of National Biography* (Oxford: Oxford University Press, 2004)

East, Edward Hyde, *Treatise of the Pleas of the Crown*, 2 vols. (London: Printed by A. Strahan, 1803)

Ellis, H. (ed.), *Original Letters Illustrative of English History*, 3rd series (London: Richard Bentley, 1846)

Elyot, Thomas, *The Boke of the Gouvernor*, 2 vols. (London: Kegan Paul, Trench & Co., 1885)

'The Examination of Q. Katherine Howard' in Burnet, Gilbert, *The History of the Reformation of the Church of England* (Oxford: Clarendon Press, 1865), pp. 504–5

'Examination of Queen Katherine' in Cartwright, J.J. (ed.), *Calendar of the Manuscripts of the Marquis of Bath preserved at Longleat, Wiltshire*, Historical Manuscripts Commission, no. 58, pp. 9–10

Finch, Andrew J., 'Parental Authority and the Problem of Clandestine Marriage in the Later Middle Ages', *Law and History Review*, vol. 8, no. 2, autumn 1990

Fox, Julia, *Jane Boleyn: The Infamous Lady Rochford* (London: Weidenfeld & Nicolson, 2007)

Foxe, John, *Narratives of the Days of the Reformation* (ed. J.G. Nichols) (London: Camden Society, 1859)

Fraser, Antonia, *The Six Wives of Henry VIII* (London: Weidenfeld & Nicolson, 1992)

Fuller, Thomas, *The History of the Worthies of England*, vol. 2 (London: Printed for Thomas Tegg, 1840)

Greene, Robert, *Mamillia, a Mirrour or Looking Glasse for the Ladies of England*, part I (1583–92)

Hall, Edward, *Chronicle* (London: Printed for J. Johnson and others, 1809)

Harpsfield, Nicholas, *A Treatise on the Pretended Divorce between Henry VIII and Catharine of Aragon* (London: Camden Society, 1878)

Hasted, Edward, *The History and Topographical Survey of the County of Kent* 13 vols. (Canterbury: Printed by W. Bristow, 1797–1801)

Head, David M., *The Ebbs and Flows of Fortune, the Life of Thomas Howard, Third Duke of Norfolk* (Athens, GA; London: University of Georgia Press, *c.*1995)

Hobby, Elaine (ed.), *The Birth of Mankind* (Aldershot: Ashgate Publishing, 2009)

Hopwood, C.H. (ed.), *Middle Temple Records*, vol.1 (London: Butterworth & Co., 1904)

Horrox, Rosemary, *Richard III: A Study in Service* (Cambridge: Cambridge University Press, 1989)

Howard, Henry of Corby, *Indication of Memorials, Monuments, Paintings and Engravings of Persons of the Howard Family* (Corby, 1834)

Hume, Martin Andrew Sharp, *The Wives of Henry the Eighth, and the Parts they Played in History* (London: Eveleigh Nash, 1905)

—— (ed.), *Chronicle of Henry VIII* (London: George Bell & Sons, 1889)

Hutton, Ronald, *The Stations of the Sun* (Oxford: Oxford University Press, 2001)

Inderwick, F.A. (ed.), *Calendar of the Inner Temple* (London: Stevens & Son, 1896)

Ives, Eric, *Anne Boleyn* (Oxford: Blackwell, 1986)

Journals of the House of Lords, Beginning Primo Henrici Octavi, vol. 1, 1509–77 (London: 1808)

Kaulek, Jean Baptiste Louis (ed.), *Correspondance Politique de MM. de Castillon et de Marillac, Ambassadeurs de France en Angleterre* (Paris: Felix Alcan, 1885)

Kelly, Henry Ansgar, *The Matrimonial Trials of Henry VIII* (Stanford, CA: Stanford University Press, 1976)

Kirkman, Francis, *The Unlucky Citizen* (London: Printed by Anne Johnson for Fra. Kirkman, 1673)

Langham, William, *The Garden of Health* (London: 1578)

Law, Ernest, *The History of Hampton Court Palace in Tudor Times*, 3 vols. (London: G. Bell & Sons, 1885)

Leadam, I.S. (ed.), *Select Cases before the King's Council in the Star Chamber, Commonly Called the Court of Star Chamber, A.D. 1509–1544*, vol. 2 (Selden Society, 1911)

Les Enseignements d'Anne de France . . . à sa Fille Susanne de Bourbon (Moulins: C. Desrosiers, imprimeur-éditeur, 1876)

Letters and Papers, Foreign and Domestic, of the Reign of Henry VIII, 1509–47 (ed.) J. S. Brewer, J. Gardiner and R. H. Brodie, 21 vols. in 33 (London: HMSO, 1862–1932)

MacCulloch, Diarmaid, *Thomas Cranmer: A Life* (New Haven, CT; London: Yale University Press, 1996)

McDonnell, Michael F. J., *A History of St Paul's School* (London: Chapman & Hall, 1909)

McLaren, Angus, *Reproductive Rituals: The Perception of Fertility in England from the Sixteenth to the Nineteenth Century* (London; New York: Methuen, 1984)

——, *A History of Contraception: From Antiquity to the Present Day* (Oxford; Cambridge, MA: Blackwell, 1991)

Martin, Charles Trice, 'Sir John Daunce's Accounts of Money received from the Treasurer of the King's Chamber temp. Henry VIII', *Archaeologica*, vol. 47 (ii), 1883

Merriman, Roger Bigelow, *Life and Letters of Thomas Cromwell* (Oxford: Clarendon Press, 1902)

Metcalf, Walter C. (ed.), *Visitations of Suffolk, 1561, 1577, 1612* (Exeter: William Pollard, 1882)

Muir, Kenneth, *Life and Letters of Sir Thomas Wyatt* (Liverpool: Liverpool University Press, 1963)

Nucius, Nicander of Corcyra (ed. J.A. Cramer), *Second Book of Travels* (London: Camden Society, old series, vol. 17, 1841)

Nichols, J.G. (ed.), *Chronicle of Calais* (London: Camden Society, 1846)

——, *Narratives of the Days of the Reformation* (London: Camden Society, 1859)

Nicolas, Nicholas Harris, *Proceedings and Ordinances of the Privy Council of England*, vol. VII (Printed by the Command of King William IV, 1837)

——, *Privy Purse Expenses of Elizabeth of York: Wardrobe Accounts of Edward the Fourth* (London: William Pickering, 1880)

Noble, Graham, 'Evil May Day; Re-examining the Race Riot of 1517', *History Today*, September 2008

Norris, Herbert, *Tudor Costume and Fashion* (Mineola, New York: Dover Publications, 1997)

Original Letters Relative to the English Reformation, written during the reigns of King Henry VIII, King Edward VI and Queen Mary: chiefly from the Archives at Zürich, 2 vols. (ed. Rev. Hastings Robinson) (Cambridge: Parker Society, 1846)

Paget, Hugh, 'The Youth of Anne Boleyn', *Historical Research*, vol. 54, issue 130, November 1981, pp. 162–70

The Parliamentary or Constitutional History of England, 2nd edn, vol. 3 (London: Printed for J. and R. Tonson, and A. Miller in the Strand; and W. Sandby in Fleet Street, 1762)

Paston Letters (ed. James Gairdner) (London: Chatto & Windus; Exeter: James G. Commin, 1904)

Percy, T. (ed.), *The Regulations and Establishment of the Household of Henry Algernon Percy, the fifth Earl of Northumberland* (Printed in 1770)

Porter, Linda, *Mary Tudor: The First Queen* (London: Portrait, 2007)

Redworth, Glyn, *In Defence of the Church Catholic: The Life of Stephen Gardiner* (Oxford: Basil Blackwell, 1990)

Reid, R.R., *The King's Council in the North* (London: Longmans, Green & Co., 1921)

Ridley, Jasper, *The Tudor Age* (London: Constable & Robinson, 2002)

Roberts, Howard and Walter H. Godfrey (eds.), 'Norfolk House and Old Paradise Street' in *Survey of London*, vol. 23, *Lambeth: South Bank and Vauxhall* (London: London City Council 1951)

Robinson, John Martin, *The Dukes of Norfolk: A Quincentennial History* (Oxford: Oxford University Press, 1982)

Roper, William, *The Lyfe of Sir Thomas Moore, Knighte* (London: Published for the Early English Text Society by Humphrey Milford, Oxford University Press, 1935)

Russell, John, Wynkyn de Worde and Hugh Rhodes (ed. Frederick James Furnivall), *The Babees Book, or The Book of Nurture* (Roxburghe Club, 1867)

Ryrie, Alec, 'Lassells, John (d. 1546)', *Oxford Dictionary of National Biography* (Oxford: Oxford University Press, 2004; online edn, January 2008)

Sander, Nicholas, *Rise and Growth of the Anglican Schism* (London: Burns & Oates, 1877)

Scarisbrick, J.J., *Henry VIII* (London: Eyre & Spottiswode, 1968)

Schofield, John, *The Rise and Fall of Thomas Cromwell: Henry VIII's Most Faithful Servant* (Stroud: History Press, 2011)

Schroeder, Joy, *Dinah's Lament: The Biblical Legacy of Sexual Violence in Christian Interpretations* (Minneapolis: Fortress Press, 2007)

Siddons, Michael Powell, *Heraldic Badges in England and Wales* (Woodbridge: Boydell, 2009)

Smith, Lacey Baldwin, *A Tudor Tragedy: The Life and Times of Catherine Howard* (London: Jonathan Cape, 1961)

Starkey, David, *The Reign of Henry VIII: Personalities and Politics* (London: Vintage, 2002)

——, *Six Wives: The Queens of Henry VIII* (London: Vintage, 2004)

State Papers published under the authority of his Majesty's Commission: King Henry the Eighth, 11 vols. (London: His Majesty's Commission for State Papers, by John Murray, Albemarle Street, 1830–52)

Statutes of the Realm (London: George Eyre and Andrew Strahan, 1810–28)

Streitberger, W.R., 'On Edmond Tyllney's Biography', *Review of English Studies*, new series, vol. 29, 1978

Strickland, Agnes, *Lives of the Queens of England*, (London: Published for Henry Colburn, 1854)

Strype, J., *Ecclesiastical Memorials under Henry VIII*, 3 vols. in 6 (Oxford: Clarendon Press, 1822)

Summit, Roland C., 'The Child Sexual Abuse Accommodation Syndrome', *Child Abuse and Neglect*, vol. 7, 1983

Surrey Archaeological Collections: Relating to the History and Antiquities of the County of Surrey (Guildford: Surrey Archaeological Society, 1950)

'The Third Report of the Deputy Keeper of Public Records' (1842), Appendix II

Thomas, William, *The Pilgrim: A Dialogue on the Life and Actions of King Henry the Eighth* (London: Parker, Son and Bourn, 1861)

Thornton, T., 'Henry VIII's Progress through Yorkshire', *Northern History*, vol. 46, no. 2, September 2009, pp. 231–44

Tusser, Thomas, *Five Hundreth Points Good Husbandry* (London: Lackington, Allen & Co., 1812)

Victoria History of the Counties of England: Bedfordshire (London: Victoria County History, 1912)

Victoria History of the Counties of England: The City of York (London: Dawson for the University of London Institute of Historical Research, 1982)

Visitations of the County of Nottingham, 1569 and 1614 (London: Harleian Society, 1871)

Visitations of the County of Surrey, 1530, 1672, 1623 (London: Harleian Society, 1899)

Visitations of Kent, 1619–1921, Camden, Philipot, Hovenden (eds.) (London: Harleian Society, 1898)

Visitations of Norfolk, 1563 (Norwich: Printed by Miller and Leavins, 1878)

'Wardrobe Accounts of Henry VIII', *Archaeologia*, vol. 9, 1789, pp. 243–51

Warnicke, Retha, *Wicked Women of Tudor England: Queens, Aristocrats, Commoners* (New York: Palgrave Macmillan, 2012)

Wayment, Hilary, *The Windows of King's College Chapel, Cambridge: A Description and Commentary* (London: Published for the British Academy by Oxford University Press, 1972)

Weever, John, *Ancient Funerall Monuments within the United Monarchie of Great Britaine, Ireland, and the Islands Adjacent* (London: 1631)

Wegg, Jervis, *Richard Pace, A Tudor Diplomatist* (London: Methuen & Co., 1932)

Weir, Alison, *Henry VIII, King and Court* (London: Pimlico, 1992)

——, *The Six Wives of Henry VIII* (London: Pimlico, 1992)

——, *Children of England: The Heirs of King Henry VIII* (London: Jonathan Cape, 1996)

Wilkinson, Josephine, *Richard III* (Stroud: Amberley Publishing, 2008)

Wilson, Derek, *A Tudor Tapestry: Men, Women and Society in Reformation England* (London: The History Club, 1972)

Wood, M.A.E., *Letters of Royal and Illustrious Ladies of Great Britain*, 3 vols. (1846)

The Works of Aristotle, the Famous Philosopher / Complete Masterpiece (London: Printed by the Publisher, 1828)

Wright, Thomas (ed.), *Three Chapters of Letters Relating to the Suppression of Monasteries* (London: Camden Society, old series, 1843)

Wriothesley, Charles, *A Chronicle of England during the Reign of the Tudors, from A.D. 1485 to 1559* (London: Camden Society, 1875–7)

Index

~

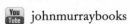
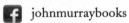
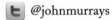